MUY MACHO

ALSO BY RAY GONZÁLEZ

ANTHOLOGIES

City Kite on a Wire: 38 Denver Poets

Crossing the River: Poets of the Western U.S.

Tracks in the Snow: Essays by Colorado Poets

The Midnight Lamp

After Aztlán: Latino Poets in the Nineties

Without Discovery: A Native Response to Columbus

Guadalupe Review Anthology

Mirrors Beneath the Earth: Chicano Short Fiction

This Is Not Where We Began: Essays by Chicano Writers

*Currents from the Dancing River: Contemporary Latino Fiction,
Nonfiction, and Poetry*

Under the Pomegranate Tree: Contemporary Latino Erotica

Inheritance of Light: Contemporary Poetry from Texas

ESSAYS

Memory Fever: A Journey Beyond El Paso del Norte

POETRY

From the Restless Roots

Apprentice to Volcanos

Twilights and Chants

Railroad Face

The Heat of Arrivals

Cabato Sentora

MUY MACHO

LATINO MEN CONFRONT
THEIR MANHOOD

Edited and with an Introduction

by Ray González

ANCHOR BOOKS
DOUBLEDAY
NEW YORK LONDON TORONTO SYDNEY AUCKLAND

AN ANCHOR BOOK
PUBLISHED BY DOUBLEDAY
a division of Bantam Doubleday Dell Publishing Group, Inc.
1540 Broadway, New York, New York 10036

ANCHOR BOOKS, DOUBLEDAY, and the portrayal of an anchor
are trademarks of Doubleday, a division of Bantam Doubleday
Dell Publishing Group, Inc.

Book design by Brian Mulligan

Acknowledgments for individual essays appear on pages (231–32.)

Library of Congress Cataloging-in-Publication Data

Muy macho: Latino men confront their manhood / edited and with an
introduction by Ray González.
p.   cm.
1. Hispanic American men—Psychology.   2. Machismo—United States.
3. Sex role—United States.   I. González, Ray.
E184.S75M89   1996
305.38′868073—dc20
95-49859
CIP
ISBN 0-385-47861-5
Copyright © 1996 by Ray González

First Anchor Books Edition: June 1996
1   3   5   7   9   10   8   6   4   2

CONTENTS

EDITOR'S ACKNOWLEDGMENTS

The opportunity to create this kind of book would not be possible without the encouragement of my agent, Susan Ginsburg. I also thank Bill Johnson Gonzales, her former assistant, for the initial idea. The gathering of these men's writings, and being able to present them in this format, came from the care and direction of Charles Flowers, my editor at Anchor Books. I dedicate this book to some men: Ramon González, my father; Bill Broadwell and Peter Ashkenaz, my childhood friends; Robert Burlingame, the first teacher to show me how poetry fit into my life; and to two friends who know how important the content of this book is to all of us—Phil Woods and George Kalamaras.

ABOUT THE EDITOR

Ray González is a poet, essayist, and editor born in El Paso, Texas. He is the author of *Memory Fever: A Journey Beyond El Paso del Norte* (Broken Moon Press, 1993), a memoir about growing up in the Southwest. He was educated at the University of Texas at El Paso and Southwest Texas State University, where he received an MFA in Creative Writing. He is also the author of four books of poetry—*From the Restless Roots* (Arte Publico Press, 1985), *Twilights and Chants* (James Andrews & Co., 1987), *The Heat of Arrivals* (BOA Editions, 1996), and *Cabato Sentora* (BOA Editions, 1997). He is the editor of sixteen anthologies, most recently *Currents from the Dancing River: Contemporary Latino Fiction, Nonfiction, and Poetry* (Harcourt Brace, 1994) and *Under the Pomegranate Tree: Contemporary Latino Erotica* (Pocket Books, 1996). He has served as poetry editor of *The Bloomsbury Review,* a book review magazine in Denver, for fourteen years. Among his awards are a 1987 Four Corners Book Award for *Twilights and Chants,* a 1988 Colorado Governor's Award for Excellence in the Arts, and a 1993 Before Columbus Foundation American Book Award for Excellence in Editing. He is assistant professor of English and Latin American studies at the University of Illinois in Chicago.

INTRODUCTION

In *Iron John,* his best-selling book about male initiation and the role of the mentor, poet Robert Bly states, "We are living in an important and fruitful moment now, for it is clear to men that the images of adult manhood given by the popular culture are worn out; a man can no longer depend on them. By the time a man is thirty-five he knows that the images of the right man, the tough man, the true man which he received in high school do not work in life. Such a man is open to new visions of what a man is or could be." *Muy Macho: Latino Men Confront Their Manhood* is the first book by Latino male writers to address how they see themselves as men within the concept of what it means to be "macho"—the catchword for Latino adult manhood. As Omar S. Castañeda has said, "Machismo is complex and multifaceted and too often, in Anglo-American interpretations, reduced to self-aggrandizing male bravado that flirts with physical harm to be sexual, like some rutting for the right to pass on genes." The men in this book have gone beyond this expected rutting to write on disturbing topics like family history and their roles as tough guys or passive men. These writers do not depend on the old stereotype of the dark, brooding head of the household, as some of their fathers may have done, to define their domestic life. The caricatures of the rebellious street punk and the Latin lover, who beds as many women as he can, no longer fit the mold being shaped by the "fruitful" time Bly talks about.

To have Latino men write about their fathers, sexuality, and the cult of silence between men is a literary task taking place for the first time. Some of these writers found it hard to create these essays because they had never written about their parents so honestly before. Others met the challenge of recalling painful childhood memories with the satisfaction that, at last, they were dealing with subjects their poetry and fiction could never directly approach. Writing about themselves as boys, teenagers, or wiser, middle-aged men gave them a different focus as to who they are as writers. Most of all, these true stories were a chance to look back on how they have dealt with issues common to any man.

When they were solicited, contributors to *Muy Macho* were asked to answer the question of whether Latino men must live with the macho, tough-guy image all their lives, or if there is room for redefining machismo. Where did the word "machismo" come from? What does it mean to be a "real man" in Latin America and the U.S.? How does the immigrant who comes in search of work to support his family understand his masculinity or his role as a father? Besides Rudolfo Anaya's " 'I'm the King': The Macho Image" and Ilán Stavans's "The Latin Phallus," long pieces on the cultural history of being macho, each essayist addresses the notion/tradition of machismo in his own style. Anaya and Stavans present examples of specific individuals whose actions influenced the development of the macho image, where it manifested itself in passive silence or aggressive domination. The two essayists show what kind of cultural and literary models young men have had when it comes to behaving the way they do. Omar S. Castañeda's "Guatemalan Macho Oratory" and Ricardo Pau-Llosa's "Romancing the *Exiliado*" balance the historical points of view with insights from outside the United States. Their Latin-American focus contributes to a more complex profile of who the Latino man is and where he came from.

The question of whether Latino males are different than other men in America is one of the central themes of this book. Do Latino men approach adulthood differently than other males in America? How does racism, poverty, and religious beliefs affect self-development and the way these men treat women? Does the cult of silence, where many Latino fathers are silent as they leave parenting to the mother, mean every son will imitate his father as be becomes a parent? Luis J. Rodríguez admits, "The patriarchal Mexican culture had helped build a wide breach between my father and I. The silent and strong man—vestiges of deceit—was revered. Waited on. Accepted."

These essays revolve around major issues Latino males have had few opportunities to discuss in book form before. One is their absence from the men's movement. Why are Latino men not part of the large gatherings of men who beat on drums and recount their problems with their emotions? Why are their similar conflicts so well hidden? A second concern is whether Latino culture allows its men to redefine the macho myth without abandoning positive role models they have. In other words, can Latino men do away with the myth of aggressive yet emotionally private males and still prosper? Another issue brings up questions about their role in a society where many American men are searching for new identities. Can Latino men keep up with the social and political gains made by their culture? During a time when male roles are being restructured in the mainstream society, will these males be able to assimilate?

The essayists in *Muy Macho* point out some of the differences in cultures that complicate any expression of manhood: the domination of a strict Catholic upbringing, language barriers that keep many Latinos from being more assertive about what they want, and the relative passivity of many Latino women. Some women, who have moved slowly toward a more feminist transformation, still reinforce the traditional roles that give the men the message that it is okay to beat them, cheat on them, or not be available for a nurturing relationship with their children. While it is true that it is not the woman's responsibility to make the man a "good man," cultural traditions have made it easy for many Latino men to stand still without change and leave everything up to the women. Latino men have been more hesitant in reevaluating their gender roles than white males, who are dramatically organizing and expressing themselves. The writers in this book know Latino men have been silent for too long about their growing alienation.

Though only a few essays refer directly to the men's movement, *Muy Macho* can be seen as a response to these large gatherings of men in which writers, storytellers, and psychologists like Bly, Michael Meade, and James Hillman conduct a mass reexamination of the male character. In recent years, books like *Iron John,* Meade's recent *Men and the Water of Life,* and various Hillman titles have influenced male self-evaluation and forced men to confront hidden emotions. These popular books have created a debate over how men get in touch with their feelings, and have encouraged both men and women to contribute to this dialogue over the male character in America.

In the midst of this dramatic cultural phenomenon, Latinos and other men of color have been left out. While leaders like Bly and Meade have worked hard to get men to be more honest about their lives, the men's movement has been seen as primarily a white-male cause. The gatherings of men and the issues confronted in the publications are not addressing minority issues, like urban crime, racism, and poverty. They are not admitting there are double standards in the educational system. Crumbling schools, high dropout rates, and lack of job opportunities are problems many Latino men are blamed for and many statistics reinforce. As with the feminist movement of the 1970s, issues of race, class, and sexual orientation have been downplayed in order to build unity—yet these very differences enlarge the dialogue and communicate a more accurate portrait of American masculinity. Can the men's movement go beyond the internal and emotional conflicts of white males and devote more time to examining how the changing role of men has to cross cultures—a male evolution that would include all men? There is an obvious absence of Asian, African-American, and Latino men at these meetings. None of the best-selling books have addressed the difference in cultures that are keeping Latinos and other men of color from speaking about their male psyches. They have not acknowledged their wants and needs and how these men have lived within and outside the stereotypes their cultures and non-Latinos created long ago. In "On Macho" and "The Puerto Rican Dummy and the Merciful Son," Luis J. Rodríguez and Martín Espada talk about how Latinos see the men's movement and the kind of direct involvement they expect.

Muy Macho is a book about what Rodríguez calls "tribal connections," those that are made on a more personal rather than a public level, as in the men's movement. These intimate essays are about examining one's own character without a large and loud support system of other men. The voices in these true stories leave a sense of aloneness, even if the insights gained were not reached in isolation. For the first time, Latino men go beyond more dramatic and familiar testimonies of ex-gang members and pintos (ex-cons), or the success stories of "having escaped the barrio for a better life," to make statements about self-identity. Those writers who had to leave their cultural trappings behind recognize the advantages of assimilation without denouncing their past entirely. Confessions by men who led destructive lives of crime have dominated the media for years and given many non-Latinos the image that most Hispanic men are antisocial misfits, even when these men have reformed and become good role models for Latino youth. Essays that do bring up this "dark" side point to the price paid, and the lessons learned, before these men were able to offer their sons an alternative.

The men in *Muy Macho* are revealing the many other ways in which the Latino male identity has been formed. These pages contain wisdom gained from good educations, thriving careers in teaching and the arts, and day-to-day experiences of new fathers. In writing about the joys of raising his first son, Martín Espada also admits, "I hope that, someday, I can explain clearly why there are those waiting for him to explode, to confirm their stereotypes of the hot-blooded, bad-tempered Latino male who has, without provocation, injured the Anglo innocents. His anger—and that anger must come—has to be controlled, directed, creatively channeled, articulated, but not all-consuming, neither destructive nor self-destructive." This book, too, then, is about anger. Yet, like Espada, these writers share their triumphs and failures as expressions of hope that they are giving the world a more complete picture of masculinity, one not destroyed by anger.

In *Men and the Water of Life: Initiation and the Tempering of Men*, Meade writes, "The most lost and dangerous people in this world are those who are not emotionally bonded to family, community, and humanity as a whole and those who have acquired personal power without being initiated to a sense of the source of that power and the value of individual life." Even though he was referring to the state of American society as a whole, Meade could easily be talking about Latino society itself. The long-standing notion that Latino communities are close-knit has also covered over a widespread alienation among its individuals, a dilemma that is universal. *Muy Macho* is about Latino men growing up and leaving childhood behind. Each of them did it in a different manner, which gave them various definitions of family and community amid the alienating forces. Some of these men had lonely childhoods. Others believed in the strong father figures they were fortunate to have, whether as an actual parent or a substitute. Several are still seeking that bond denied to them in their youth. What kind of initiation rites did these men go through, if they had different kinds of fathers? Were racial confrontations at school part of this initiation? How did early sexual adventures affect their relationships with women? Leroy V. Quintana's "Bless Me, Father" and Luis Alberto Urrea's "Whores" recount how, as young men, they participated in timeless rites of initiation. Their need to steal or drink, or learn about sex for the first time, is part of any universal coming-of-age story. Yet, as Latinos, they had to come to terms with the consequences of growing up in a society that produces a high rate of substance and sexual abuse. How did these incidents affect the way these men played out the process of reaching maturity? How did education, racism, and the country they grew up in affect their values and heighten their skills at self-preservation?

In his startling memoir, *Always Running: La Vida Loca, Gang Days in L.A.,* Luis J. Rodríguez writes, "As an ex-gang member, I know I could have looked at myself with more self-esteem if I had had a sense that the men around me—my father, uncles, brothers, and homeboys (gang members)—also felt good about themselves. Latinos need that strong tribal connection that does not emphasize the destructive forces of men bonding with one another." Some of the essays in *Muy Macho* contain writing about the Latino child-men—homeboys who dominate the cultural image of Latino youth. Others deal with drug addiction and alcoholism, wife batterers, boys raised in single-family homes, and school dropouts. In recent decades, men with these backgrounds have grown in numbers while influencing the way Latino males behave, treat women, and deteriorate their own culture. Some of these negative aspects of life were forced upon Latino men by mainstream society and social policies that influenced the environment in which many of these young men grew up. Racism is a major factor in the way the individual and collective characters of Latinos have been shaped. These essays contain lessons and road maps on overcoming these social ills. They are written in an environment that takes the achievements and blessings of individuals, and reminds us about the fact Latino men are also thriving today.

Artistic, political, and economic gains among Hispanics are giving Latino men more opportunities than in past decades. These writers have set some criteria for evaluating the dark forces that overcome many Latino males in their younger years. By writing these essays they are allowing very personal confessions and experiences to set the tone for a new manner of defining their inner selves. *Muy Macho* leaves the message that it is now okay to talk about the many versions of machismo and the lasting impact fathers leave on their children. The sense of "feeling good about yourself," which Rodríguez was seeking, is evident in what is being written here. Not every inner conflict has been resolved, but the composite character of the Latino man that has been constructed in these pages presents a communal portrait from which to embark on further revelation and debate.

Another issue that is addressed is the fact there are many good role models among Latino men. Often, they get overlooked in favor of the sensational notions of the tough guy or the destructive father figure. How can Latinos look up to positive role models like César Chávez, Edward James Olmos, or Henry Cisneros? What can young men learn about self-identity from these famous figures, while attempting to live new lives in a time that is challenging many men to start over again?

Several writers in *Muy Macho* discuss their lives outside their familiar literary careers, share emotions and memories about fathers they never knew, or fathers whose dominating presence affected every family member during childhood. Some of the contributors recount their close relationships with a male of the family, not always their fathers. Dagoberto Gilb celebrates being a father to two sons, while Alberto Álvaro Ríos mourns a dying parent. This is also a book where gay Latino men reveal their spiritual and physical bonds with other males—a rare subject in Latino nonfiction. Elías Miguel Muñoz, Rane Arroyo, and Ilán Stavans talk frankly about the conflict of sexual identity and how it too defines the Latino man.

The publication of this collection does not mean these issues have been resolved. It is the beginning of public self-expression on topics that have been at the heart of these men's literary work. By writing about their inner lives, these men have learned a number of lessons and have pondered what it means to be macho, or how a certain parent letting them down repeats a timeless cycle between fathers and sons. They have traced their stories back from childhood to the present and have learned more about who they are now, and where they came from. They have new things to say to their sons, their male friends, their wives and lovers, and to their audience. The fear and anxiety of confessing too many personal things have changed to relief and enlightenment.

When Elías Miguel Muñoz writes, "I'll never be able to justify the way Papi tainted my childhood, but I can cease to see him through the gaze of a hurt and frightened child," he is speaking for those men who have obtained a deeper understanding of their fathers by dealing with the past. Years of fear and denial have turned toward introspection and long-overdue self-evaluation. Rudolfo Anaya states that "We learn not only how to talk, act, respond, and think like men from the intimate clan of males in which we are raised, we also learn an attitude toward life." In writing about young men lucky to have strong bonds with the older men around them, Anaya explores numerous insights into Latino identity that comes from these traditional, macho bonds. What lies between these two contrasting views of growing up makes up a large portion of this book.

How can men with varied backgrounds move from weak bonds to ones that are constructive and energize their people in a positive manner? The debate, the emotions, and the personal stories in these pages attempt to answer that question. By admitting there are spiritual and emotional places to go beyond gang brotherhood, or the stereotype of the Latin lover, these writers have enlarged the personal environment in which men like themselves can thrive in, as well as a new perspective on the state of American manhood.

—Ray González

MUY MACHO

ME MACHO,
YOU JANE

Miriam Berkley

DAGOBERTO GILB is the author of a book of stories, The Magic of Blood, and a novel, The Last Known Residence of Mickey Acuna, both from Grove/Atlantic Monthly Press. The Magic of Blood received a Hemingway Foundation Award in Fiction. He was also awarded a 1993 Whiting Award in Fiction and a 1995 Guggenheim Fellowship. He lives in El Paso, Texas.

I'VE BEEN ACCUSED of suffering from involuntary macho spasms most of my life. Usually not to my face. Very few got the *cojones* for that! Okay, maybe a couple of people have mentioned it. Tell you the truth, I don't know what it is they're talking about. To me it's a lot like my astrological sign. Which is Leo. I remember this party a long, long time ago. "A Leo, of course he's a *Leo,* what else would he be?" My sign had pissed these people off. I was pissed off back. What're you gonna do about it? I snorted, my chin up, the muscles in my hands twitching to knot up, feeling light and quick. I don't remember what I'd done or said, if that was it. Was I too wasted? I didn't belong at that party. Too pseudo-hippie for me (real hippies were too stoned to make accusations). Another one I've often heard is that it's Mexican blood. A hot, spicy *colorado.* Now you see what I'm getting at? That it's usually a complaint about some behavior, or perceived potential for, these people don't approve of. Sort of like when I'm saying I like cockfights. Not as much as certain friends of mine, but I do. I hear the moaning already. People on low-fat, boneless-chicken-is-okay diets. Somehow roosters fighting is a lot worse than football or boxing. But I've sat in stands with all kinds of people, men and women, at all kinds of sporting events, and to me it's the same screaming noises in all of them.

I was raised by my mom. My father lived in the same house as me, maybe my first year or two. My first stepfather lived there when I was thirteen. I was not too fond of this first stepfather. He did not teach me to like manhood. Did my mom teach me to be macho? She had a mean temper, that's true. And I know I got my temper from her. She was a wild, beautiful woman, though. So I'm telling you the truth, I'm not really sure what being macho is. Except sometimes when I see how some wuss behaves.

Is it risk-taking? Danger? Women who take physical risks, look for danger, aren't they being "macho"? Or the threat of violence. Shooting guns. Killing animals. Or men talking about women. Especially a naked woman, real or imagined.

————

I've come to this office because I need a machine she has offered me the use of, for free. Time and place, from a long time ago to now, from L.A. to El Paso and between or a few miles east or north, I will not specify for reasons of security. Though I barely know her, I sense this woman is interested in me. Twitch, twitch. Okay, score that remark as macho evidence for the prosecution. I know I'm right, though (go ahead, score that one too). I'm not interested in her, though, haven't been. In fact I've avoided her a few times because I don't want the trouble. I'd rather we be friends (score that for the other side?). She's into the local power movement, is playing that sport. I imagine how someday she'll run for a public office. A Chicana superstar. I'm thinking this as she's talking to me, all these papers strewn everywhere, paper clips and staplers, dirty telephones with long cords all tangled up, posters and bulletin boards, take-out boxes, coffee cups, beer bottles, ashtrays. I'm listening to her quietly, sitting across from her, not really following a story she's telling me about political capital, those who have what and where and how much and the arguments each have about accumulating more and positioning for it, the difficulties she has, as a woman, an attractive woman, elbowing her way in. She is really a nice-looking woman, too. At certain angles, she's unquestionably sexy. She's got a husky laugh because she's large-boned, maybe on the heavy side. She's tough, as fearless and aggressive about her opinions as her desires. Her appetite for fun is as big and loud as she is. Big breasts too. Which all adds up to say that she's not the type I've usually known in a biblical respect. Which is what I'm considering as I'm paying the most superficial attention to what she's saying. Why not? is what I'm thinking. Maybe we ought to get drunk, laugh, take off our clothes in the dark. For the sake of acting bad, to play, not be romantic. Suddenly she says something that startles me into the flow of her monologue:

"... doesn't like a woman, a tough bitch like me, on stage getting attention. He's so macho. Like you." Who she's talking about is this *político* I don't know personally but can't not know of because he's always news. I ask for an explanation. "You know what I mean," she says. No, I don't. I don't at all. I've never run for any political position. I've never been or even wanted to be anybody's boss. "Yours isn't bad like his," she explains, laughing. Flirting. I don't know *her* well, so how come she decides she knows *me,* knows my "good" or "bad" machismo? In the past I've been nothing less than a gentleman in all respects, and even now, haven't I been sitting here quietly, practically without moving, waiting, listening politely to her about this *pedo* I could care less about so I can use a machine? I have said or done absolutely zero that would give her any knowledge of who I am or how I behave. *Ni una cosa,* nothing.

I worked this four-story in Newport Beach, California, a building so close to Pacific Ocean saltwater that it pushed against a parking structure sheerwall like an aquarium, above which was a view of uncountable masts of million-dollar yachts and catamarans lining the curving bay's piers. All the other carpenters were Anglo. I'd become the Chicano from Texas. From no less than mythical El Paso: the Rio Grande, adobes, Rosa's Cantina, Tony Lama cowboy boots, Juárez whorehouses. I wasn't just me, in other words. I was an embodiment. I was especially as wild as the west Texas wind because I was living in a motel room and I didn't want to continue to work for the company once this job ended. I was even planning to leave sooner than that. Once I'd earned enough, I was outta there, thanks, *hasta la próxima,* and "later"s. The boys knew this about me because I was still there, the only one who'd come out of the union hall still around. The superintendent called men from the hall when some walls had to be formed up in a hurry for a large cement pour; then, a week later, almost two, they were down the road. But he liked my work, and leaving me on was like a long-term employment offer. He kept company men busy all over L.A. and Orange counties. These were guys who talked about which company jobs they'd been at, how many years. It seemed like a good outfit, too, but, complimented as I was, I was there for the money to be made on this job site alone.

I told guys I lived in Texas because I didn't want to live on California freeways and in stucco tract houses. That I had plans to go my own way. I mentioned side jobs I got in El Paso and implied that eventually they would lead to something, or, if not, I just didn't care. No, I did not mention my writing. It wasn't like I had to hide it, since it was not a topic that ever popped up. I didn't and wouldn't want it to, anyway, and wouldn't have blinked if it did. With over ten years in the trade at the time, I was a carpenter both to myself and to everyone I worked with, nothing more, nothing less. It's how I wanted it, too. What I inwardly prized about construction (most of the time) was you were judged not by your talk, but what you did, on time, right. What I liked about construction was that, at the end of the day, when you were joint and bone sore, when your feet throbbed, when you required cold beer to numb the pain, you knew you were tired from really working. You rubbed the yellowed calluses, hard as fingernails on your index finger and thumb of your hammer hand, picked at feathery splinters in your palms that seemed to grow hormonally like body hair, wiped away dribbling tie-wire cuts you discovered where you didn't feel them happen. What I liked was that at the end of the day you felt like a man, and at the end of the week you got your check, and at the end of a job you knew you'd *earned* your money.

Now I'm ready to tell you about The Asshole. The caps are important in my opinion, descriptive of his transcendent dimension. He's a kid. Looks seventeen, though may be nineteen. Probably twenty-one since he could buy beer. He is pudgy, a soft though unblubbery fat cushioning his belly and wrapping his arms, where there ought at least to be a little muscle tone (we're talking about men in the building trades, you know?). He's a third- or fourth-period apprentice carpenter, meaning he was in his second year of four. He rides what sounds like an uncorked Yamaha. He's got on a black helmet, with black-tint visor, and a black leather jacket. He thinks he is all things bad, and in the morning he struts into work with the attitude. He's a biker. He's a champion football player. He's a sex machine. He's a "lots of lines" doper—meth and coke, but he's done 'em all and can anytime—and he gulps white lightning. He's a musician and an asskicker and killer, if he has to be. His dog is a Doberman, and he's saving for a Harley. He carries a buck knife, owns a Luger, wants a magnum.

He does not have a toolbox in the lockup, just hard hat and bags—hammer, tape, tri-square, pencil (often no pencil)—and so one of the first specifically irritating things about him is that he asks to borrow tools the company doesn't supply, but that any carpenter is supposed to carry. A crescent wrench, a cat's paw, a flat bar, a level, a chisel, screwdrivers, handsaws. At first the loan was made, like it would be to anyone who asked. When he didn't give a tool back for days, once he was asked, usually it hadn't been lost yet. Usually, though a few times already. Tools getting lost on a job is nothing new, and it's part of the expense. But nobody liked guys who borrowed his shit, and nobody liked anyone who lost it. That was just one particular reason the carpenters on the job shook their heads about him.

Mine was different, though. I already couldn't stand him after the first breaktime I sat down, new on the crew, and he opened his mouth. It wasn't just the boot-high bullshit. It was the whiny, lazy, slow, dumb, loutish American audacity of it. The seeming privilege of it. I didn't like him because he was a punk, and what made my dislike unique was that I was upfront about it. I said so to anyone and most of all to him. Right in his face. "Go away. Go. Away. I do not want you to work anywhere near me. Good-bye." Guys would find this hysterical. The first few times he'd smile like I was kidding, even though it was clear to anyone with a two-digit IQ I was not, and he would bob between staying and leaving. The superintendent told him to help here, he whimpered. "I don't care. You do not work here. You work over there, you find anything else to do somewhere else. Away from me. Leave." If he wavered, I was unhesitant. "Now!" I'd yell to make my meaning less complex.

I had tried to work with him a few times. He was one of those who'd stand there forever if you didn't suggest he do *something,* watching me do everything, all alone, like this was his job description. Okay, I was a journeyman, he was an apprentice, so I'd only shake my head: I'd suggest he lift up the end of this four-by-six—but too heavy for him because it was too wet, or cement-logged, or he'd been out too late, or he didn't work out last week. *Measure that*—he'd stare at the tape, and stare, then give a few numbers, remeasure, and it'd be wrong. I'd even gotten real simple and asked him to get nails, or plywood—that was what laborers did! Or he'd be gone so long I could've forged or glued my own. If he didn't forget, if he came back. He was enthusiastic only when the lunch wagon blew its horn, though he even had bad taste in food. Old wrinkled hot dogs on stale yet wet buns, packaged burritos, Twinkies. He savored these like a gourmet. Quitting time was the only part of the day he was quick. No, I could not understand why he was on the payroll at all. I told him so. And I told him he should learn to take a shower, with soap, and to use deodorant, and to brush his teeth, and to wash his stinking underwear and socks and probably the rest of his clothes once in a while too, told him he should hang baking soda from his neck. I was dead serious, too.

The more insulting I got, the more he began to admire me. Yes, you read that correctly. I'd never heard of such a thing either, and certainly had never experienced anything so twisted like it. Would this be unwanted, obsessive macho-bonding? I was wild, hooting Texas. I was outlaw Mexican El Paso. To extinguish the chance of having to sit with him at break or lunch, I'd often go over with the laborers, all *mexicanos,* who usually sat a distance away from the English-speaking carpenters. Once or twice I caught him peering at me with the metaphorical equivalent of his mouth wide open, tongue limp on his lower lip (I'd move so my back was to him). I was so exotic! Oh, how could *he* become exotic like *me?!* I was a Doberman with Great Dane size, or a custom Harley. He did finally come to understand that I was serious about not wanting him near me, not even within my sight. But he came around anyway, like I was an irresistible force, and I'd have to sling more contempt. You wouldn't believe the words I used to send him off! And he'd say and do nothing. He'd disappear, maybe a day or two, maybe come back hours later to talk to another guy, until he thought, I guess, I'd forgotten or forgiven, and then I'd hurl more paeans of loathing. Did the power of them, their threat and fearsomeness and bravado, sting his wimpy psyche until it was testosterone-numb with envy and fascination for me?

It was like some warped Beauty and the Beast tale. Disgusting. Pathetic. Bizarre. I was not seeking any happy ending. Did I hate the dude? No. I only wanted him to go away, to not be anywhere near me. About his existence I felt an active indifference. That once I was gone, I wouldn't care what his future held, good or bad, and wouldn't care to know. I'd be grateful to never be around the weirdo asshole again, grateful I wouldn't have to.

When that last day came, I'd already said good-bye to the crew, was about to step off the dust and dirt and paraphernalia of the job site, my hard hat on backward, my tool bags looped over one shoulder, the other sagging from the weight of my toolbox, when he struts up. And I can tell he's wanting to act like a man. Like one out of a World War II movie or something.

"You're a real good carpenter," he says with a respect verging on I-don't-want-to-know. And then he puts out his too plump, too soft hand for a handshake.

Graduate seminar, Tucson, Arizona, fall 1992. The subject was books of fiction. I sat at the head of the table—six tables shoved together to make one in a nondescript room in the halls of the English department. The color of the room was manila, as in folders. It was a one-semester appointment in the creative writing program. I'd assigned a few writers I valued—John Fanté, Langston Hughes, Juan Rulfo, Naguib Mahfouz, Cormac McCarthy. An initial list also included Paul Bowles, and I was considering Hubert Selby, Jr. Note the shortage of female names. And I was taking over an established, and pre-enrolled, seminar from a professor whose course title was "Women Writers and the World of Their Invention." I hadn't been told this small detail when I accepted the employment. When she sent me her course description, I knew very quickly I was the wrong construction worker for the duty. I had to think and act fast to order books I knew, and I did consider retitling the course "Men and Their Books." With Selby as a possible (my sincere hesitation with him was that a movie had been made; I was interested in the linkage of style and story, and movies cheat close reading), all I'd have to do was add Bukowski and the tanks would be gassed. So I didn't. I wasn't there yet, and they didn't know me, and I was afraid nobody'd laugh. I did have three other books on the list. Ones by Pat Little Dog (Pat Ellis Taylor), J. California Cooper, and Leslie Marmon Silko. Who are women. Since people didn't recognize but one of them, they thought they were men names and men books.

When I arrived there was much less laughter than I could've imagined. Upset students, nervous faculty. A sexual harassment charge draped everyone like a trenchcoat, and, I was to learn, hiring me, a male and a man like I was, was met with such disapproval, it was as though all I wore was a trenchcoat. I was asked to add more books by women, and so I added two, an anthology of stories about and by bad girls, and a novel by Jean Rhys. I'd already decided to pass on Selby, and I dropped Bowles. It wasn't like doing this troubled me in the slightest. I wanted to joke and say how I really, really liked women. How I'd teach any they wanted me to, and I'd read them too! But I left my sense of humor out of it. My physical presence did not seem to inspire too much confidence, either. After my first meeting with those in charge, eyes stumbling around like the words were, after I said I had absolutely no discomfort adding and subtracting books for this course, that I even sincerely agreed with the student complaints (they enrolled for a course for and about women, and this large and loud guy shows up), after that, standing in the busy hall with my first-day escort, I just couldn't hold back one *bromita,* one small crack. "Where's the men's room? They do allow them here still, don't they?" I thought it was a little funny. My escort pointed, unsure, without smiling.

I sat at the head of the tables, a couple of months into it. One woman in the class was the most bitter, unhappy student with the state of Arizona (she was from the east), unhappy with the department's MFA program (evidence my visiting, substitute presence), unhappy specifically with several professors (her unconventional thesis not being received enthusiastically). Since there was much grumbling going on with many students, I didn't know if this was simply a common by-product of all writing programs, or even all graduate schools, or not. I'd read none of her creative work, but she was bright, and most of all she was hardworking, a trait that went a long way with me.

The book assigned to discuss that week was by Rick DeMarinis, a writer whose work I admire as much as I like him. An extremely rare combination. Though DeMarinis is highly regarded among fiction writers, I teased the students, warning them that he lived in El Paso and was my friend. The book, *The Burning Women of Far Cry,* is a comic, coming-of-age novel set in Montana. The women are smart and sexually wild and they drink. The men scam and pine for women and drink.

Usually the student was quiet and needed prodding to speak. This evening she opened the seminar. She picked up DeMarinis's novel by a corner and held it in the air. Picked up the novel like it wasn't a book, with a thumb and finger, at the farthest corner. Like it was soiled. Smelled. Like her fingers would be smeared by it. Holding the very least possible. She turned her eyes away like it didn't deserve their contact. Picked up the novel, eyes averted, held her arm out toward the center of the tables, dropped it, and said, "I can't believe we're expected to read a book like this in a graduate-level seminar." Her tone was contemptuous, defiant, fearlessly in the right.

Her complaint? The portrayal of women. Especially the excessive depiction of them possessing glorious breasts.

To be honest, I hadn't especially noticed the breasts in the novel. And I'd still say that they do not dominate any character description, are not part of even a motif. What interested me in the story was the broken family, the stepfathers, the jobs. What consumed me was the commanding, simple beauty of DeMarinis's prose. Yet the student seemed to have a good, quality argument. I could see how tasteless, how male-fetished the subject might be. So if talking about women's breasts is an inappropriate fixation, how much should be attributed to the writer's character, how much to the character's? Is it breasts in general? I'd have to confess that I like women's breasts. I mostly keep this to myself, but is it wrong to admit it openly? When I hear guys talk about them (about tits, to put it bluntly) with other guys, I think so. Is it generalizing? I don't like all women's breasts, or only breasts, not even mainly, just as I don't like all women. Or is it size? Criticize the consistent description of size? When we criticize, do we criticize the writer for willful obsession, or for what is written unaware? Which are his character's flaws, which are his, and how ought they be controlled or not? All of these, and many angles I'm sure I haven't thought of, great topics for discussion in a graduate creative writing seminar.

I say that now. Because when the book plopped on the table, as the room went silent, so did I. I lost sentence consciousness. There was, indeed, only one word left in me, yet inchoate, spiritually forming, physically germinating: *kill*.

As there are differences between men and women, there are differences between men and men. They are bulk and muscle, and they begin to be sensed at an early age. Eventually one boy consciously recognizes another's, and we get in fights to test boundaries. As young men we act more or less on these, bulking and muscling, or not, to a level of satisfaction and resignation. We learn who we are going to be physically smaller than. We accept the larger and smaller distinctions between us. When we are in a dispute with another man, we silently scale one another. At the construction sites where I've so far spent most of my adult work hours, which is where lots of *those* guys go after high school, arguments are too often not subtle. When there's verbal screaming, a real nonverbal howl kicks.

Whereas, in a world of ideas, at universities, words are king. Arguments are supposed to be bulky and muscular, not the person advancing them. Even ad hominem attacks are too physical in nature. It is the very condition that I love about a university environment. It is a paradise where brutishness is the bottom, where civility and manners are high tools of learning.

No *guy* would have dared done what that student did. Unless he thought he could kick my ass. When male students look me in the eye, and I look back, we've opened a discussion. We have either mutually decided to accept the rules of the idea world, or we have scaled. And we *have* scaled. Because we always scale each other, no matter what. There is no other possibility. He would never have done this without being afraid of me or being ready. But this didn't even occur to the student. She felt right, plain and simple, and self-righteous outrage and behavior never lead to anyone smacking her in the fucking face, which parallel activity on a construction site would lead to almost assuredly. Men don't hit women. The rudeness of dropping the book, my friend's book, a book I assigned for a course with only good intentions, that insult to me, *at* me—a male student would have known the wordless realm he tossed it into.

So what did I do? Nothing. We had none of the potential conversations I spoke of above. I think I tried to maintain some professorial decorum. I don't remember if I achieved any. I have no memory of what anyone else said to this day. Stunted conversations, or that was my attention? I do remember how I told myself I was being paid. This was a mental game I learned from miserable construction jobs. I dismissed the class very early. I remember my rage and disgust, seeing around a hot desert light glaring in my eyes as the sun was setting. I remember it as my last class, even though I sat at the head of those tables a few more times.

Several years earlier, I'd taken up coaching because I couldn't stand it anymore. Coaches were either overpraising baby-sitters or Nazis. I picked up a team of seven- and eight-year-olds, which included my youngest boy, but I was too late to get an eleven to twelve group. Meaning my oldest son, Tony, had to find a team, and quick. Which turned out to be one coached by a man I knew because I'd coached his son several times. I will tell you this honestly: His son was not so good an athlete. To put it even more bluntly, he sucked. He was a kind boy with a good and gentle heart who didn't like sports. Not really. He may not have been able to say so in words, but his body wrote clear sentences. It was his dad who wanted sports for him.

There were a few reasons I didn't like this coach very much. A lot had to do with him being an overbearing Christian. A new Christian. One of those who didn't understand that someone else could have a belief that was as well-considered as his. If he wasn't loud, which he was sometimes, his sanctimonious moralism was always screaming. He'd been a foster parent, and now his job, an admirable one, too, was as a houseparent for a larger group of boys at a home. He thought they should behave like they were sixty-year-old men, grateful for any conversation. Line up politely and be quiet. Listen to him. Listen when he's talking! It was like school, day and night, and the main lesson was that lessons were to be learned. No time for art or music or any parallel waste of time. Almost all the boys were Chicanos. They spoke Spanish, and their English was strongly accented, often broken. He didn't like that. Not at all. He'd shake his head. What *is it* you're trying to say? he'd snap, intolerant, like stupidity was an accent or a mispronounced word. He didn't think there was anything valuable enough about Mexican culture that wasn't already better in the USA.

His son was to be their example. In all things. I'd coached lots of these boys, just as I had his son. I liked his son, and I liked the boys. And the boys, including his, liked me and our teams because we had fun when we played and we still mostly won and if we lost, no big deal. All of which was why he didn't like me. He didn't say so. It was a sense I had, is all. An instinct. I was inferior, he was sure of it. Something about me. And so, I swore he didn't think these boys ought to like me. I swore he took up coaching because he didn't want someone like me, and my influence, ever again around his boys and his lessons. He didn't want to let it be said that I was a better coach than him.

These were my oldest son's peak years for basketball, and he had quickly become the star of the team, unquestionably the best player. I loved that it was true. I was proud of my Toño. I loved it for him, and I loved him for it, and I loved it because I didn't like the coach. This was true—underneath, I felt I was a better dad and coach and man because my son played basketball better than his. I was proud in larger ways too. Because of how he thought, because my son was a Chicano.

They were winning this game quickly. When Tony got the ball, he scored. It wasn't like he was hogging it, wasn't like he was trying to hot dog. That was never his style. When he got the ball, he tried to get it to others, but they wouldn't shoot it, or missed, or would send it back to him. He shot it and usually made it. The other kids didn't mind. They liked the winning part a lot.

And they were winning easy, and big, when the coach shouted. Games before, he'd been yapping at his son for not taking charge, for not shooting, not rebounding, for standing around doing nothing. He was mad at that deeper level too, as disappointed as I was proud. Then I heard him go after Tony again. It was about not putting it up so much, for having the ball too much. The coach was wrong. In principle, as an idea, he was right, but not in this circumstance. It definitely wouldn't have been true if it were his son, is what I'd say. His logic and principles and understanding would have altered then. There was a kid like Tony on everybody's team, and most boys were closer to his son. But really it wasn't about either boy. No, I'd say. It was about me. It was about me and him. That's what I'd say.

It was when the coach barked at Tony again, told him he had to sit down, even, that I leaped out of my chair across the court. Something uncontrollable gripped me. Even stronger than anger. Pride. Respect. Fairness. Not that I was working around those concepts clearly. "Motherfucker, you leave him alone!"

My hot voice echoed off the hardwood floors and high ceiling of the gym, bounced louder and more rude off east and west walls—a proverbial echo, unobstructed, magnified by cool, whispering autumn air. I couldn't believe it'd come out of me, either, since moments before I'd been sitting there, watching little kids playing ball in a game I sincerely didn't think slightly important. Tony didn't either. He didn't even care that he was being yelled at.

The coach glared at me, appalled. Worse yet, I caught something else too. An I-told-you-so smirk. Now he had confirmed that I was from the crass, violent, low-class, vulgar, gang-ridden, unfit-to-lead culture he so clearly was not from. I'd justified him and his self-righteous fundamentalism. But I was shamed equally about being an American, the ugliest kind. *Abuelitas,* sitting gracious and gently near me, dressed with Sunday shawls over their shoulders, watching their sweet *nietecitos* playing, being nothing but young and sweet, leaned forward, stunned, disgusted, like I'd hocked one onto the foot of the Virgen de Guadalupe. Two little girls on the other side of them got off their seats to step out onto the court to look at the face of a goon. Their innocent mouths were open, and even their eyes wanted to keep their distance. If I could've left I would have. It was that I was in a corner and the door was at the other end, and I couldn't.

Spasms. Twitches. Juice. Blood. Alignment of moon and stars and sun and planets. Hormones. Sex or violence. Meat. Or manners. Nobility, or a lack of. What you're embarrassed about, what you're proud of.

Here's a list: I like women. I like women better than men. I think some people deserve to get their ass kicked. I don't go to bullfights. Well, I've been to a couple, but only because they're in Juárez and it's something to do. My current drink is tequila and grapefruit juice, or vodka and tonic with two squeezes of lemon. I don't drink beer very often, and I love baseball and basketball and I really don't care for football much. You don't like that, screw you. I love my family. I love walking the streets, or up a mountain, or a desert trail, alone. I eat beef. And serrano chiles.

FROM
THE LAND OF MACHOS:
JOURNEY TO OZ WITH
MY FATHER

ELÍAS MIGUEL MUÑOZ was born in Cuba and came to the U.S. as a young child. He has published two novels, <u>Crazy Love</u> and <u>The Greatest Performance,</u> both from Arte Publico Press, and two books of poetry. His work has appeared in numerous fiction and poetry anthologies, including <u>Iguana Dreams,</u> <u>Currents from the Dancing River,</u> and <u>Paper Dance.</u> He lives in Silver Spring, Maryland.

I DRIVE; HE SLEEPS. Violin music makes him feel drowsy. He doesn't like the arias and concertos I love; he finds them depressing, impenetrable. So he shuts down. And I must resist the temptation to wake him and force him to listen. It's the opera *Don Giovanni,* Mozart's secret homage to his father. The obvious symbolism of this music betrays my hidden agenda: Can my father and I finally face the past, *our* past, and go on from there? Is it too late?

He is snoring, thanks to Wolfgang Amadeus. I'm enthralled by the endless desert and the ghost towns, all so different from the Cuban landscapes of his youth. Exhausted, I drive the rented truck to a rest area. My load consists of five boxes of books (my graduate school collection), wood shelves, my twin bed, an obsolete stereo with eight-track, and my ancient rolltop desk. And memories, which can also weigh you down.

"Thank you for coming along with me, Papi." This is what I should say to Don Elías, using the word most Cubans use for their fathers: *Papi.* A word that reeks of obedience and submission. An embarrassing, obligatory form of endearment. I hate it, but I don't know what else to call him.

Truth is, I'm grateful, and I promise myself that I will thank him at the end of our journey. On this hot and cloudless August day, 1984, I'm heading for Kansas, Land of Oz, heart of the Bible Belt. An academic position awaits me at an obscure university. I've deluded myself into thinking I'll begin a new life there. For one thing, I'll be far from California. Far from my family, from this man who sleeps beside me.

Watching him, I feel something like pity or compassion. He seems so defenseless. In an hour or two he'll wake up and ask, impatiently, "Do we have a lot further to go?" And I'll tell him a lie, "No. We're almost there." And he'll be the same old Papi, with no doubts about himself, no revelations from his dreams. No questions.

What or whom does my father dream about? What does he think about when he's at work painting walls? His job since he quit the factory, after the accident: painting houses and apartments. He loves having his own business. A far cry from his sales job in Cuba, but nonetheless a perfect occupation for someone who likes to be alone. My father can spend hours without any human contact. How does he fill all that time? I wonder. He probably thinks about all his responsibilities. The bon mot for Papi, indeed: *responsabilidad.*

There are phrases from my childhood, things he said to my mother, that haunt me: "I make all the decisions here! Don't you ever raise your voice to me again! No woman is going to ride *my* horse!" She was his doll, the little woman of the house. Did she love him? I'll never know. However, now I have words to name what in those days was only an intuition: He was selfish, aggressive; never giving, never tender with her. Mami obeyed him silently, moving aside whenever his fists fell on my face. Instead of confronting my torturer, she cried. The fear paralyzed her.

Many years later Gladys, my mother, would go from total paralysis to a passionate quest for her redemption. As she began to push sixty, she'd become a warrior of her freedom. Pent-up rancor, countless reproaches sprang from Mami, flooding our home. It was a poisoned stream: water from a past that refused to run a silent course. She would defy my father, confront him, humiliate him. But all of that would be much later—later than now, I mean. Because in the present of this trip to Kansas, my image of her was still that of a gentle, passive creature.

In this present of our trek to Oz, my father and I are away from our common, known places. We'll be able to talk, I hope. This is our first and last chance. I will relate my memories, the painful ones. And he will have no choice but to listen. Who knows, we might even reach a truce. It's hard to never have found the space and time to be alone with him. It's hard to go through life holding a grudge against your father, unable to tell him how you feel.

THE MEMORY GAME

For now let us invent a game. It'll be an easy one to play: All you have to do is answer my questions. What was the name of that guy who used to sell us plantains? And that other man, the Spanish curmudgeon you used to work for, did he stay in Cuba? What about Lalia and Raimundo, our dear old neighbors, what happened to them? (I keep a thought to myself: They must be dead by now.)

Do you remember what I remember, Papi? Our carriage rides down Calle Independencia, our promenades at Parque Juanita. We spent one month each summer at Varadero. Every year, on January 6, the Reyes Magos packed our house full of presents for my brother and me. Do you remember the corner store in Vista Alegre? We called it El Kiosko Bolita, although it had no sign showing its name. There was a jukebox at the kiosk, a *traganíquel* (literally, "swallow-nickels"). It played languid, heartrending boleros that you knew by heart: *"Nosotros," "Lágrimas Negras," "Cuatro Vidas."* Have you forgotten those songs, Papi?

Our game ends abruptly when a disturbing memory pushes forward, making me lose control of the wheel momentarily. Papi and I are riding the bus home from the park. My father is trying to protect me from the onslaught of passengers who push and shove and press against us. One of these people is a shoeshine boy we've often seen downtown. Through the eyes of my remembrance he looks like a weary old man, though he couldn't have been more than fifteen. He storms onto the bus and bumps me with his box as he passes by me. It's not a big blow, but it surprises me and I let out a slight moan. My father is furious. He attacks the young man verbally and the shoeshine boy retaliates with a threat: "I'm going to break your neck when we get off!"

Papi and I get out at the stop near our house. I know we're in danger, but I also know I have to trust my father. He's a macho; he flaunts his big *cojones* all the time. My valiant Papi will defend me.

The next scene happens too fast. I've lost track of the time between the moment we stepped down and the onset of combat. Who attacked whom first? Was it a punch, a shove, a kick? All I remember is the sight of my father and the stranger locked in an embrace! They were moving in unison, in circles, not letting go of each other. What kind of a brawl was this? It made no sense! At one point I looked around and noticed the crowd, the bus that hadn't left, a man who was pulling the fighters apart. And a woman who asked Papi, gently, "What are you doing, Elías? Why are you getting involved in something dirty like this?"

Strange, how vividly one recalls phrases, gestures, voices from such a remote past. I was only five or six, but I can still hear that woman's words as if she were whispering them now in my ear. (Who was she?) I can see Papi's face, puffy and contorted; the way he inspected his arm and discovered a patch of bloody skin. Was he more of a man now, more of a macho? I wondered then. His actions, he must've thought, should speak for themselves. What did those actions tell me? I remember thinking that I'd never want to be a father, not if you had to do what Papi had done. Not if it meant being willing to fight and risk getting killed.

I should've felt pride and admiration for him. *¡Viva el valiente Papi!* I should've wished to emulate him. *¡Que viva!* Yet the only truth I'd gleaned from his display of heroism was that I would always be a coward.

PIPELINE TO HEAVEN

Dawn. We're on the road again. One full day of driving ahead. "Where did you say we're going?" he asks, half asleep and half jokingly. "To Wichita, Kansas," I repeat. "We'll arrive tomorrow morning."

Today my father is a man who feels worn out and restless. My father is an exhausted body that snores and farts and aches. The first time he's traveled since our exodus; maybe that's why he seems a little frightened. Twenty years of predictability and repetition. And then this bizarre trip.

I detect his discomfort. Time is harder to kill than we thought. We should stop at a McDonald's and have lunch, take a leak, and recoup, prepare for the next stretch of silence. Or we could just play the Memory Game. (That is, after all, my secret plan.) Does he remember how he proved God's existence to me? How he showed me that the almighty *Dios* was on his side?

We were vacationing in Varadero. The movie *Aladino* (a Mexican version) was showing at a local theater; I was dying to see it, enticed by the fantasy of having my own personal genie and a flying carpet. Papi told me he'd take me on one condition: I had to say, *"Si Dios quiere,"* "God willing." I refused to. He warned me: "If you don't say 'God willing' you won't get to see the movie." I continued to say no, just to annoy him, trusting that *Dios* would be too busy to notice Papi's out-of-character attempt. Why did my father wish to make a God-fearing believer out of me, when he wasn't a believer himself? He never prayed, he never went to Mass. Papi wasn't religious at all!

That afternoon we went to the matinee show and found that the film had been canceled. A trio of roving guitar players was entertaining the people who'd been waiting to see *Aladino*. Suddenly, for that multitude, the movie was not as immediate, not as wondrous as the boleros the street musicians played. They were all singing. All happy, except me.

I asked myself questions that were much too profound for a child of ten: Do I deserve the magic of a miracle? Is this supposed to be a message from God? I was dumbfounded, convinced of my father's mysterious pipeline to Heaven.

"Did you know they were going to cancel the movie?" I ask him now, during our trip, but he can't recall the incident. I insist: "Did you have contacts in the theater, people who informed you? Was it just coincidence?" He doesn't know what I'm talking about.

Needing closure, I conclude that the fateful event served my father perfectly. He gave me overwhelming proof of his *poder*. Yes, he had a special power for imposing his will and creating the world—my reality—at his whim. God and my father became the same entity. An omnipotent being with two faces: that of an old man with a white beard, and that of my progenitor; accomplices who incarnated the same stereotype. Both destined to propagate the seed of fear and obedience. Both fated to be machos.

I took communion shortly after that incident, and I was confirmed. But my faith, my devotion, and my prayers were a farce, an unconvincing simulacrum. I didn't deserve the protection of our Father, creator of the universe. In fact, I dared to repudiate him, secretly reproaching him for his *machista* rules. His Heaven was founded on a hierarchy of men, in which women had no voice. This *Padre nuestro* couldn't be a true god, I told myself. Because if he were real, there would be no place for me in Heaven.

Miguelito would eventually burn in Lucifer's cauldrons, I was sure. Surprisingly, though, this prospect didn't scare me. The Devil, in my young imagination, seemed much more plausible and attractive than his counterpart in the Catholic pantheon. I imagined the *Demonio* as a mischievous and fun-loving angel. Only such a creature could protect and welcome a "deviant" male like me.

For the boy I was detested all typical boys' activities. He didn't play baseball and he refused to whistle at the girls—known in Cuban macho circles as *jevitas*, "little broads"—who passed by his house. The boy I should've been, according to my father, would never have spent his afternoons in his room, drawing, writing poems, or just daydreaming. "Boys are supposed to play ball!" Papi would shout, loud enough for the neighbors to hear him.

He wanted a healthy, handsome *niño*. But then I turned out to be something he didn't expect, an oddity with no hope for a dignified future. The boy he'd engendered was an aberration, someone my adolescent father couldn't define or recognize as his own. He looked at me and hated himself because he'd helped create a monster. Worse yet: a *mariquita*.

Yes, I would go to Hell to pay for my crimes. One of these was a mortal sin: not wanting to act like a man, not assuming the authority of my gender. Papi, on the other hand, would probably wander through Purgatory first. Then he'd be tried by a jury of male angels, and by a judge clad in full patriarchal garb; a very masculine and just and normal judge. Amen.

THE LITTLE DEVIL

"Do you want to drive?" I ask him, hoping he'll accept. In Cuba he owned a Chevrolet Belair, a classy, stylish vehicle painted green and silver. (The car was confiscated by the state soon after the revolution.) As a salesman for a clothing company, my father spent a great deal of time on the road, putting miles on his '55 Chevy. Riding with him, one felt safe. Which is not the way I feel now as I watch him grab the wheel reluctantly. He endures the task because he thinks I'm tired, because he has no other choice.

But he does have a choice. He could say no and I'd gladly take over. Driving is not the reason he came along. Not *my* reason, anyway. He's here because we have old debts to settle, some unfinished business.

"Why did you punish me so much when I was a kid, Papi?" I ask him, knowing he'll deny everything. "I didn't," he says through clenched teeth. I insist, "Why did you beat me till the blood ran down my face? Why, *coño!*"

He recoils, defensively, and stares out the window. There's only barren terrain, but looking beyond it is better than looking at me. Better than having to meet my eyes. Slowly, painstakingly, he alleges that I was a *diablito* (a rascal; literally, a "little devil"). He says I was disobedient and had a foul mouth, that I talked back and called him names. I wasn't a good son, he says. He punished me only when it was necessary, when there was no other alternative, and neither more nor less than any typical father.

Bullshit! I cry to myself. There *were* other alternatives! There always are. The hurtful exchange resumes in my head: Tell me the truth, Papi. You didn't feel any pleasure when you punished me? When you gave me every bruise, every mark on my skin, on my soul? No pleasure? Not just the beatings. I'm also referring to those days—entire days—that you forced me to spend naked in bed. One of your favorite punishments: exposing me to the glances of my cousins and the neighbor kids, letting them have fun at my expense as they laughed at my shame and my nudity. Why did you invite them to our house, to come and see me, Papi? Why did you torture me this way? I'll bet I know the answer. By doing this, you castigated me for my "effeminate" manners, right? So that I'd get on a "straight" path (your words: *entrar en camino*). At the same time you proved to the observers—to the world—that I had the proper anatomy, big *cojones* like yours; that I, your *machito,* was a "normal" boy.

It is true that I was an unreachable child, that I was reluctant to participate in my father's life. I wouldn't share his joys and daily triumphs. I wouldn't commiserate with him about his burdens. My attitude and my voice and my conduct didn't fit within the molds Papi had envisioned for me. I rejected him passionately. We were dangerous strangers to each other. Enemies. Yet my "mischiefs"—such small crimes!—did not deserve the pain my father caused me.

You might as well admit it, Papi. You took a bizarre kind of pleasure in bending my will, in stripping me of my dignity, in crushing me. Admit it.

DAYS OF AQUARIUS

I play a tape I recorded especially for him. It's a compilation of old songs from scratchy records, the greatest hits of Orquesta Aragón, Beny Moré, Daniel Santos. The music of his adolescence that revives him and propels him. I hear him hum, then sing. He steps on it, commanding the truck like a pro. And it pleases me to watch him take us through the sleepy villages of New Mexico.

This sky is the most intense blue I've ever seen. (Or was my father's Cuban sky more blue and more intense?) A vast and arid landscape appears; it overpowers us. Desert, rocks, hills of a dusty yellow, caves that used to be someone's refuge.

"We're so far, Miguel," I hear him murmur. "Far from where?" I ask. His response: "From everything."

Far from the world as he knew it. Days of Aquarius, a trip with no return in 1969. We were supposed to have arrived in paradise, but Eden was a sad, desolate planet. The empty sidewalks, the endless freeways. Where did one town end and another begin? We couldn't tell. They all merged into one long, indistinguishable country.

The great northern land would never feel like home. My father was to live longing to return. The younger ones—my brother and I—would be easy converts, slipping with little effort into this new, alien culture. (Or so we thought.) Papi would remain anchored in Cuban soil, oblivious to the language and customs and ideas pulsating around him. He'd learn to speak English unwillingly. He'd fade in and out of our present, ill at ease, like a self-conscious shadow. And I, I would reap the fruit of his effacement.

I saw him cry for the first time after our arrival in Los Angeles. My image of the impassive macho was banished temporarily and that of a weak, vulnerable being emerged. He'd cry about anything: a word, a gesture, a song. His siblings' letters made him weep profusely. He got home every day bedraggled and greasy after assembling thousands of parts at the *factoría*. Papi began to look sickly, wilted.

Few chores made him happier than grocery shopping. Such joy to have enough money to buy steaks, all the rice and beans you want, the fancy sauces, coffee, cheese, and rich desserts. No rationing. No shortages. A blissful abundance of every imaginable product. He'd come home from the market loaded up with American goodies for his family: cottage cheese with pineapple, my mother's weakness; ham, a mythical meat; soda crackers, one box per person; glazed doughnuts, a delicious gringo pastry; Coca-Cola, a sweet, purifying potion; and cornflakes (can't grow up to be a true American without them).

We lived in a spacious, two-bedroom apartment, and my father had managed to buy an almost-new car; it was a cream-colored Impala convertible. There is a photo from those days that shows him in the driver's seat, proudly displaying his machine. Things were finally working out. His sons went to school in Hawthorne, the white people's area, and both he and their mother had jobs. Some day they'd buy a house and he'd have his own business. No more factory work for Gladys. No more greasy parts for Elías.

The photo of him at the hospital vividly depicts his next phase. Papi suffered an accident at work, hurt his back—a pinched disc—and had to stay at home, prostrate, for weeks. Long days stuck in a solitary bed while my mother went off to her *factoría*. He must've done a lot of thinking in those days, a lot of staring at the walls, or at the carpet with its revolting olive color. He must've cursed his decision to come to this city of fenced-in lawns and vacant boulevards.

The accident ordeal left him limping, but a richer man, with a lawyer. He sued the company and got some money (a measly sum) out of it. Well-deserved compensation, he probably thought.

By now he'd realized that we weren't going back to Cuba. His children didn't long for his tropical haven, nor did they share his wrenching nostalgia. This was the phase of resignation; our roots had been permanently severed. But he wouldn't give up his dream of *el regreso* without a fight. Resentful, thriving on his uprootedness, he unleashed his wrath against us. A maniac was set loose in our house with his fist in the air. *"¡Castigo!"* he shouted. He resolved to punish the weaklings like my mother and the unruly dissidents like me. *"¡Castigo!"* Punishment for those who dare forget where we came from!

I was already in my late teens and I had stopped fearing his wrath. He couldn't hurt me anymore; I felt strong enough to fight him. This was a time when the desire for vengeance consumed me. I dreamed of torturing and killing him. I begged my mother to divorce him. At the slightest sign of abuse, I'd start slamming doors and screaming loud enough for the neighbors to hear me: "Why did you have a family, *coño*?! So you could mistreat us?" I'd head him off at the pass with a fit of my own. An eye for an eye and a scream for a scream. *¡Coño!*

I started wearing makeup and dying my hair. I'd come home from school barefoot, carrying flowers, wearing colorful necklaces of beads and seashells. I'd be gone for days, staying with friends, while he waited for me at home, worried and ashamed and raging. His son was a hippie! It felt great to defy him. A disgusting *maricón*! It was a pleasure to be different from him.

The young man I turned into wasn't solely the by-product of a macho upbringing; I'm quite aware of that. My actions—and my thoughts and my beliefs and my desires—were not just a result of my rejection of Papi. That would be too simple and deterministic. Yet I surprised myself, during my phases of most intense rebellion, thinking: Fuck you, Elías. *¡Jódete!* I'll show you!

CALIFORNIA DREAMING

He grabs the map and scrutinizes it. "We're doing okay, don't worry," I reassure him. "We're not lost. This is the only way to Kansas." He makes a face like a spoiled, impatient kid. "I'm sick and tired of this truck," he whines. So I suggest we take a long break from driving and have a picnic.

We stop at a roadside park. The span of grass before us is dry and unappealing, but there are tables with benches and some trees. We could sit in silence, observe the other travelers. Or perhaps we could just talk. Is he game?

Papi listens distractedly while I describe one of my recurring dreams. Its meaning is blatantly evident: I'm always a lost child. I find myself in the midst of an unfamiliar scene, a city, a desert, or often a tunnel through which a train runs swiftly. There are people around me, but I feel alone. My parents aren't with me. They've abandoned me. I run and run, though I don't know where I'm going.

"I never dream," he says, crossly, before I have a chance to interpret my nightmare.

"Everybody has dreams," I declare, "but some people forget them." He adds: "I must be one of those cases. When I wake up, all I can think about are real things."

The intangible world of the subconscious—with its frightening, uncontrollable scenarios—is of no import to him. (Or does he negate his nightmares in order not to face what they show him?) No. Real men don't indulge in dreams and illusions.

Once I asked him to go to the cemetery with me. I thought we could put flowers on his mother's grave. Josefina, my paternal grandmother, was the first of our family to die in the United States. Even if only for that reason we should do something in her honor, I thought, a small ritual like lighting a candle or visiting her grave some Sunday.

"I won't do anything like that," he said. "Why not?" I asked. "Because," he replied, "I did everything I could for my mother when she was alive. When it counted."

For Papi, Josefina had ceased to exist completely. There was nothing tangible about her, nothing that needed tending to. Because his world exists—or is worthy of existence—only when he can touch it, shape it, or destroy it. Meanings could never be found here, in the mind, or in one's heart. There is no room for anything *real* in there.

And yet my telling of the dream has made Papi introspective. How could it not? He turns to me and asks, "Do you regret that we left Cuba?" I believe what he really wants to ask me is: Do you regret that I got you out of Cuba? He needs to know that all the good he's done for me—our exodus, this trip to Wichita—is solid and lasting.

Yes, getting us out of Cuba was a big job. Yes, his good deeds have been considered; the great, unselfish acts are all accounted for. I should tell him that I'm grateful for his efforts and his sacrifices. But I won't, can't bring myself to say a simple *gracias*. Instead, I respond: "No, I don't regret having left."

OVER THE RAINBOW

So much rolling through flat, unwelcoming places. Truck stops with names like "Eats" and "Restaurant" where the best dish is soggy, bland meatloaf and the rest rooms are raunchy. Barren towns like Barstow, California; Kingman, Arizona; Gallup and Tucumcari, New Mexico; Liberal, Kansas. So much driving on forsaken routes to arrive here, in Mid-America. A brand-new exile; only, this one is mine. Miguel alone will invent it.

I resist the temptation to sing "Over the Rainbow." It is an easy-to-resist temptation because Wichita looks nothing like Dorothy's Emerald City. Vast wheat fields extend from the outskirts of this urban enclave that aspires to be a metropolis. We drive along its main artery, Kellogg Street, a nondescript strip where a handful of typical establishments thrives: hamburger chains, hotels, some office buildings.

I resist the temptation to tell my father, "Papi, I don't think we're in Cuba anymore." An enormous truth: *No estamos en Cuba*. Yet there are parallels between the myth of Oz and the myth of our exodus. We, too, were brought here by a tornado. Many of us left behind an Auntie Em. Some of us came here not knowing how or why.

Fifteen years after our flight from communism, my father and I are standing in an empty house where I will be living. Papi seems impressed. "What luxury!" he exclaims. My new home belongs to a professor on sabbatical and is located in Eastborough, an affluent community. (The police will stop me several times to ask me what I'm doing there and where I'm from.) The whole area is a welcome oasis in the Kansas flatness: towering trees, flowers, birds, ponds. Locus Amenus that has nothing to do with the realities I'll have to face Monday, at the university.

But academia belongs in a future unbeknownst to me today. At the moment of this present, my father and I are unloading the truck. He came along in case I needed a hand, so he could help soften the blow of separation, my so-called uprootedness from family and friends. This is his responsibility; he's fulfilling his role of provider. I observe him taking my books out of boxes. Together we install the old stereo, assemble the shelves, and build all my domestic bridges.

Our voyage has ended. Whatever wounds didn't get healed will remain open, bleeding. Did we manage to suture any of them? I tell myself that the journey has been helpful. I'll have to remember it and narrate it some day. Will there be, in my story, a magical yellow brick road and a loving, wise wizard to save us from our worst fears? I wonder. Beyond the rainbow, will there rise an emerald-green enchanted castle? Will the mischievous, friendly munchkins and the benevolent Witch of the North help us find our way?

My optimistic heart wills the Wizard of Oz to exist. I ask the powerful magician to give my father the courage to admit his mistakes, to talk about the damage he did to his family. (He'll be rewarded for this with unconditional love.) For me, the Wiz will concoct the wisdom of oblivion, the power to forgive and forget.

I must forgive him. Love him? He couldn't connect with me, see the world through my eyes. What models were available to a young, uneducated Cuban male in 1954? What could be expected of him? He inherited a mentality founded on absolute patriarchal rule, a legacy of pernicious taboos and absurd notions. To name just a few: masturbation causes stupidity; a man's "milk" (his semen) floods his brain when he doesn't fuck regularly; a healthy, normal penis is a *pinga* with a big head and plenty of foreskin; the man is the boss in his home; women are weak; homosexuality is a vice and a sickness; homosexuals are inferior human beings.

Papi, too, was a victim. He, too, had to endure humiliation, beatings, undeserved suffering. His father was a Spanish patriarch who ran his house with an iron fist. Like father, like son. Or, as we say in Spanish, *de tal palo, tal astilla*—"from such a stick, such a sliver." Until I became the sliver and the stick of machismo was crushed. Torn into pieces.

I will never emulate my father. And yet without him, Miguel wouldn't be who he is. The irony doesn't escape me; I wouldn't be obsessed with the ancestral curse of machismo, with the idea of what it means to be or not to be a man. Perhaps I should thank my father also for this: His attitude and his mentality have served me as important lessons. It's as though he's been saying, "Look at me, son, observe my actions carefully. Never be the type of man I've been."

My father will always incarnate machismo, while I will always try to deconstruct the macho archetype. (Yes, even as I listen to Mozart's rewriting of the Don Juan myth.) I'll seek new ways of defining my identity; I'll let alterity "corrupt" me. And my father will always reject those who aren't like him. He'll awaken each morning and know himself to be a true *cubano,* 100 percent *hombre.* As he opens his eyes, he won't remember his dreams.

PAPI'S SHOES

He'll be leaving tomorrow on an early flight. He's not looking forward to taking a plane, he says. Proudly, my father informs me that his painting and his responsibilities await him. Soon he'll be back in his world: Mami's cooking and the *café criollo* that he drinks three times a day; his car, in need of repairs; his grocery shopping at the Cuban market; the Mexican *telenovelas;* the old records, songs he still listens to but never sings.

I will write several books (one of them a disguised version of our past) while living in the Emerald City. I'll spend my time—the future that is

now upon me—writing, reading, teaching. While my father still struggles
to survive in a foreign country.

I'm not sure what I expected to accomplish during this trip. One fact
has become absolutely clear: I had never, until now, tried to walk in my
father's shoes. Not those of the oppressor, nor the ones worn by the torturer. Not the glamorous slippers whose heels you can click together to
transport you. But the shoes of a man who left the world he knew—with
a one-way ticket—for the sake of his children. A man who was willing to
start over at thirty-five, having no marketable profession and no English
skills, so that I would be free. So that I would one day have the freedom
to take this job in Kansas and leave my family behind.

Those shoes don't fit me, yet I must wear them. They are invisible but
tangible: the shoes of an immigrant. I'll never be able to justify the way
Papi tainted my childhood, but I can cease to see him through the gaze of
a hurt and frightened child. I must stop thriving on that pain, on that hatred. Only in a black-and-white world can Papi be my eternal enemy. In
the multilayered space of our relationship, nothing is cut and dried. Nothing simple. Only in a one-dimensional universe can I avenge myself, destroy my tormentor.

I remember how tall he used to be; his hair perfectly parted on the left
and his thin mustache à la Clark Gable. I remember his strength, his powerful voice when he called me. A young and handsome father, a powerful
and abusive father remains there in the bruised corners of my heart. Like
a thorn. An image now juxtaposed to the one of a tired old man at a Mid-
western airport.

This other father is giving and defenseless; he has tried, in his own way,
to undo the wrongs. He's a parent who won't threaten me or hit me, who
doesn't want to mold me. This is a father who remembers, even though
he denies everything. Forgetting is not easy for him, either. And he
doesn't even have the comfort of words. Words to name the love between
a father and a son. Words that by naming it could make this emotion a reality.

Two different fathers have taken over the space of my memories. One
is virile and manly and is still determined to shape me in his likeness. The
other one is learning to express his regrets. This new, kinder image is
fragile. Maybe it has arrived too late?

We give each other an uneasy hug at Midcontinent Airport. "Take care of yourself, *mi hijo!*" he whispers, and starts moving clumsily down the jetway. Will he turn around to see me one last time? I have something to tell him, something I forgot to say. He's almost gone. Can he still hear me? "*¡Gracias!*" I yell seconds before he disappears.

GUATEMALAN
MACHO
ORATORY

Bleu Castañeda

OMAR S. CASTAÑEDA was born in Guatemala and moved to the United States at age three and grew up in the Midwest. His books of fiction include the novels <u>Cunuman, Among the Volcanoes</u> and <u>Abuela's Weave,</u> a children's book. His book of short stories, <u>Remembering to Say Mouth or Face,</u> received the 1993 Charles H. and N. Mildred Nilon Excellence in Minority Fiction Award from The Fiction Collective and the University of Colorado. He teaches literature at Western Washington University in Bellingham, Washington.

Hermosa encuentra la vida
quien la consruye hermosa.
—Otto René Castillo

MACHISMO IS COMPLEX and multifaceted and, too often in Anglo-American interpretations, reduced to self-aggrandizing male bravado that flirts with physical harm to be sexual, like some rutting for the right to pass on genes. *Pues,* there is another machismo that is quite different.

This is not to say that there is a sense of machismo in common parlance that should be supported, or ignored. When I was growing up, I perceived of it in simplistic ways. I saw the "dress" of it and the machismo of simple men (those for whom it might be said maturity was desirable only as a last resort). In other words, I saw the strut of men, the "bad boy" image, as means and end together. Then as now, there is no lack of "grown" men who perpetuate this belief because they are too isolated from cause to find machismo's true place, too dim-witted to go beyond it, or too lost in some way that makes them slaves to surfaces. And there is no lack of "grown" women who are also disempowered, isolated, or dim-witted, and who foolishly prefer these superficial depictions. To complain about this machismo is easy, though not discriminating if this is all one conceives of as machismo.

I went through the macho stuff that is superficial and abhorrent (sexism, male-to-male competition, violence, swagger over the most trivial things, etc.) in the way that nonadults everywhere act out simplistic visions—and thus make a mockery—of their culture's "adulthood." And every culture has its men, as well as its women, who will never grow up, but will continue in adolescent visions of the roles optioned by their society.

In my own life, I have been called macho for a variety of reasons, but the most interesting to me is what vaguely has been called a "certainty of expression," a "confidence in speaking," a "loudness in voice and in presence." I have been "accused" of being macho by many Anglo-Americans in a variety of relationships to me, including students, colleagues, friends, and lovers. The usual charge associated with being "macho" is that I am arrogant and full of self-interest, opinionated and unwilling to listen to others. How odd, then, to believe that I am just the opposite (except opinionated; *that,* I am).

I have seen that my ways of speaking and of acting, labeled macho, are not simply my own. My brothers, father, and even my mother and sister can carry themselves in similar ways. I have relatives and friends in Guatemala who act similarly. This macho attitude, by virtue of being spread throughout my family and non-family Guatemalans, seems more of a cultural mode than a personal one. Although more easily applied to men, machismo is not limited to men. If machismo is attitude, then women can have it. Indeed, I know several macho women, family and otherwise. Perhaps because men historically have had more freedom to express themselves and to move about, the attitude can be more readily visible in males. Perhaps, too, machismo in women is identical to that of men, but it is merely prejudicially labeled something else (e.g., *bitch, nag, castrator,* or other offensive terms).

> "The fact that those in power label others negatively seems common enough that it should never surprise us, only challenge us."
> —Cassandra Mateo

It has taken me years to understand the positive side of macho discourse, given the fact that I was raised in the USA. This country is dominated by speaking styles that have a distaste and rejection of many Latino modes of speaking. I know that it sometimes rejects my Guatemalan, familiocentric style of speech. In the end, I am left feeling compromised in nearly every interaction. My impulse is to speak with fervor, loudly, state things clearly and without hesitation, expecting a vigorous exchange of ideas that has no winners or losers but solutions to problems communally obtained. Often, I speak energetically and am misunderstood or "pinned" with incorrect motivations. There are times I have forgotten to keep a taut leash on my way of speaking and launch into an impassioned discussion of fictive techniques, or the politics of techniques and of publishing, and that one has to write as if driven by a fever, forgetting fame and fortune, and dive deeply into the fathomless pool of one's soul to write with *duende* . . . and so on. There are students who think I'm intimidating, frightening because of my "energy." I often imagine students in this 84 percent Anglo-American university avoiding me because they think I am not "nurturing"—I tell myself to go about with a muzzle, so as not to turn some student to ash. Turn some student to ash. In actuality, there *are* students with their own internal fires, Anglo-American and otherwise. And thank goodness it rains often in the Northwest, we may think. What a horror: the snap and crackle of tumbleweed students set afire.

Still, this way of speaking is not something I am always aware of doing. In other words, there are many times when I believe to my bones that I am holding back, acting timid and effaced (as in this essay), yet discover that I am perceived as in "macho oratory." It must be cultural. There is, of course, a macho discourse that is the equivalent to "I'm too sexy for my clothes," with its bright spotlight on an elevated self. True macho oratory, however, may seem similar, yet it is a bravado that appeals to something "transcendent," through the individual as a conduit, and thus perhaps is misunderstood as focused on that individual. It may be that, in the case of Guatemala, this macho oratory has several histories and many manifestations.

My own family has two roots: My maternal side is middle-class, urban Guatemalan; my paternal side is lower-class, rural Guatemalan. Both sides are Ladino. My mother's family is generally educated and privileged; the sprawl of kin covers territories in Flores, Petén, and Guatemala City, where my closest family lives. My father's side of the family is mostly situated in Zacapa and Chiquimula, particularly in the isolated villages of San Vicente and Cabañas. This is the Guatemala that Paul Theroux thought of as not worth a minute of any visitor's time. It is an area not often visited by tourists, who usually seek the Maya or the *garifano*. It is also an area with a fair number of light-skinned, brown-haired people, like me. *Canches,* as they say in Guatemala; *güeros,* in Mexico. It is known for pistol-carrying, hard-drinking, incessantly joking "frontiersmen." And for "aggressive" women. Just into Zacapa on the highway to the coast, one begins to see Castañedas everywhere. My paternal family names—Castañeda, Paz, Calderón—spread out through the hotlands and scrubby hills between the highway and Honduras. Though I am closest to my maternal family, I think I have more traits of my paternal family.

My paternal grandfather was a man I knew only after he had debilitating strokes. I have seen pictures of him when he went around with bandoliers and pistols. He was known for being a very macho man. But it was the surface kind of machismo: The stories about him talk of violent exchanges; fierce individualism in farming inhospitable lands; snatching women as they washed clothes in the river; little talk—lots of physical stuff. This is not mostly positive commentary. One such snatched woman was my grandmother, Sara. She was taken at the age of fourteen. Sara gave birth to my father at fifteen years of age. My grandmother was the third or fourth of Ezikiel's "wives" brought out to the stand of huts on a bend of the San Vicente River. There, about half an hour by horse from the village of San Vicente, the huts are made of cornstalks lashed together and topped by palm-leaf roofs. San Vicente is a village above a river valley. Running water and electricity came very late, and not at all to my grandfather's house as of three years ago (now used by my uncles and aunts). My grandfather, like most men of frontier fortitude and of that ilk of machismo, rarely struggled for anything but self-interest, or for survival as far removed from the company of others as possible.

My grandmother left San Vicente under cover of night with my father and aunt in hand. They walked the river's edge for miles, up to meet relatives with horses, and then rode for hours to the road, where they took a bus into the capital, some ten hours away back then.

My father grew up in the capital and later went to school in Costa Rica. During the brief taste of democracy in Guatemalan history, in the late 1940s until the 1954 CIA-backed installation of military rule, my father studied in the USA under a scholarship. When he finished his Ph.D. in philosophy he and the family returned to Guatemala, with the intent of staying, in the fall of 1954, days before I was born. Within three years, my father was offered a job in Michigan and the whole family migrated. It wasn't for another eight years that we became U.S. citizens.

Since then, I have grown up in Anglo-American neighborhoods, becoming *agringado*, seemingly losing everything Guatemalan, even what color my flesh had. No doubt this makes my oratory seem displaced and thus more individual rather than cultural, since it comes from a body that strikes so many as not Guatemalan. But the oratory has remained. It seems that much of one's culture remains no matter how far away one drifts. Thus, recovery is an act of building histories and of weaving possible influences, and an act of assertion.

In Guatemala, people perform *actos,* highly oratorical presentations for any number of occasions, secular and religious. During Festival Days of Santiago Atitlán, as with festival days in virtually all Guatemalan communities, different leaders and young adults will give speeches full of gesture and passion, which, if taken straight to heart, would incite to noble action. I'm convinced that some of the most impassioned speakers in the world are Guatemalans. What a sight: a young man or woman standing up high on some wooden stage planked together, laced with wire, creaking, itself a kind of miracle of stability under heavy traffic and bric-a-brac construction techniques. Chins lifted, chests thrust out, these young speakers rail against complacency, raise a great sermon for community, honor, *orgullo del pueblo.* In true Guatemalan fashion, these macho orators cleave the air with an arm as if to machete through space the true path of dignity and hope. Below them, next to no one will seem to listen. Festival days bring a flood of people, jamming the narrow streets, overcrowding the open spaces. Hawkers of cheap fair rides and carnival entertainments nearly, almost, drown out the impassioned *acto.* Children scrabble about noisily. *Pues,* it hardly matters. Only a fool would think that the performance was unimportant to the community, or that there wasn't another kind of listening going on.

Speakers say what they feel needs to be said as if everyone on the planet were listening, finish, then return to nonoratory with perfect ease. *Ladino* events also have their *actos.* In all spheres, the speakers speak, yet those within earshot don't have to respond. The oratory is an invitation to join in some higher purpose than just passing time or earning one's keep. That higher purpose, or transcendence, can be religious fervor, political action, striving for intellectual excellence, discipline for worthy goals, etc. The individual uses a strong voice not for self-glorification, but as invocation of some ideal.

The decade of the 1980s was one of contemporary Guatemala's worst sieges of terror as the military tortured, murdered, and "disappeared" the populace with impunity. My own family, as did virtually every

Guatemalan family, lost members to the brutalities. Despite the facade of civilian presidents in recent years, the demon of human rights abuses has remained in power and waits to come bounding into full view from its catacombed citadel like some hound of the anti-Christ. For instance, General Rios Montt, a past president responsible for numerous mass assassinations of men, women, and children, for dictatorial overthrow of the constitution, for turning civil patrols into agencies of torture, for developing secret hit squads . . . in short, a man who should be imprisoned for life—or worse!—in any true democracy for his unspeakable horrors against humanity is now, in March 1995, the president of Congress. He will, no doubt, do anything imaginable to be president of Guatemala in the next election despite a constitutional ban.

It is extremely common to see *ladino* and indigenous men (and some women) sloppily drunk to ease for just a few hours the madness that daily emasculates them and butchers their families. I have seen many a man rip open his shirt and cry out against the military—screaming that he has had enough and that if the soldiers don't come right this minute to kill him, that he will hunt the soldiers down like the beasts that they are; he declares that he is a guerrilla and that the time has come to stand and fight for justice like a man. Bystanders and friends make ambivalent attempts to hush such drunken bombast: Such outcries mean certain death, yet the poor man's bravado voices everyone's sentiment, everyone's need. That suicidal machismo is not arrogant self-proclamation, but oratory that lifts everyone out of oppression for a moment and places them on a higher moral plane, full of strong purpose, hope, and the possibility of good winning out. It shouts what it knows is right and lets those around join in or not, depending upon their own impulses. *Pues,* in Guatemala such men *would* be found murdered and, of course, there would be no suspects and no investigation. This cultural heritage of oppression and lurking violence by "authorities" is very foreign to most Anglo-Americans. Kidnapped and "disappeared" people in this country are sought through television, milk cartons, direct-mail coupons. In Guatemala, the government actively—often murderously—represses information about the tens of thousands of *desaparecidos* since the 1954 invasion.

I have spent a great deal of time in Santiago Atitlán and Cerro de Oro, traditional lands of the Tzutujil Maya. As should be expected, these neighboring places are very distinct. They tease each other with names: *tejoy ch'oy* and *tejoy cumatz* ("rat eaters" and "snake eaters"). The Atitecos think those from Cerro are yokels; those from Cerro think the Atitecos jaded urbanites. Most Anglo-Americans would think both equally "colorful," "exotic," the "real" Guatemala because of a "primitiveness," and other such condescensions. Many might also think that the Tzutujil are "innocent."

Such simplistic labeling can arise from misidentifying surface features, from taking isolated behavior for whole cultural codes, from simple racism, or from other sources.

The Tzutujil have a certain fame for being tough fighters, strong defenders of their traditions, virile, attractive, and very spiritual. Of the three Maya groups dominating the highland region of pre-Columbian power, including the ruling Quiché and competing Cakchiquel, the Tzutujil were always the smallest in number and at the bottom of the hierarchy; however, they were not meek or docile tribute payers, nor collaborators with the invading Spanish, but fiercely independent, though always militarily restrained. In pre-Columbian times, this meant an uneasy division of Lake Atitlán, with the Cakchiquel taking the north side and outward, and the Tzutujil taking the south under the shadows of two powerful volcanoes, Volcán Tolimán and Volcán Atitlán. South of these giants lie the coastal plains, with their vast plantations and intolerable working conditions. Perhaps it is the martial fame of the Tzutujil that brought more brutal military acts in contemporary times, purported guerrilla bases in the upper reaches of the volcanoes and deliberate difficulty for terrestrial access to the southern shore, where rich Ladinos own chalets. Perhaps it was the spiritual fame of the Tzutujil that made Santiago one of the most important places of religious activity (with numerous thriving *cofradías*), and the home of Guatemala's most powerful idol, Maximón. To this day, healers from all regions of Guatemala make pilgrimages to this "trickster" deity.

One can enter this important *cofradía* quite easily. *Pues,* since the military base was removed from Santiago after the December 2, 1990, massacre, tourism to the town has increased and it is virtually impossible to enter Santiago without someone offering to take you to Maximón. It is usual to see many foreigners taking photos and sitting around as ardent *costumbres* (prayer and ritual) take place. Initially, Anglo-Americans can experience discomfort for violating what to them is a very private and sacred event. A common reinterpretation under Anglo-American codes of meaning, then, is that the rituals are "touristy" or faked. Before them, a healer gives a long prayer on behalf of a supplicant, who kneels silently before the idol for as long as two hours. Maximón stands in the center of a small room, incense-filled, candle-strewn, the eaves festooned with cut paper and fruits.

Within the *cofradía*'s syncretism of ancient and new beliefs, it would not be odd for the *telenel* or *alcalde* (two *cofradía* "priests") to get up noisily and shout over the heads of the people in ritual as if they were engaged in nothing more than everyday conversation. Moreover, the *Aj kun,* a healer and intermediary between supplicant and idol, continues with his ardent prayer without batting an eye as mundane matters are shouted across the room: invitations to foreigners to sit, to take photos, to drink *cuxa;* or raucous chatter to family members. The *Aj kun* gestures broadly, recites loudly, pleads with great devotion as censers fume, offerings are laid out.

The oratory is not disturbed, really; the conviction and higher intent not compromised by the lack of attentiveness around the ritual. Or by the misinterpretations.

It is easy to see inflamed speech taking place during festivals, ceremonies, or under political urgencies. Yet the underlying cultural code for this way of speaking manifests itself in daily conversations with enough frequency that Anglo-Americans often believe Latinos are aggressive, arrogant, or blustering speakers. Contrast this macho oratory with what is more common in Anglo-American speech, the kind that happens between friends, colleagues, or between teachers and students. In this mode, the speaker is purported to be "nurturing," "diplomatic," "warm," "self-effacing," "not arrogant."

From a more macho perspective—my Guatemalan macho perspective—this mode of talking is actually the opposite of all those descriptions and, finally, just plain insulting and *aggressively* intrusive. Never mind the intangible issue of being "real" by saying exactly what one means. More bothersome is the fact that a speaker who dances around an issue or will not speak frankly is a speaker who believes in the frailty of the listener, the inability of the listener to deal with truth, or, worse, believes that he or she knows the psychology of the listener and is in a position to manipulate responses. Sometimes this "nurturing" style is nothing more than fear, but that's another issue. Underlying the nonfearful speaking style is the belief that the speaker has a right or a duty to either take care of the listener's emotional health or to manipulate the listener's responses. *Pues,* from a macho oratory perspective, this is the height of arrogance and presumption. I shot pool with a colleague—once!—and he spoke very diplomatically. In his "kindness" he complimented me on virtually every shot I made and exclaimed how impossible the shots were that I missed. This insulted my skill by his inability to distinguish good shots from bad shots; it would have been a much worse insult had he been a better shot than me. He thus placed all my made shots on equal footing, effectively saying that I was lucky all the way around since difficult and easy shots were all the same. He also insulted me by placing me in a "needy" situation that he felt compelled to nurture. Nurturing is fine, I suppose, if a person asks for it. For the most part, however, the Anglo-American speaking style is *arrogant,* by psychoanalyzing the listener, and it is *aggressively intrusive,* by attempting to manipulate the listener.

In contrast, macho oratory lays out belief in full view, with a sweep of the hand, perhaps, as if to say, "There I am, right or wrong, and now it is your turn." This bravado assumes the listener as an equal, able to hear anything and able to respond freely. Macho oratory says, "I take my right to speak and assume your power and right to do the same." Furthermore, it says, "I will not insult you by pretending I can manipulate you."

Anglo-American discourse can seem, as a consequence, to value the material world above the transcendent, even as it pretends human kindness. In fact, it seems by its manipulations and contrivances and Machiavellian circumlocutions to place the material world of personal success at the highest value. Macho oratory, on the other hand, calls people to act in a more noble way, more bravely against injustices, more disciplined in seeking goals, reaching for moral strength, striving for excellence, aspiring to greatness. Its "aggression," if it is to have any, is against the status quo that belittles people and makes them ashamed of strong will and presence; in comparison, Anglo-American discourse seeks to maintain the status quo by shaming noncomplacent individuality and making difference of opinion an egotism or aggression. Such shame can only result in more easily controlled people.

I believe "entering the word"—using language to construct reality and to praise transcendence—has developed as the single most powerful trope of Guatemala. The roots of this come from *Pop Wuj,* through the arabesques within the heritage of invading Christian Spaniards, and extend to the *mestizo/ladino* labyrinth of contemporary political upheaval. *Pop Wuj* (a.k.a. *Popol Vuh*), the K'iche Maya cosmology, is an elaborately plotted journey from the initial "speaking into existence" of the deities, to the correct use of language to honor the gods in the proper way, to a disguised cosmology for a non-Maya audience. The major task throughout the text is to have individuals speak as individuals in their particular "calling" on behalf of community and with respect to the realm of the divine. Like ornate lines in arabesque "decorations," language use in *Pop Wuj* is simultaneously overwrought on the surface, as if convolution is itself a form of praise, and, on a deeper level, plain-speaking praise for a transcendent order. In traditional arabesques, the intricate calligraphy is basic and direct adoration for Allah—sometimes no more than "Praise be to Allah"—yet it can be so entwined that it can seem no language at all. The complexity in Arab calligraphy is bold, highly ornate praise that might seem to call attention to the individual, but the message is from an effaced self about the divine. Its "audaciousness," as defined by flair or the baroque, invites others to efface themselves before the divine. The Arab influence is everywhere in Spanish heritage, but perhaps most visible in the literary traditions of Latin America. The "good" or "true" machismo, in the form of speaking, has its analog of both these cultural currents.

In this scheme, individuals speak with passion and dynamism in a way that places them center stage. Yet they speak of issues and with an embraciveness that includes everyone around them. An audience may or may not listen (*escuchar* more than *entender*) to the individual. The oratory is an invitation to join, not an attempted manipulation of response. As well, there is no need to respond if one is of a like mind with the speaker: The sea of language, of oratory, washes over the audience and enters its pores, drenches guts and souls, plays and replays high principle, community good, revitalizes, and, at worst, ritualizes moral vision in oratory performance. At best, this kind of macho speaking reminds one or two in the audience—those who heard a bit more this time, because it struck closer to home—that they *want* to lift up out of everyday living, out of complacency, out of the pressures of subsistence to find that plane of moral imperatives—and *act!* If there is any challenge in macho discourse, it is this challenge to resist weakness of will and ruinous humility, that which is more low esteem than humbleness.

When Guatemalans encounter this "good" machismo, the listener and speaker are both ennobled. There is sometimes a curious posture or gesture when a person acknowledges another's "true" machismo. I have seen it in men and women in my family. It involves a slight stiffening of the upper body—a similar yet smaller bracing than that of flamenco dancers—perhaps a cocking of the head, an angling, with chin lifted minutely, and one of the hands moving to the chest while cupped stiffly. This gesture is part of complimenting another, but in such a way as to bring the good of the other into the body of the one making the compliment. The hand by the chest is half fist, half cupped hand: the fist as a sign of strength, the cupped hand as holding the other's strength and bringing it inward. When speaking about or encountering the "bad" machismo, the body is not held up nor empathic with the "other," but mocking, perhaps, or tight with disgust.

I have had people say that I "come on too strong" or "intimidate" by the way I speak. These kinds of descriptions often come from Anglo-Americans with very different patterns of speech. For instance, a friend was mortified by the "loud, aggressive, attacking" conversations within my family. In her family, people spoke quietly, with gestures close to the body, and they never contradicted anyone, no matter how patently wrong. Indeed, it seemed that the more wrong someone was, the less likely a "correction" would be made. To do so was a great insult. My friend and I could not have come from more divergent cultural modes of expression. To her, our family conversations were extraordinarily macho.

In my familiocentric culture, at least, conversations are more or less empty unless addressing some larger issue. Perhaps it was due to my father's philosophical training, which turned every "please pass the salt" into a quasi-humorous discussion about cause and effect, the nature of propositions, claims to authority, the right to civil disobedience, or other abstractions. Of course, there is value in social chitchat, if nothing else to establish or reaffirm relationships, but basically our family considered this a *pérdida de tiempo*. One brother, the most macho of us, can seem nearly preverbal, he is so disinterested in social chitchat, or "polite and nurturing" talk. Unless there is discussion of larger issues—moral, social, intellectual, or political—there is only the possibility of condescension because of the mind-reading "politeness" that purely social interactions inevitably involve. To a certain extent, chitchat that reaffirms relationships can be another condescension, since it may be one person controlling the other by "knowing" appropriate patterns and/or assuming the emotional need for the reaffirmation. In other words, "polite" speakers usually think that the listener is needy or frail in some way. Macho speaking assumes the listener is as strong and aware as the speaker, perhaps more. It assumes that nothing the speaker says will be insurmountable to the listener and that straightforwardness is the highest compliment to a centered will. By saying things directly—indeed, *con machismo*—you signal your strong will and presence, and your very flair (that hand stuff that Latinos do) points to the assumed strong will and presence of the audience. If no one returns the macho oratory, the original speech is left for all to savor. If it is returned, then a joyful discussion can ensue. The more continuous the macho exchanges, the more "real" and satisfying the communication. I have to laugh to recall my friend's reactions to such dialogues. Her first encounter made her think the family was about to come to blows. Silence, noncommunication, high deference . . . these are the signs of distrust.

In contemporary, strife-ridden Guatemala, machismo has as one important, transcendent plane visions of justice and social duty. This sense of social justice easily translates to these united states called America, with its patterns of social discrimination and paternalistic or empirialistic foreign policies. Even so, this country acts and feels at ease. With its long history of military and capitalist abuses, and rewritten histories, Guatemala cannot pretend as the USA can that there is a separation between the personal and the public. Individuals are reminded every day of how individual acts have political repercussions. Most important, how individual *inaction* can have grave political consequences. Anglo-Americans, by contrast, usually resist the joining of the two and go to elaborate means to blind themselves with absurd notions like the separation of the individual and the political, church and state, politics and art, personal responsibility and social construction. Perhaps it is the affluence and the distance from personal strife that allows such complacencies. It is no wonder that the Anglo-American speaking style is so passifying and supportive of the status quo. Rupture of the status quo for most Anglo-Americans would surely mean a serious reduction in power. Over people of color, for one. In this context, macho oratory can seem very wrong, primarily because it assumes nonhierarchical communication.

Everyone is equal in macho oratory and has an equal right to make assertions, ask questions, doubt, challenge authority, and, most important, to be wrong. Entering the word is vigorous and invigorating, and is a communal appeal to higher aspirations. It invites participation, passes judgment only on those who pass it first or wield it unfairly, and asks for reciprocated dignity. That's something to praise.

In truth, working for a pluralism of styles goes hand in hand with developing a multicultural society—that is, if multiculturalism means an *equality* among diverse cultures living together. For the most part, we have barely approached such a reality. Anglo-American systems of interpretation, of value, of "history," etc., still form the standard by which all other behaviors are measured and deemed useful or not. The default modes of this greater society are yet to be changed in any significant way.

As a rule, dominant culture will place prejudicial meaning systems upon another mode long before it tries to accept and understand another mode on its own terms. A crude comparison can be made with the fact of urban-Midwestern-white English as Standard American. All other ways of speaking, from New York City, to Mobile-Alabamese, to Border Texan, to Seattle Vietnamese-American, to Memphis Black English, to San Francisco Chinese-American, and so on, are considered to be "accents." We recognize their accents on television, in the movies, in classrooms, and mostly—confess it!—make fun of them. Yes, there are accents that are even more privileged than Standard American, such as French-English, British-English, Old-Family Bostonian. Think of the implications of that! Not until Standard American is as easily and automatically considered an accent as are other accents will there be evidence of real change in that language arena. Until then, there will be only affected acceptance or intellectual curiosity or academic exploitation of difference. Never true acceptance.

It may be some time before different modes of speaking and their rhetorical implications are given equal footing in this America. It is an ideal to strive for, this vision of a less-condemning attitude for those behaviors or modes of speaking that are not within the "norm" of this country. There is much that needs to be changed here and elsewhere before we reach equality and mutual respect.

In the meantime, *pues,* there will be those wishing we would just get over macho, and others who see political and social needs as worth getting macho over.

HOW TO LIVE WITH A FEMINISTA AND (STILL) BE A MACHO: NOTES UNABRIDGED

Mayela Padilla, © 1994

JUAN FELIPE HERRERA received a Before Columbus Foundation American Book Award for <u>Facegames,</u> a book of poems. His other collections include <u>Rebozos of Love,</u> <u>Akrílica,</u> and <u>Zen José.</u> His most recent book of poems, <u>Night Train to Tuxtla,</u> was the inaugural volume in the Camino del Sol series from The University of Arizona Press. He is also the author of a memoir, <u>Mayan Drifter,</u> an account of his travels to Chiapas, Mexico, forthcoming from Temple University Press. He teaches in the Chicano Studies Program at Fresno State University in Fresno, California.

THERE ARE SEVEN WAYS.

The first involves the ability to be a *payaso*—a nimble clown with the eyes akimbo as a Chicano Charlie Chaplin's or, even better, a Hispanic legislative type—let's call him Cristóbal.

Cristóbal with a three-piece suit of propriety, hard Catholicism, and a well-defined leaning toward apologia. "Have you been there?" he asks her. "Have you eaten shoelace potatoes made out of leather and never winced?" Cristóbal utters bitter reprisals in a sweet munchkin voice.

"I've cut my long hair, shaved my mustache," he says, "just for you." Sometimes he wears tight *puto* jeans, drives upstate in the snow, and buys her fancy fuchsia-colored undergarments thinking he's on the right track—on the way to a skewed but tasty what-can-you do-for-me *Paraíso*.

Marlon Brando for the second way.

Are you ready to graduate into true testosterone leather?

Maybe you've been in Venice, California, wearing an *Easy Rider* helmet that Raoul, a good acid buddy, gave you. Got the jacket in the outskirt boutiques of Beverly Hills for twelve dollars, café-latte-colored boots from Greenwich Village (got them when you purchased the fuchsia stuff on an earlier jaunt). For the Brando effect you speak slow, with a twang, and you burn internally, mutter the inadequacies of conjugal romance, kick domesticity backward, and eat very small tortes while you smolder on your lover's locked journals. This stuff can get you places fast—too fast.

For the third road you go holy.

I said *holy,* carnal.

Holier than the typical middle-class-hamster-maharishi-iconoclast. You go into 100 percent cotton, no *calzones,* no underwear, no T-shirt. Like I said, you just go. One pair of pointed huaraches, one pair of golfer khakis pilfered from an army surplus store—if they still have them. A male anorexia mode. The idea is to put everything on a diet except your cock. Even the cock strikes a different pose. It wants to appear docile, easy to handle, silky, if possible. This particular way requires mixed meditations. One part, a critique of gender politics and homoerotic art. Part two: a critique of Super Bowl as American power performance, mucho Murine for the eyeball. The woman in your life drinks a lot of Bancha tea and (still) reads de Beauvoir. This is how you communicate.

Che Guevara speaks in your ear in the fourth way. In a fancy Spanish, an Argentinean sing-along where you go gravely through the city streets in search of a coin from Lesbos; a neo-grunge boy with Vietnam boots and no cologne on the pits. "This is the jungle," you tell her. "This is this." You quote your other leader, Robert De Niro in *The Deer Hunter*. You want to quote Visconti but it rubs against your seduction mobile. You want to quote Paglia but you are too Dionysian to utter a woman's language. "This is this," you repeat at the kitchen table as you devour lox, capers, and bagels. Anything goes. Cold cream on fresh-picked cranberries. No post-mod cultural bull. Just pure vision—the Marxist Blendinist Epicurean kind. You are atomic and nuclear, solar and parabolic. She knows you have the semiotic scope and the androgynous look. Most of all, with a swish gesture, you can prove yourself in a minute. All your followers lean on you for change. True change. *"Cambio es cambio,"* you write in your shredded notebook.

The next boy is the Taco Boy.

Yes, I hate to admit it. El Taco Muchacho is most appropriate. He comes on light. He comes on light-colored and light-spoken. Gentle boy with the handbook of Elizabethan-Hispano manners. This is his charm and most of all his sadist-masochistic weaponry. She can't tell if she met him in the barrio over a *raspada,* cherry flavor, of course, or at a Wimin's Mural inaugural. She just can't tell where he's going to end up (of course, we know where). Genuflection, the inflection of piety and sobriety; all this is what catches the fly-girl. His sensuality and personal spice is effusive; an overkill in the form of stuttered underdog poetics and a facade of suave nurturance that filters through his melancholia and slight, hooked face.

Of course, the most post-post-modern and politically correct is the whiny, crabby, crappy, mid-potbellied and wise-beaked fellow you come to know as El Trucha.

El Trucha says he's been through the mill, he's walked up Movimiento Hill, he's seen the pumiced land, no longer idolizes Sam the Sham (you remember "Wooly Bully"). In other words, he's made ideological sacrifices. For one, he's finally let go (it required Rolfing and a relapse into Shakti yoga) of his oldies collection. El Trucha goes shopping with her and doesn't really mind it. He drives her son to prep school on occasion and argues about the need for Trigonometry II. Her colleagues appear and he serves them amaretto with chips and salsa. You see, he's come this far. El Trucha has arrived at a quixotic, Zen fullness.

The Organic Poet sees things.

He's always saying that.

He tells her he's taking care of business, that he doesn't need anything. This is what is alluring. He doesn't need anything (we know about this one). Not even words. He works on pure gas. When he flatulates by cocking one leg over the beige sofa or in front of the half-collie that he keeps in the back yard of his suburban studio, he reminds her that poetry is "a constant flow." This fellow doesn't play games. He offers wind, that is all. No more arduous barbecues in the name of Family, Culture, and Revolution. No more addendums and grammars for a tractatus on the Meaning of Blurred Sexual Roles. "Who wants wind?" he posits as he pours garlic shards over his spinach quesadilla. Socrates and Deleuze couldn't have done better. But, the ripened Poet sees things, this is what he says.

I almost forgot: Science, the coiled shapes in the quarks and pro-stars, these are the jewels of the quantum lover—JQ.

JQ is in love with Señorita Números—bank accounts, cashier receipts, old gas bills, cuneiform integers of (her) spending power. The credit cards in her purse, for example. Her revisionist (mainstreamed) feminist résumé is secondary. He measures her documents for frayed edges every other Saturday. No astrology, no literary mumbo jumbo, no Kama Sutra bath crystals, no-nonsense for this *carnal*. Just these torso shaped *S*'s with stripes running down the belly button. JQ is up-to-date. Shaved, saved, and made. Johnny Quantas is always asking her, *"¿Cuánto? ¿Cuánto? ¿Cómo, cuánto?"* After an average sexual thrust, he throws his head back twice to look at the ceiling, where he has placed the Periodical Table of Upwardly Mobile Feminist Elements. This is the cellular boy of the millennia, the push-button member that promises her pragmatism without pregnancy and nontoxic furniture.

The Magnificent Macho Seven (plus one).

For decades, I have studied their behavior. I've used agents. Sentries and mirrors. These are preliminary charters of their desires, symbolic elements in their clothing—the space and culture coordinates of their habitats. Even their penchant for late-nineteenth-century art is fascinating, especially the unexplained obsession for German woodcuts; these qualities seem to speak of potential turns in their lives. Yet, the macho ecology remains fragile. This I haven't solved. The constructions of the internal landscape have always escaped me; its tiny trees, the lack of rivers, its odd shape, tied so intimately and yet intrinsically readied for fatal rejections.

"I'M THE KING":
THE MACHO IMAGE

Marion Ettlinger

RUDOLFO ANAYA is the author of several novels, plays, memoirs, and collections of short stories. He is best known for his first novel, <u>Bless Me Ultima,</u> which was recently reprinted in mass paperback by Warner Books. Selections from his novels, plus essays and stories, are collected in <u>The Rudolfo Anaya Reader,</u> also by Warner. His two most recent novels, <u>Zia Summer</u> and <u>Alburquerque,</u> are part of a trilogy set in New Mexico. <u>Alburquerque</u> received the 1993 Pen/Faulkner Award for Fiction. In 1992, he retired from teaching at the University of New Mexico and lives in Albuquerque.

WHAT IS MACHO?

The word *macho* has one of the shortest definitions in the Spanish language dictionary, and yet the cult of macho behavior (machismo or the macho image) is as ambiguous and misunderstood as any aspect of Hispanic/Latino culture. To be macho is to be male, that's simple, but when the term is applied to Hispanic male behavior, then the particulars of the role are defined according to the particular culture. From Spain to Latin America, from Mexico to the Chicanos in the USA, one gets a slightly different definition of the macho image at every turn.

Being macho is essentially a learned behavior; as such it is a conditioned behavior. We males learn to act "manly" from other males around us; the "macho" that preceded us was learned from the cultures from which it evolved. Many forces impinge on the Hispanic/Latino cultures, so throughout history, machismo—or the conditioning of male behavior—has attracted all sorts of positive and negative elements.

Many cultural forces (from literature and religion to the latest musical fad, movies, MTV, or car styles) play a role in promoting the behavior of the macho, and these influences are the issue here. Still, beneath the conditioned behavior, the essence of what maleness means remains largely unchanged across time. We can describe conditioning and its effects; it is more difficult to describe the essence of maleness, especially today, when males seem to be retreating from describing, or laying claim to, a positive macho image.

Drunkenness, abusing women, raising hell (all elements of *la vida loca*) are some mistaken conceptions of what macho means. And yet the uninformed often point to such behavior and call it machismo. In fact, much of this negative behavior is aped by a new generation, because as young men they are not aware that they are being conditioned. Young men acting contrary to the good of their community have not yet learned the real essence of maleness.

SEX

One generation passes on to the next its ideals and rituals, and important behavior that has to do with our sexuality. People have always composed games about sexuality. In this respect, the macho image has a history. The cock-of-the-walk behavior is game playing. Games and sex go hand in hand.

The game can be spontaneous and fun, reflecting the courtship and mating we see in the natural world. Part of the purpose of gender games is to reflect nature's dance of life, evolution playing itself out in each new encounter. Animals, insects—high and low organisms—engage in this dance of life. We are caught up in "nature's game," this vast and beautiful dance that is part of the awe of life. We feel love in the harmonious flow of nature, the movement of birth and death, and we take meaning from our sexual natures.

But the game has taken on a manipulative aspect. The assertion of one over another is part of our conditioning. The game has turned ugly in many ways, and we are numbed by the outcome of the conditioning factors. But we can still be in charge of the game, and change the negative aspects of the game. We can choose not to play a power game that hurts and demeans women.

Macho behavior, in large part, revolves around the acting out of sex roles. The games the macho plays may be part of nature's dance, with the goal of procreation imprinted on the cells long ago, but the power to subjugate is also inherent in our relationships. When the male gets caught up in superficial power plays that have to do with sex, he is acting against his community. It's time to analyze the social forces that condition negative behavior and toss out the ones that destroy family, friendship, and community.

For the Chicano, the roots of the idea of maleness extend not only into the Mediterranean world but also into the Native-American world. We still act out patterns of male behavior emerging from those historic streams. To fully understand our behavior requires a knowledge of those literary and cultural histories. The Don Juan image and how it sets the tone for a pattern of behavior from Mediterranean Spain to the present day is only one aspect of a behavioral legacy. We need to know the role of the Native-American warrior and how he cares for the community. The Chicano is a synthesis of those, and many more, streams of influence.

"I CAN PISS THE FARTHEST"

Little boys like to brag about the length of their penises, or they have contests to see who can piss the farthest. Acting out "I'm bigger, I'm better," the game begins to have its built-in power aspect. Later, boys will brag about having scored with a girl, and in the boast is contained a hint of the power they have exercised. Those who haven't yet scored have less power. They're virgins in the game. Those who don't see girls as the goal to be conquered have even less power. A hierarchy of needs and behavior begins to define the male role, and the power inherent in it. The truer essence of male and female doesn't need this hierarchy, for hierarchy implies the use of power over others. And why should that which is most natural to our nature, our sexuality, require us to deal with others as objects?

Macho needs partners, not objects.

Until my father's generation, the men of the Mexican culture of the southwest U.S. could continue to speak Spanish and interact within the parameters of their history. That is, they set the code of behavior, one that was communal and focused on survival in an often harsh land. As Anglo-Americans moved into the territory, a wrenching of male relationships took place. As Anglos moved in, the language of domination shifted from English to Spanish. The Anglo-American law came to New Mexico in the mid-nineteenth century, but the rule of law in daily life and most communal enterprises remained Spanish. It was not until after World War II that the ways of my ancestors were overwhelmed. And therein lies an epic tragedy.

My father's generation *had* to adjust to the new language, the new man in town, the new laws. To be a man under Anglo domination was difficult if you didn't have the tools. I saw men broken by the new time, the new space. If they didn't adjust to the new language, they were demeaned. I now better understand my father's behavior, why he gave up. He didn't have the language, the tool with which to protect his own dignity, his own concept of macho. An excellent example of this meeting of cultures is shown in the movie *The Ballad of Gregorio Cortez,* a film that takes its story from a real legend.

In some areas the males did absorb one another's concept of maleness. For example, the New Mexican land owners, lawyers, and politicians (those generally known as *los ricos* or *los patrones*) quickly learned to work with their Anglo counterparts. The Mexican vaqueros taught the Anglo cowboys the trade, so there existed some camaraderie on a macho level in those endeavors. But overall, the power of law and language was too vast and overwhelming. The Anglos could dictate roles; they could piss the farthest, so to speak.

"I'M THE KING"

"Sigo siendo el Rey. I'm the king" are the lyrics from a popular Chicano rap song I hear on the radio. The words and rhythm are catchy. I listen to the song and find myself repeating the lines.

Macho behavior is instilled in us as children. Both father and mother want their boys to grow up to be manly. Usually, the more traditional the rules of behavior are for the macho, the stricter the behavior the child learns. When he becomes a man the child sings, "I'm the king. I rule the family, like my father before me, and what I say goes." The child is the father to the man. But fathers at home are more and more rare. The child turns to the gang in the streets. A new style of being king is learned.

My parents knew a wonderful couple, old friends, who came to visit. My mother and her *comadre* would cook up big meals, my father and his *compadre* would buy the wine. It was fiesta time. The old man would have a few glasses of wine and start acting like the king. *"Yo mando,"* he would tell his wife, and the teasing about who ruled, the man or the woman, would go on. Visiting across the kitchen table and drinking wine, they were all caught up in discussing the roles of man and woman.

It has always been so. In that space of the family fiesta in the small kitchen, they could define and redefine their roles. The mask of gaiety put on for the fiesta allowed them to speak freely. But beneath the surface a real dialogue was going on, defining and refining the roles of the men and the women. Do we have that dialogue about machismo going on in our community today? Or have we accepted old roles conditioned by forces beyond our control? Are we too programmed to see the light?

The male child observes and learns to be the king, how to act as *número uno,* how to act around men and women. In a community that is poor and often oppressed there is much suffering, so he is taught *aguantar:* to grin and bear it. *"Aguántate,"* the men around him say. A macho doesn't cry in front of men. A macho doesn't show weakness. Grit your teeth, take the pain, bear it alone. Be tough. You feel like letting it out? Well, then let's get drunk with our *compadres,* and with the *grito* that comes from within, we can express our emotions. Lots of essays could be written on *aguantar.* The women also learn *aguantar:* Bearing it crosses the gender boundary. How women express the floodwaters of the *aguanto* is now being documented by Chicana writers.

The macho learns many games while learning to be *número uno.* Drinking buddies who have a contest to see who can consume the most beer, or the most shots of tequila, are trying to prove their maleness. From the pissing contest to drinking, the wish to prove his manliness becomes antisocial, dangerous. The drunk macho driving home from the contest he won can become a murderer.

The car in our society has become an extension for the macho. The young male hungers for the most customized, flashiest car. It replicates him. It is power. The car is used in the mating ritual. As in our small villages generations ago the young vaqueros came into town to show off their horses and their horsemanship, the young now parade the boulevard showing off their cars. The dance is the same; the prize is the same.

To other males, the *vato* with the best car is saying, "I'm bigger, I'm better, I'm the king." Exactly the lyrics to the rap song. *"Sigo siendo el Rey,"* he sings, "I continue being the king." The song describes one goal of the macho, to be king, to be *número uno,* to answer to no one. The message is aimed not only at other males, it is also for the female of the species.

OUTSIDE INFLUENCES

But guns have entered the game. Perhaps they've always been there, because certainly the Mexican *charro* and the cowboy of the movies both carried pistols, both fought it out with the bad guys, and the fastest draw won. In the rural areas hunting is most often male behavior. The gun extends the power and the sexuality of the young men. Now you can strike farther and deadlier.

It is time to call that behavior that is good, good. And that which is negative to the self and the community, not good. To be unkind and violent is not macho. The *vato* in the song who wants to be the king needs to find positive ways of acting for his community.

In my generation the "attitude" of James Dean influenced young male behavior, as did that of black musicians and black talk. Today, parents worry about the violent influence of the movies. The characters portrayed by Arnold Schwarzenegger (and other such exaggerated macho images) and the Power Rangers have become symbols of violence in our society. Machos seem to solve problems only through violence, and quickly. Discourse and problem solving, which take time, are not honored in such movies. Parents worry about the influence such media are having on the young. Macho has really gotten out of hand; in fact, it's been perverted by those who use a false idea (ideal) of manliness to achieve their goals. We need to stand up and say, loud and clear, that violence and oppression are not macho.

As more Chicano families become single-parent families, the traditional role of the father and the extended-family males will not be as influential in shaping the behavior of boys. The boys are being conditioned instead by the behavior they see on TV, in movies and music videos. Boys loose in the hood are being shaped by the gang instead of the father.

La ganga shapes behavior, provides initiation, belonging. (Life in the gang—whether it's a neighborhood group of boys; an athletic fraternity ("the jocks"); or a gang into *la vida loca,* cruising, drinking, drugs, and guns—is a subject that requires a book to itself.) In the traditional culture, we didn't practice drive-by shooting as initiation into maleness. Young Chicanos moving into the maleness of the gang now practice a more violent form of initiation.

Young Chicano males learn from the past generations (drinking is often learned from brothers or close relatives), and such behavior is greatly influenced by the mainstream society. The influence of the Anglo-American culture on the Chicano culture cannot be overlooked. We can no longer speak of a continuum of learned behavior that is solely Mexican macho, because young males are greatly influenced by the totality of the culture around them. MTV, music, movies, television, and the behavior of other cultural groups *all* influence the behavior of the young Chicano male. To truly understand himself, and his maleness, the young male *must* ask himself: Who is affecting me? What do they want of me? How can I take charge of my own life?

There is a lesson to be learned here. Let us *not* repeat the loss of the prior generation, a loss we see today in the streets. Let us *not* be "powerless" as men. Let us *not* act out negative behaviors. We have within us the power to change. We have the future of our community at stake, so macho behavior has to be used positively for the community.

LOS CHUCOS

Each new generation becomes a new link in the group's tradition, but also transforms behavior. My adolescent years saw the advent of the *pachuco,* a radical departure in the male behavior of the small New Mexican town I knew. Who were *esos vatos locos* imitating in the forties when they invented the *pachuco* argot, the dress, sexual liberation in attitude and action, use of drugs, use of cars, etc.? Was there a continuous line of macho behavior in which the *chucos* were a link? Or was the behavior so spontaneous and new that the *pachucos* initiated a new definition of what it meant to be macho? After all, being macho does mean to defend the territory, and the *chucos* did defend their barrios against mainstream encroachment. Were the *pachucos* a reaction to the growing oppression by Anglo America? Partly, but once the warriors defined themselves, they spent as much time fighting each other as they did fighting the enemy, *el gabacho.*

The *pachuco* became a new model of behavior, breaking with the past, and yet in his role vis-à-vis *la chuca,* the male-female dance contained the same old elements embedded in the Mexicano culture. The power play was definitely at work. *La chuca,* as liberated as she was from her contemporary "square" sister, who remained a "nice" girl, was still subservient. The *pachuco* loved to show off *his* baby doll.

This makes us question if breaks with the past are really radical, or does only the surface dress of the macho change? Beneath the zoot suit of the *pachuco,* old cultural forces and conditioned behavior continued to define the relationship between the macho and *his* woman. *"Esta es mi ruca,"* he said proudly, introducing the woman as property in which he was pleased.

The *pachuco* practicing *la vida loca* continued to influence the definition of macho behavior into the nineties. They were the early lowriders. They spawned the baby chooks and those Chicano males who today are acting out roles, sometimes unknowingly, with roots in the *pachuco* lifestyle. (The Chicano rapper borrows from the black rapper, but in his barrio, in his strut and talk, he is borrowing as much from the old *veteranos.*) This role of an "unconscious energy" in the community is something we can't measure, but it's there. History is passed on not only in stories and books, but by osmosis.

It makes us ask: Is behavior only learned? Or is there real maleness, a golden rule not only in the blood but in the myths? I look at the young machos parading down the street, acting out their roles, and I wonder how much of their behavior comes from that unconscious influence, something inherent in maleness itself. There is something in that dignity of maleness we don't want to give up. But what is it? We know those negative forces that condition us have to be repudiated. But we also yearn to be noble men, and to act in a noble fashion for our families.

LA FAMILIA

The *pachuco* macho behavior, while very visible in the barrio (and introduced to a larger audience by the U.S. Navy anti-*pachuco,* anti-Mexican riots during the early forties in Los Angeles, and made more visible through the Valdez "zoot suit" film), was not the only model of maleness in the community. A far greater percentage of the men of the barrios went about their work, raising families, trying to do the best they could for them. Macho means taking care of *la familia.* Perhaps this is the most important definition of macho, the real, positive meaning of the word. And yet it is often given short shrift. Critics often look at the negative behavior of the macho and forget the positive.

In the villages and barrios of New Mexico when I was growing up, being manly (*hombrote*) meant having a sense of honor. The intangible of the macho image is that sense of honor. A man must be honorable, for himself and for his family. There is honor in the family name. *Hombrote* also means providing for the family. Men of honor were able to work with the other men in communal enterprises. They took care of the politics of the village, law and order, the church, the *acequia,* and the old people.

The greatest compliment I could receive as a child when I did a job well was to be called *hombrote.* I was acting like an *hombre,* a man. This compliment came from both males and females in the family and in the extended family. By the way, this compliment is also given to the girls. They can be *hombrotas,* as well as *muy mujerotas,* "very womanly." Either way, the creation of male and female roles are created and rewarded with the appropriate language, and the language is male-centered.

Much is now written about male bonding, how the father and other males in the community shape the macho image. In Hispanic culture the role of the *compadres* is such a role. (The *compadres* are the godfathers, for lack of a more thorough definition.) The *compadres* bond at marriages, baptisms, or other family celebrations. Their goal is to ensure the welfare of the child that one of the *compadres* has baptized or confirmed. The best man at the wedding becomes a *compadre. Compadrazgo* has a very positive role to play. The *compadres* act "manly" toward one another, and the children of the *compadres* learn male behavior through those interactions.

Still, it's not just the males that are in charge of shaping the macho image. Women play an important role.

THE WOMAN CREATES THE MACHO

Talking about being macho also means talking about the role of women in our lives. In a traditional setting, the Mexican mother raises the male child and has a great influence on the learned macho behavior of the child. We learn a lot about the sexual behavior from the males of the clan, but the mother, if she does the raising of the male child, is a most crucial ingredient in the evolving macho role.

Food, warmth, protection, the first sounds, and all that has to do with the tactile sense of the first years on earth are provided by the mother. In our culture the mother is the first confidante of the male child. If the Catholic Church says, Give me the child for indoctrination for the first six years of life and I will mold a lifelong Catholic, the mother has already imprinted her femininity on the child and the child's response to that feminine aura in the womb. No wonder mothers exclaim at birth, "I have created."

In her novel, *Face of an Angel,* Denise Chavez explores the role of women in the formation of macho. By exploring the lives of women in the culture, she gives us an excellent, uninhibited view of the woman's influence on the life of the male. Other Chicanas are also doing this in their writings. Ana Castillo in her essay on machismo (in *Massacre of the Dreamers: Essays on Xicanisma,* University of New Mexico Press, 1994) has much to tell us of the history of the macho image. We need to listen to the ideas of such writers as the role of the macho is transformed. By us, by them.

Oedipal complexes and fears aside, we are our mother's creation, and so early macho behavior will be shaped actively and by nuance by the mother. Perhaps this is what we recognize when we attribute great value to the family. A mother who is active in shaping the maleness of her child will produce a more integrated man; if the mother is not there or if her behavior has been conditioned by an oppressive patriarchy, a more dysfunctional child will emerge. (This role of the woman who has historically been controlled by the demands of a male-oriented society has been amply analyzed by Castillo.)

Chicano males brought up in a positive atmosphere do not hesitate to say they love their mothers. Embracing (*el abrazo*) is as common for the mother as for the father. A continuing relationship with the mother as a guide who provides warmth, love, strength, and direction is integral to the culture. Our community did not traditionally initiate a cut-off age when the young male had to leave the household, i.e., leave his mother's side. Both father and mother remain confidantes—thus a description of the closeness of the family. Only recently, as we copy Anglo-American behavior, and as the status of the culture has changed from rural to urban, do some Chicanos begin to practice readying the child to be completely independent.

As we grow we begin to leave the mother's side. I learned about the male's role in the family and society from my father and his *compadres,* men who worked and drank with him. And I was fortunate to have three brothers who were around long enough in my adolescent years to allow me to learn from them. I learned from my boyhood friends. Playing together we created and acted out the mythology of boyhood. Sexuality played an important part in those years of definition.

We learn not only how to talk, act, respond, and think like men from the intimate clan of males in which we are raised, we also learn an attitude toward life. We learn that intangible which lies beneath behavior. Part of that essence is how we carry ourselves as men, the dignity and honor we exude. Men who don't have this dignity are *sinvergüenzas,* men without shame. They have a tough time holding their heads high, a tough time being macho. We learn to carry ourselves as men in our families, in the community, and in respect to women and men. And because we are members of a different cultural group living within the boundary of Anglo America, we learn to carry ourselves in respect to the Other, in this case, other white males.

MYTH AND MACHO: LA LLORONA

There are deeper currents to wade in when we speak of our maleness. For me, myths and their inherent messages are integral to a definition of our humanity. Myth and legend shine in our folklore; folklore is a reflection of myth when there is no written text. The stories of the people also define our maleness. Let me propose a few areas of interest that don't have their history in a Eurocentric past. For example, let's look at one of our most persistent legends, which I believe also describes the macho image.

Part of the underpinning of our worldview, our values, is indigenous. The indigenous myths are part of our inheritance, working most often quietly in the cells, in memory, in dreams, and appearing as stories in the folklore. Our male relationship to the female can be better understood if we understand such pervasive legends as that of *La Llorona.* Every Chicano I know has heard of *La Llorona.* Some have actual experiences of the wailing woman, i.e., they claim to have met her. (Who knows how many times we have met her in our dreams and our *pesadillas,* but contemporary psychologists have not been trained to listen to our mythology. They have not paid attention to that body of work and therefore lack interpretations intimately useful to us.)

Briefly, *La Llorona* is a young woman who is taken advantage of by a man. She has a child (generally out of wedlock) by the man. But the man does not stay home; he goes off seeking a new adventure (and usually a new woman). The young mother goes insane, or into a jealous rage. To get revenge on the man who has jilted her, she kills the child (or children) and throws the body in the river, into a pond or lake. She is returning the flesh to the primordial water, the ooze of primal creation.

This is not so much the replaying of the Medea tragedy. It has closer kinship in myth to the pre-Greek, Mediterranean world. When the Egyptian Osiris is killed by his brother, it is Isis, Osiris's sister, who wanders along the Nile, collecting the pieces of the dismembered body to "reconstitute" Osiris. (She symbolically gives birth to her brother, i.e., the virgin has delivered the male child who will be God.)

La Llorona of our legend also seeks the pieces of the (male) child she has murdered. Or sacrificed? To date, the legend has been too narrowly analyzed. Has *La Llorona* really sacrificed the child to re-create him in the waters of the river (the earth womb) and thus raise him symbolically to the status of God? Perhaps *La Llorona* realizes the child has to die to be reborn a better male. That is, the consciousness of the child has to be reshaped to fit the time. Consciousness is evolving, and in this case the mother (*La Llorona*) is a key player in that new consciousness. Put another way, *La Llorona* is creating a new humanity.

Another interpretation would question if it is *La Llorona* who really kills the child. In the Osiris myth, Osiris is killed by his brother, a male. It seems to me that feminist Chicana critics need to dig deeper into this paradigm. In my novel *Zia Summer,* my main character, Sonny Baca, a thirty-year-old understanding his maleness (and his cultural identity) more and more, is told the story of *La Llorona* by his grandmother. In the grandmother's story it is a man who kills *La Llorona*'s child.

What if it *is* the man who kills *La Llorona*'s child, a child she would raise to a new consciousness, thus defeating the father's old macho ways? The woman has the power to create the new male, not Nietzsche's Superman, but a child more closely aligned to the feminine sensibility, which is the mother's inheritance. The man kills the male child not because he fears an Oedipal ending (after all, in the legend the father is going off searching after a new woman), but because he fears the status quo and his macho role in it will be supplanted by the son.

Therein lies new hope. We can constantly re-create the child, raise the child in a new way, so the macho image of yesterday need not be a prison to us, especially its dysfunctional aspects. *La Llorona* knows this, and so like Isis she searches along the river's bank, the lake, the sacred springs of myth in search of the pieces of the child she can bring back to life. What incredible power lies in this woman of legend that we have dismissed as a bogey woman of the river. We've used her to frighten children, when we should be using her to raise them—the new children of a new era who understand that each one carries the hope of the future.

Children, both male and female, can put aside old, destructive ways of behavior and define maleness in a new way. *La Llorona,* the mother of the sacred lake, can play a role in describing the new macho. (The lake image represents the unconscious, that creative energy from whence rise new images.) In our time, the greatest change taking place in the macho image and its behavior is the influence of a new generation of liberated Chicanas. Their cry is not a cry of despair, but voices insisting that they are taking a greater role in defining male/female relationships, and so they *are* redefining macho. These contemporary *Lloronas* can be liberating mothers creating new concepts and behaviors by which to live. Or they can be shortsighted and engage in old gender accusations that don't move us toward the definition of a new paradigm. A lot rides on their thoughts, their stories, their actions.

So, *La Llorona* has pre-Greek, Egyptian, Semitic roots. Roots in ancient civilizations. Blame men, the pillars of the morality of the community, if she has been given a bad rap. Blame ourselves if we do not reinterpret the old myths and give them new meaning for our violent time. There's hope in new interpretations, a hope that will bring new understanding to our roles as men and women. We don't have to be stuck with old stereotypic roles of behavior that define dysfunctional machos.

LA VIRGEN

La Virgen de Guadalupe is another mother figure. She is the Aztec goddess Tonantzin, the indigenous New World answer to the goddess religions that were destroyed during the Neolithic Age around the fringes of the Mediterranean world. *La Virgen de Guadalupe* exists because Quetzalcóatl (the monotheistic feathered-serpent god who can fly and is of heavens) could not erase the goddess worship in indigenous America. Perhaps the cult of Quetzalcóatl chose not to erase the goddess cult, after all, Quetzalcóatl was not like the Yahweh of the Old Testament. He was not a thundering god of vengeance, he was a god of the fields and civilization.

Quetzalcóatl and the cult of goddess worship went hand in hand. But Quetzalcóatl flew too high. One reason for his banishment is that he mated with his "sister," a heavenly sister of the starry skies. The feathered energy of his nature drew him toward the heavens, and thus separated him from the earth energy, the intuitive energy wound up in procreation and nurturing. He should have mated with the Earth goddess and thus preserved his serpent earth energy and procreative powers. Or at least he should have kept the energy of these polarities in balance, in harmony, able to wed the intuitive with the rational, the earth-creative with the aspirations to the spiritual. In a sense, Quetzalcóatl deserted the fields, the earth, and his people, and as such, except for the words of a few Chicano writers and poets, he passed out of our consciousness. In Mesoamerica he was easily replaced by the Catholic Cristo. But not the earth goddess Tonantzin. She lives on in *La Virgen de Guadalupe*.

Quetzalcóatl was banished. He traveled east to be absorbed into flames, into Venus as the morning star, into the sunlight of dawn. Tonantzin, the earth goddess, did not flee, nor was she banished from the hearts of her people. The Spanish friars knew they could not destroy the adoration of the goddess. The ties to the earth were too deep in the ancient Mexicans. The church could stamp out Quetzalcóatl (after all, the god had already forsaken his people just before the arrival of the Europeans), and so Cristo did not have the competition of a strong, indigenous male god. But the natives would not let go of the goddess of the earth. She is incorporated into the pantheon of the Catholic Church as *La Virgen de Guadalupe*. The smartest move the Church ever made in the Americas was not to fight this syncretic impulse.

The female goddess was imprinted in the psyche of the people of the Americas. The goddess created, nurtured, provided. She is seen in corn, the sustenance of much of the New World. She spoke to the god of rain on behalf of the farmers. All attributes of *La Virgen*. And so the female (anima) of the human psyche remains represented as an active force in our lives. Take whatever route you like to the past, you will discover the prototypes of *La Virgen*. Her role remains the feminine sensibility with which we identify. For the male she is a living presence of the anima within, the female within.

Is being macho *only* learned behavior? Well, mostly, but what of this stream of myth? What part of this inheritance describes the history of our blood? What whispers do we hear from the collective memory, and how can it describe a new way of being macho? Perhaps the old macho image has to die when it does not engender the community. The essence of maleness doesn't have to die, it merely has to be understood and created anew. To re-create is evolution's role. We can take an active role in it, but to do so we have to know the history of false behavioral conditioning.

Nature dictates much. The chemicals, hormones, and elements in the blood and in the psyche are elements she needs for the job of procreation of the species. But she also provides a fantastic interplay of forces within the essence of the human, within the soul. The soul exists as a motivating, energizing force within. We can transform ourselves, and in that transcendent encounter, or epiphany, we become more than the humans whose feet are bogged down in the mud.

To do that we need to pay full attention to the forces within. We are not all male at any given time, nor are we all female. We need to find balance and give harmony to the deep currents of our nature. Macho need not be all male, *puro hombre*. Nothing is pure one thing or the other, especially when we speak of human nature. The old dictates of the fathers have to be transformed to create a new macho, and for that we need to listen to the feminine sensibility. To listen within.

THE PUERTO RICAN
DUMMY AND THE
MERCIFUL SON

Terry Pitzner

MARTÍN ESPADA is the author of five books of poetry, most recently City of Coughing and Dead Radiators and Imagine the Angels of Bread, both from W.W. Norton. He is also the editor of Poetry Like Bread: Poets of the Political Imagination, from Curbstone Press. His awards include two NEA Fellowships, the PEN/Revson Fellowship, and the Paterson Poetry Prize. A former tenant lawyer, he teaches literature at the University of Massachusetts-Amherst.

I HAVE A FOUR-YEAR-OLD SON named Clemente. He is not named for Roberto Clemente, the baseball player, as many people are quick to guess, but rather for a Puerto Rican poet. His name, in translation, means "merciful." Like the cheetah, he can reach speeds of up to sixty miles an hour. He is also, demographically speaking, a Latino male, a "macho" for the twenty-first century.

Two years ago, we were watching television together when a ventriloquist appeared with his dummy. The ventriloquist was Anglo; the dummy was a Latino male, Puerto Rican, in fact, like me, like my son. Complete with pencil mustache, greased hair, and jawbreaking Spanish accent, the dummy acted out an Anglo fantasy for an Anglo crowd that roared its approval. My son was transfixed; he did not recognize the character onscreen because he knows no one who fits that description, but he sensed my discomfort. Too late, I changed the channel. The next morning, my son watched Luis and María on *Sesame Street,* but this was inadequate compensation. *Sesame Street* is the only barrio on television, the only neighborhood on television where Latino families live and work, but the comedians are everywhere, with that frat-boy sneer, and so are the crowds.

However, I cannot simply switch off the comedians, or explain them (how do you explain to a preschooler that a crowd of strangers is angrily laughing at the idea of *him?*). We live in western Massachusetts, not far from Springfield and Holyoke, hardscrabble small cities that, in the last generation, have witnessed a huge influx of Puerto Ricans, now constituting some of the poorest Puerto Rican communities in the country. The evening news from Springfield features what I call "the Puerto Rican minute." This is the one minute of the newscast where we see the faces of Puerto Rican men, the mug shot or the arraignment in court or witnesses pointing to the bloodstained sidewalk, while the newscaster solemnly intones the mantra of gangs, drugs, jail. The notion of spending the Puerto Rican minute on a teacher or a health care worker or an artist in the community never occurs to the television journalists who produce this programming.

The Latino male is the bogeyman of the Pioneer Valley, which includes the area where we live. Recently, there was a rumor circulating in the atmosphere that Latino gangs would be prowling the streets on Halloween, shooting anyone in costume. My wife, Katherine, reports that one Anglo gentleman at the local swimming pool took responsibility for warning everyone, a veritable Paul Revere in swim trunks wailing that "The Latinos are going to kill kids on Halloween!" Note how 1) Latino gangs became "Latinos" and 2) Latinos and "kids" became mutually exclusive categories. My wife wondered if this warning contemplated the Latino males in her life, if this racially paranoid imagination included visions of her professor husband and his toddling offspring as gunslingers in full macho swagger, hunting for "gringos" in Halloween costumes. The rumor, needless to say, was unfounded.

Then there is the national political climate. In 1995, we saw the spectacle of a politician, California Governor Pete Wilson, being seriously considered for the presidency on the strength of his support for Proposition 187, the most blatantly anti-Latino initiative in recent memory. There is no guarantee, as my son grows older, that this political pendulum will swing back to the left; if anything, the pendulum may well swing farther to the right. That means more fear and fury and bitter laughter.

Into this world enters Clemente, which raises certain questions: How do I think of my son as a Latino male? How do I teach him to disappoint and disorient the bigots everywhere around him, all of whom have bought tickets to see the macho pantomime? At the same time, how do I teach him to inoculate himself against the very real diseases of violence and sexism and homophobia infecting our community? How do I teach Clemente to be Clemente?

My son's identity as a Puerto Rican male has already been reinforced by a number of experiences I did not have at so early an age. At age four, he has already spent time in Puerto Rico, whereas I did not visit the island until I was ten years old. From the time he was a few months old, he has witnessed his Puerto Rican father engaged in the decidedly nonstereotypical business of giving poetry readings. We savor new Spanish words together the same way we devour mangoes together, knowing the same tartness and succulence.

And yet, that same identity will be shaped by negative as well as positive experiences. The ventriloquist and his Puerto Rican dummy offered Clemente a glimpse of his inevitable future: Not only bigotry, but his growing awareness of that bigotry, his realization that some people have contempt for him because he is Puerto Rican. Here his sense of maleness will come into play, because he must learn to deal with his own rage, his inability to extinguish the source of his torment.

My father has good reason for rage. A brown-skinned man, he learned rage when he was arrested in Biloxi, Mississippi, in 1950, and spent a week in jail for refusing to go to the back of the bus. He learned rage when he was denied a college education and instead struggled for years working for an electrical contractor, hating his work and yearning for so much more. He learned rage as the political triumphs of the 1960s he helped to achieve were attacked from without and betrayed from within. My father externalized his rage. He raged at his enemies and he raged at us. A tremendous ethical and cultural influence for us nonetheless, he must have considered himself a failure by the male career-obsessed standards of the decade into which I was born: the 1950s.

By adolescence, I had learned to internalize my rage. I learned to do this, not so much in response to my father, but more in response to my own growing awareness of bigotry. Having left my Brooklyn birthplace for the town of Valley Stream, Long Island, I was dubbed a spic in an endless torrent of taunting, bullying, and brawling. To defend myself against a few people would have been feasible; to defend myself against dozens and dozens of people deeply in love with their own racism was a practical impossibility. So I told no one, no parent or counselor or teacher or friend, about the constant racial hostility. Instead, I punched a lamp, not once but twice, and watched the blood ooze between my knuckles as if somehow I could leech the poison from my body. My evolving manhood was defined by how well I could take punishment, and paradoxically I punished myself for not being man enough to end my own humiliation. Later in life, I would emulate my father and rage openly. Rarely, however, was the real enemy within earshot, or even visible.

Someday, my son will be called a spic for the first time; this is as much a part of the Puerto Rican experience as the music he gleefully dances to. I hope he will tell me. I hope that I can help him handle the glowing toxic waste of his rage. I hope that I can explain clearly why there are those waiting for him to explode, to confirm their stereotypes of the hot-blooded, bad-tempered Latino male who has, without provocation, injured the Anglo innocents. His anger—and that anger must come—has to be controlled, directed, creatively channeled, articulated—but not all-consuming, neither destructive nor self-destructive. I keep it between the covers of the books I write.

The anger will continue to manifest itself as he matures and discovers the utter resourcefulness of bigotry, the ability of racism to change shape and survive all attempts to snuff it out. "Spic" is a crude expression of certain sentiments that become subtle and sophisticated and insidious at other levels. Speaking of crudity, I am reminded of a group organized by white ethnics in New York during the 1960s under the acronym of SPONGE: The Society for the Prevention of the Niggers Getting Everything. When affirmative action is criticized today by Anglo politicians and pundits with exquisite diction and erudite vocabulary, that is still SPONGE. When and if my son is admitted to school or obtains a job by way of affirmative action, and is resented for it by his colleagues, that will be SPONGE, too.

Violence is the first cousin to rage. If learning to confront rage is an important element of developing Latino manhood, then the question of violence must be addressed with equal urgency. Violence is terribly seductive; all of us, especially males, are trained to gaze upon violence until it becomes beautiful. Beautiful violence is not only the way to victory for armies and football teams; this becomes the solution to everyday problems as well. For many characters on the movie or television screen, problems are solved by *shooting* them. This is certainly the most emphatic way to win an argument.

Katherine and I try to minimize the seductiveness of violence for Clemente. No guns, no soldiers, and so on. But his dinosaurs still eat each other with great relish. His trains still crash, to their delight. He is experimenting with power and control, with action and reaction, which brings him to an imitation of violence. Needless to say, there is a vast difference between stegosaurus and Desert Storm.

Again, all I can do is call upon my own experience as an example. I not only found violence seductive; at some point, I found myself enjoying it. I remember one brawl in Valley Stream when I snatched a chain away from an assailant, knocked him down, and needlessly lashed the chain across his knees as he lay sobbing in the street. That I was now the assailant with the chain did not occur to me.

I also remember the day I stopped enjoying the act of fistfighting. I was working as a bouncer in a bar, and found myself struggling with a man who was so drunk that he appeared numb to the blows bouncing off his cranium. Suddenly, I heard my fist echo: *thok*. I was sickened by the sound. Later, I learned that I had broken my right ring finger with that punch, but all I could recall was the headache I must have caused him. I never had a fistfight again. Parenthetically, that job ended another romance: the one with alcohol. Too much of my job consisted of ministering to people who had passed out at the bar, finding their hats and coats, calling a cab, dragging them in their stupor down the stairs. Years later, I channeled those instincts cultivated as a bouncer into my work as a legal services lawyer, representing Latino tenants, finding landlords who forgot to heat buildings in winter or exterminate rats to be more deserving targets of my wrath. Eventually, I even left the law.

Will I urge my son to be a pacifist, thereby gutting one of the foundations of traditional manhood, the pleasure taken in violence and the power derived from it? That is an ideal state. I hope that he lives a life that permits him pacifism. I hope that the world around him evolves in such a way that pacifism is a viable choice. Still, I would not deny him the option of physical self-defense. I would not deny him, on philosophical grounds, the right to resistance in any form that resistance must take to be effective. Nor would I have him deny that right to others, with the luxury of distance. Too many people in this world still need a revolution.

When he is old enough, Clemente and I will talk about matters of justification, which must be carefully and narrowly defined. He must understand that abstractions like "respect" and "honor" are not reasons to fight in the street, and abstractions like "patriotism" and "country" are not reasons to fight on the battlefield. He must understand that violence against women is not acceptable, a message which will have to be somehow repeated every time another movie trailer blazes the art of misogyny across his subconscious mind. Rather than sloganizing, however, the best way I can communicate that message is by the way I treat his mother. How else will he know that jealousy is not love, that a lover is not property?

Knowing Katherine introduced me to a new awareness of many things: compassion and intimacy, domestic violence and recovery. Her history of savage physical abuse as a child—in a Connecticut farming community—compelled me to consider what it means to heal another human being, or to help that human being heal herself. What small gestures begin to restore humanity?

WHEN THE LEATHER IS A WHIP

At night,
with my wife
sitting on the bed,
I turn from her
to unbuckle
my belt
so she won't see
her father
unbuckling
his belt

Clemente was born on December 28, 1991. This was a difficult birth. Katherine's coccyx, or tailbone, broken in childhood, would break again during delivery. Yet only with the birth could we move from gesture to fulfillment, from generous moments to real giving. The extraordinary healing that took place was not only physical but emotional and spiritual as well. After years of constant pain, her coccyx bone set properly, as if a living metaphor for the new opportunity represented by the birth of this child.

WHITE BIRCH

Two decades ago rye whiskey
scalded your father's throat,
stinking from the mouth
as he stamped his shoe
in the groove between your hips,
dizzy flailing cartwheel down the stairs.

The tail of your spine split,
became a scraping hook.
For twenty years a fire raced
across the boughs of your bones,
his drunken mouth a movie
flashing with every stabbed gesture.

Now the white room of birth is throbbing:
the numbers palpitating red on the screen of machinery
tentacled to your arm; the oxygen mask wedged
in a wheeze on your face; the numbing medication
injected through the spine.
The boy was snagged on that spiraling bone.

Medical fingers prodded your raw pink center
while you stared at a horizon of water
no one else could see, creatures leaping silver
with tails that slashed the air
like your agonized tongue.

You were born in the river valley,
hard green checkerboard of farms,
a town of white birches
and a churchyard from the workhorse time,
weathered headstones naming women
drained of blood with infants coiled inside
the caging hips, hymns swaying
as if lanterns over the mounded earth.

Then the white birch of your bones,
resilient and yielding, yielded again,
root snapped as the boy spilled out of you
into hands burst open by beckoning
and voices pouring praise like water,
two beings tangled in exhaustion,
blood-painted, but full of breath.
After a generation of burning
the hook unfurled in your body,

the crack in the bone dissolved:
One day you stood, expected again
the branch of nerves
fanning across your back to flame,
and felt only the grace of birches.

Obviously, my wife and son had changed me, had even changed my poetry. This might be the first Puerto Rican poem swaying with white birch trees instead of coconut palms. On the other hand, Katherine and I immediately set about making this a Puerto Rican baby. I danced him to sleep with blaring salsa. Katherine painted *coquís*—tiny Puerto Rican frogs—on his pajamas. We spoon-fed him rice and beans. He met his great-grandmother in Puerto Rico.

The behavior we collectively refer to as "macho" has deep historical roots, but the trigger is often a profound insecurity, a sense of being threatened. Clemente will be as secure as possible, and that security will stem in large part from self-knowledge. He will know the meaning of his name.

Clemente Soto Vélez was a great Puerto Rican poet, a fighter for the independence of Puerto Rico who spent years in prison as a result. He was also our good friend. The two Clementes met once, when the elder Clemente was eighty-seven years old and the younger Clemente was nine months. Fittingly, it was Columbus Day, 1992, the five-hundredth anniversary of the conquest. We passed the day with a man who devoted his life and his art to battling the very colonialism personified by Columbus. The two Clementes traced the topography of one another's faces. Even from his sickbed, the elder Clemente was gentle and generous. We took photographs, signed books. Clemente Soto Vélez died the following spring, and eventually my family and I visited the grave in the mountains of Puerto Rico. We found the grave unmarked but for a stick with a number and letter, so we bought a gravestone and gave the poet his name back. My son still asks to see the framed photograph of the two Clementes, still asks about the man with the long white hair who gave him *his* name. This will be family legend, family ritual, the origins of the name explained in greater and greater detail as the years pass, a source of knowledge and power as meaningful as the Book of Genesis.

Thankfully, Clemente also has a literal meaning: "merciful." Every time my son asks about his name, an opportunity presents itself to teach the power of mercy, the power of compassion. When Clemente, in later years, consciously acts out these qualities, he does so knowing that he is doing what his very name expects of him. His name gives him the beginnings of a moral code, a goal to which he can aspire. "Merciful": Not the first word scrawled on the mental blackboard next to the phrase "Puerto Rican male." Yet how appropriate, given that, for Katherine and me, the act of mercy has become an expression of gratitude for Clemente's existence.

BECAUSE CLEMENTE MEANS MERCIFUL
   —for Clemente Gilbert-Espada
      February 1992

At three AM, we watched
the emergency room doctor
press a thumb against your cheekbone
to bleach your eye with light.
The spinal fluid was clear, drained
from the hole in your back,
but the X ray film
grew a stain on the lung,
explained the seizing cough,
the wailing heat of fever:
pneumonia at the age
of six weeks, a bedside vigil.
Your mother slept beside you,
the stitches of birth still burning.
When I asked, "Will he be OK?"
no one would answer: "Yes."
I closed my eyes and dreamed
my father dead, naked on a steel table
as I turned away. In the dream,
when I looked again,
my father had become my son.

So the hospital kept us: the oxygen mask,
a frayed wire taped to your toe

for reading the blood,
the medication forgotten from shift to shift,
a doctor bickering with radiology over the film,
the bald girl with a cancerous rib removed,
the pediatrician who never called, the yawning intern,
the hospital roommate's father
from Guatemala, ignored by the doctors
as if he had picked their morning coffee,
the checkmarks and initials at five AM,
the pages of forms flipping like a deck of cards,
recordkeeping for the records office,
the lawyers and the morgue.

One day, while the laundry
in the basement hissed white sheets,
and sheets of paper documented dwindling breath,
you spat mucus, gulped air, and lived.
We listened to the bassoon of your lungs,
the cadenza of the next century, resonate.
The Guatemalan father
did not need a stethoscope to hear
the breathing, and he grinned.
I grinned too, and because Clemente
means merciful, stood beside the Guatemalteco,
repeating in Spanish everything
that was not said to him.

I know someday you'll stand beside
the Guatemalan fathers,
speak in the tongue
of all the shunned faces,
breathe in a music
we have never heard, and live
by the meaning of your name.

Inevitably, we try to envision the next century. Will there be a mens'
movement in twenty years, when my son is an adult? Will it someday

alienate and exclude Clemente, the way it has alienated and excluded me? The counterculture can be as exclusive and elitist as the mainstream; to be kept out of both is a supreme frustration. I sincerely do not expect the mens' movement to address its own racism. The self-congratulatory tone of that movement drowns out any significant self-criticism. I only wish that the mens' movement wouldn't be so *proud* of its own ignorance. The blatant expropriation of Native American symbols and rituals by certain factions of the movement leaves me with a twitch in my face. What should Puerto Rican men do in response to this colonizing definition of maleness, particularly considering the presence of our indigenous Taíno blood?

I remember watching one such mens' movement ritual, on public television, I believe, and becoming infuriated because the drummer couldn't keep a beat. I imagined myself cloistered in a tent with some Anglo accountant from the suburbs of New Jersey, stripped to the waist and whacking a drum with no regard for rhythm, the difference being that I could hear Mongo Santamaría in my head, and he couldn't. I am torn between hoping that the mens' movement reforms itself by the time my son reaches adulthood, or that it disappears altogether, its language going the way of Esperanto.

Another habit of language that I hope is extinct by the time Clemente reaches adulthood is the Anglo use of the term "macho." Before this term came into use to define sexism and violence, no particular ethnic or racial group was implicated by language itself. "Macho," as employed by Anglos, is a Spanish word that particularly seems to identify Latino male behavior as the very standard of sexism and violence. This connection, made by Anglos both intuitively and explicitly, then justifies a host of repressive measures against Latino males, as our presence on the honor roll of many a jail and prison will attest. In nearby Holyoke, police officers routinely round up Puerto Rican men drinking beer on the stoop, ostensibly for violating that city's "open container" ordinance, but also as a means of controlling the perceived threat of macho volatility on the street. Sometimes, of course, that perception turns deadly. I remember, at age fifteen, hearing about a friend of my father's, Martín "Tito" Pérez, who was "suicided" in a New York City jail cell. A grand jury determined that it is possible for a man to hang himself with his hands cuffed behind him.

While Latino male behavior is, indeed, all too often sexist and violent, Latino males in this country are in fact no worse in that regard than their Anglo counterparts. Arguably, European and European-American males have set the world standard for violence in the twentieth century, from the Holocaust to Hiroshima to Vietnam.

Yet, any assertiveness on the part of Latino males, especially any form of resistance to Anglo authority, is labeled macho and instantly discredited. I can recall one occasion, working for an "alternative" radio station in Wisconsin, when I became involved in a protest over the station's refusal to air a Spanish-language program for the local Chicano community. When a meeting was held to debate the issue, the protesters, myself included, became frustrated and staged a walkout. The meeting went on without us, and we later learned that we were *defended,* ironically enough, by someone who saw us as acting macho. "It's their culture," this person explained apologetically to the gathered liberal intelligentsia. We got the program on the air.

I return, ultimately, to that ventriloquist and his Puerto Rican dummy, and I return, too, to the simple fact that my example as a father will have much to do with whether Clemente frustrates the worshipers of stereotype. To begin with, my very *presence*—as an attentive father and husband—contradicts the stereotype. However, too many times in my life, I have been that Puerto Rican dummy, with someone else's voice coming out of my mouth, someone else's hand in my back making me flail my arms. I have read aloud a script of cruelty or rage, and swung wildly at imagined or distant enemies. I have satisfied audiences who expected the macho brute, who were thrilled when my shouting verified all their anthropological theories about my species. I served the purposes of those who would see the Puerto Rican species self-destruct, become as rare as the parrots of our own rain forest.

But, in recent years, I have betrayed my puppeteers and disappointed the crowd. When my new sister-in-law met me, she pouted that I did not look Puerto Rican. I was not as "scary" as she expected me to be; I did not roar and flail. When a teacher at a suburban school invited me to read there, and openly expressed the usual unspoken expectations, the following incident occurred, proving that sometimes a belly laugh is infinitely more revolutionary than the howl of outrage that would have left me pegged, yet again, as a snarling, stubborn macho.

MY NATIVE COSTUME

When you come to visit,
said a teacher
from the suburban school,

don't forget to wear
your native costume.

But I'm a lawyer,
I said.
My native costume
is a pinstriped suit.

You know, the teacher said,
a Puerto Rican costume.

Like a guayabera?
The shirt? I said.
But it's February.

The children want to see
a native costume,
the teacher said.

So I went
to the suburban school,
embroidered guayabera
short sleeved shirt
over a turtleneck,
and said, Look kids,
cultural adaptation.

The Puerto Rican dummy brought his own poems to read today. *Claro que sí.* His son is always watching.

OF **CHOLOS** AND SURFERS

Patricia Geary

JACK LÓPEZ is a graduate of the MFA program in writing at the University of California at Irvine. His short stories have appeared in literary journals, as well as in several Latino literature anthologies, including <u>Iguana Dreams and Pieces of the Heart</u> He teaches literature at California State University at Northridge.

THE ONLY STORE around that had this new magazine was a Food Giant on Vermont Avenue, just off Imperial. *Surfer Quarterly,* it was then called. Now it's *Surfer Magazine* and they've celebrated their thirtieth anniversary. Sheldon made the discovery by chance when he'd gone shopping with his mother, who needed something found only at Food Giant. Normally we didn't go that far east to shop; we went west toward Crenshaw, to the nicer part of town.

We all wanted to be surfers, in fact called ourselves surfers even though we never made it to the beach, though it was less than ten miles away. One of the ways you could become a surfer was to own an issue of *Surfer Quarterly.* Since there had been only one prior issue, I was hot to get the new one. To be a surfer you also had to wear baggy shorts, large Penney's Towncraft T-shirts, and go barefoot, no matter how much the hot sidewalks burned your soles.

That summer in the early sixties I was doing all sorts of odd jobs around the house for my parents: weeding, painting the eaves, baby-sitting during the daytime. I was earning money so that I could buy Lenny Muelich's surfboard, another way to be a surfer. It was a Velzy-Jacobs, ten feet six inches long, twenty-four inches wide, and it had the coolest red oval decal. Lenny was my across-the-street neighbor, two years older than I, the kid who'd taught me the facts of life, the kid who'd taught me how to wrestle, the kid who'd played army with me when we were children, still playing in the dirt.

Now we no longer saw much of each other, though he still looked out for me. A strange thing happened to Lenny the previous school year. He grew. Like the Green Giant or something. He was over six feet tall and the older guys would let him hang out with them. So Lenny had become sort of a hood, wearing huge Sir Guy wool shirts, baggy khaki pants with the cuffs rolled, and French-toed black shoes. He drank wine, even getting drunk in the daytime with his hoodlum friends. Lenny was now respected, feared, even, by some of the parents, and no longer needed or desired to own a surfboard—he was going in the opposite direction. There were two distinct paths in my neighborhood: hood or surfer.

I was entering junior high school in a month, and my best friends were

Sheldon Cohen and Tom Gheridelli. They lived by Morningside Heights, and their fathers were the only ones to work, and their houses were more expensive than mine, and they'd both been surfers before I'd aspired toward such a life. Sheldon and Tom wore their hair long, constantly cranking their heads back to keep their bangs out of their eyes. They were thirteen years old. I was twelve. My parents wouldn't let hair grow over my ears no matter how much I argued with them. But I was the one buying a surfboard. Lenny was holding it for me. My parents would match any money I saved over the summer.

Yet *Surfer Quarterly* was more tangible since it only cost one dollar. Lenny's Velzy Jacobs was forty-five dollars, quite a large sum for the time. The issue then became one of how to obtain the object of desire. The Food Giant on Vermont was reachable by bike, but I was no longer allowed to ride up there. Not since my older brother had gone to the Southside Theatre one Saturday and had seen a boy get knifed because he wasn't colored. Vermont was a tough area, though some of the kids I went to school with lived up there and they weren't any different from us. Yet none of them wished to be surfers, I don't think.

What was needed was for me to include my father in the negotiation. I wasn't allowed to ride my bike to Vermont, I reasoned with him. Therefore, he should drive me. He agreed with me and that was that. Except I had to wait until the following Friday when he didn't have to work.

My father was a printer by trade. He worked the graveyard shift. I watched my younger brother and sister during the day (my older brother, who was fifteen years old, was around in case anything of consequence should arise, but we mostly left him alone) until my mother returned from work—Reagonomics had hit my family decades before the rest of the country. Watching my younger sister and brother consisted of keeping them quiet so my father could sleep.

In the late afternoons I'd go to Sportsman's Park, where I'd virtually grown up. I made the all-stars in baseball, basketball, and football. Our first opponent on the path to the city championships was always Will Rogers Park in Watts. Sheldon and Tom and I had been on the same teams. Sometimes I'd see them in the afternoons before we'd all have to return home for dinner. We'd pore over Sheldon's issue of *Surfer* while sitting in the bleachers next to the baseball diamond. If it was too hot we'd go in the wading pool, though we were getting too old for that scene, since mostly women and kids used it.

When Friday afternoon arrived and my father had showered and my mother had returned from work, I reminded my father of our agreement. We drove the neighborhood streets up to Vermont, passing Washington High School, Normandie Avenue, Woodcrest Elementary School, and so on. We spoke mostly of me. Was I looking forward to attending Henry Clay Junior High? Would I still be in accelerated classes? My teachers and the principal had talked with my parents about my skipping a grade but my parents said no.

Just as my father had exhausted his repertoire of school questions, we arrived at the Food Giant. After parking in the back lot, we entered the store and made for the liquor section, where the magazines were housed. I stood in front of the rack, butterflies of expectation overtaking my stomach while my father bought himself some beer. I knew immediately when I found the magazine. It looked like a square of water was floating in the air. An ocean-blue cover of a huge wave completely engulfing a surfer with the headline BANZAI PIPELINE. I held the magazine with great reverence, as if I were holding something of spiritual value, which it was.

"Is that it?" my father asked. He held a quart of Hamm's in each hand, his Friday night allotment.

"Yes." I beamed.

At the counter my father took the magazine from me, leafing through it much too casually, I thought. I could see the bulging veins in his powerful forearms, and saw too the solid bumps that were his biceps.

"Looks like a crazy thing to do," he said, finally placing the magazine on the counter next to the beer. My father, the practical provider, the person whose closet was pristine for lack of clothes—although the ones he did own were stylish, yet not expensive. This was why he drank beer from quart bottles—it was cheaper that way. I know now how difficult it must have been raising four children on the hourly wages my parents made.

The man at the counter rang up the purchases, stopping for a moment to look at the *Surfer*. He smiled.

"*¿Eres mexicano?*" my father asked him.

"*Sí, ¿cómo no?*" the man answered.

Then my father and the store clerk began poking fun at my magazine in Spanish, nothing too mean, but ranking it as silly adolescent nonsense.

When we got back in the car I asked my father why he always asked certain people if they were Mexican. He only asked men who obviously were, thus knowing in advance their answers. He shrugged his shoulders and said he didn't know. It was a way of initiating conversation, he said. Well, it was embarrassing for me, I told him. Because I held the magazine in my lap, I let my father off the hook. It was more important that I give it a quick thumb-through as we drove home. The *Surfer* was far more interesting for me as a twelve-year-old than larger issues of race.

I spent the entire Friday evening holed up in my room, poring over the magazine, not even interested in eating popcorn or watching *77 Sunset Strip,* our familial Friday-night ritual. By the next morning I had almost memorized every photo caption and their sequence. I spoke with Sheldon on the phone and he and Tom were meeting me later at Sportsman's Park. I did my chores in a self-absorbed trance, waiting for the time when I could share my treasure with my friends. My mother made me eat lunch before I was finally able to leave.

Walking the long walk along Western Avenue toward Century and glancing at the photos in the magazine, I didn't pay attention to the *cholo* whom I passed on the sidewalk. I should have been more aware, but was too preoccupied. So there I was, in a street confrontation before I knew what had happened.

"You a surfer?" he said with disdain. He said it the way you start to say *chocolate. Ch,* like in *choc—churfer.* But that didn't quite capture it, either.

I stopped and turned to face him. He wore a wool watch cap pulled down onto his eyebrows, a long Sir Guy wool shirt with the top button buttoned and all the rest unbuttoned, khaki pants so long they were frayed at the bottoms and so baggy I couldn't see his shoes. I wore Bermuda shorts and a large Towncraft T-shirt. I was barefoot. My parents wouldn't let hair grow over my ears. *Cholo* meets surfer. Not a good thing. As he clenched his fists I saw a black cross tattooed onto the fleshy part of his hand.

His question was *not* like my father's. My father, I now sensed, wanted a common bond upon which to get closer to strangers. This guy was Mexican-American, and he wanted to fight me because I wore the outfit of a surfer.

I rolled the magazine in a futile attempt to hide it, but the *cholo* viewed this action as an escalation with a perceived weapon. It wasn't that I was overly afraid of him, though fear can work to your advantage if used correctly. I was big for my age, athletic, and had been in many fights. The problem was this: I was hurrying off to see my friends, to share something important with them, walking on a summer day, and I didn't feel like rolling on the ground with some stranger because *he'd* decided we must do so. Why did he get to dictate when or where you would fight? There was another consideration, one more utilitarian: Who knew what sort of weapons he had under all that baggy clothing? A rattail comb, at the least. More likely a knife, because in those days guns weren't that common.

At Woodcrest Elementary School there was a recently arrived Dutch-Indonesian immigrant population. One of the most vicious fights I had ever seen was the one when Victor VerHagen fought his own cousin. And the toughest fight I'd ever been in was against Julio, something during a baseball game. There must be some element of self-loathing that propels us to fight those of our own ethnicity with a particular ferocity.

Just before the *cholo* was going to initiate the fight, I said, "I'm Mexican." American of Mexican descent, actually.

He seemed unable to process this new information. How could someone be Mexican and dress like a surfer? He looked at me again, this time seeing beyond the clothes I wore. He nodded slightly.

This revelation, this recognition verbalized, molded me in the years to come. A surfer with a peeled nose and a Karmann Ghia with surf racks driving down Whittier Boulevard in East L.A. to visit my grandparents. The charmed life of a surfer in the midst of *cholos*.

When I began attending junior high school, there was a boy nicknamed Niño, who limped around the school yard one day. I discovered the reason for his limp when I went to the bathroom and he had a rifle pointed at boys and was taking their money. I fell in love with a girl named Shirley Pelland, the younger sister of a local surfboard maker. I saw her in her brother's shop after school but she had no idea I loved her. That fall the gang escalation in my neighborhood became so pronounced my parents decided to move. We sold our house very quickly and moved to Huntington Beach and none of us could sleep at night for the quiet. We were surrounded by cornfields and strawberry fields and tomato fields. As a bribe for our sudden move my parents chipped in much more than matching funds so I could buy Lenny Muelich's surfboard. I almost drowned in the big waves of a late-autumn south swell, the first time I went out on the Velzy-Jacobs. But later, after I'd surfed for a few years, I expertly rode the waves next to the pier, surfing with new friends.

But I've got ahead of myself. I must return to the *cholo* who is about to attack. But there isn't any more to tell about the incident. We didn't fight that summer's day over thirty years ago. In fact, I never fought another of my own race, and don't know if this was a conscious decision or if circumstances dictated it. As luck would have it, I fought only a few more times during my adolescence, and did so only when attacked.

My father's question, which he'd asked numerous people so long ago, taught me these things: The reason he had to ask was because he and my mother had left the safe confines of their Boyle Height upbringing. They had thrust themselves and their children into what was called at the time the melting pot of Los Angeles. They bought the post–World War II American dream of assimilation. I was a pioneer in the sociological sense that I had no distinct ethnic piece of geography on which my pride and honor depended. Cast adrift in the city streets. Something gained, something lost. I couldn't return to my ethnic neighborhood, but I could be a surfer. And I didn't have to fight for ethnic pride over my city street. The neighborhood kids did, however, stick together, though this was not based upon race. It was a necessity. The older guys would step forward to protect the younger ones. That was how it was done.

The most important thing I learned was that I could do just about anything I wished, within reason. I could be a surfer, if I chose, and even *cholos* would respect my decision. During my adolescence I went to my grandparents' house for all the holidays. They lived in East Los Angeles. When I was old enough to drive I went on my own, sometimes with a girlfriend. I was able to observe my Los Angeles Mexican heritage, taking a date to the *placita* for Easter service and then having lunch at Olvera Street. An Orange County girl who had no idea this part of Los Angeles existed. I was lucky; I got the best of both worlds.

WHORES

LUIS ALBERTO URREA received a Western States Book Award and The Colorado Book Award for <u>Fever of Being,</u> a book of poems from West End Press. He is also the author of the widely acclaimed memoir <u>Across the Wire: Hard Times on the U.S.-Mexican Border,</u> from Anchor Books, and a novel, <u>Searching for Snow,</u> from Harper-Collins. He lives in Tucson, Arizona.

Let me burn you, let me burn you,
let me burn you Down.
—Front 242

IT'S TWELVE HUNDRED miles south of Tijuana and about an hour inland from the sea. It lies on the western lip of the town, near a small cemetery and the old rail line. The town itself is a classic rural Mexican community, with cobble and dirt streets, a small square with a gazebo, and such new developments as marijuana and *cholos* and graffiti. Sometimes, gringos make their way here, but few stick around long enough to be impressed. Once in a while, they even make their way to this place, called *El Club Verde Para Hombres*—"The Green Club for Men."

It's not as exciting or evil-hearted as some of the places in Tijuana. Most of the clients here are skinny farmhands or well-fed minor urban functionaries or fat off-duty cops. A few of the women are too old for work in a more fancy house, and the other ones are just lucky that this is as far down as they'll go.

It's a big structure, and it presents a blank wall to the street. Concrete blocks slathered over with slapdash Mexican stucco and a green paint job last touched up in the 1950s. The relentless sun has faded it a sort of watercolor yellow. If you listen at the wall, at night, you will hear the forced sounds of partying emanating from within—trumpets, laughter, jukeboxes, bad live *rocanrol*. And the women, every night, can be heard shouting naughty jokes and risqué insults.

I am in a car with the most macho young men of the Urrea family, cousins I first met when my father decided I was queer. Third grade, perhaps. Tough Mexican boys brought up to the United States because I was being raised gringo. I was speaking Spanish in too *pocho* a manner: not enough rough edges in the words, not enough disdain and wit inherent in my pronunciation. My *R*'s were not hard enough, the *G* and *J* sounds lacked the heft of phlegm at the back of the palate to really sizzle. I had learned, to my utter shock, that the wrong emphasis on the wrong consonants could lead to humiliation, insults, even violence. I remember one of these cousins giving me tequila in fifth grade, then cigarettes, in order to roughen the far borders of my words. I, apparently, had a garden on my tongue, and the men were demanding a desert.

They were doubly worried about me because I had made the deadly error of announcing, in first grade, that I wanted to be a priest. My father said, "But you won't want to have women." What did I know of women? I'd had visions of the plaster Christ on the cross opening His eyes and looking at me. I wanted the stigmata. I wanted to work miracles and save the sick. "You want to wear a black dress? You'll be a faggot!"

What's that? I remember wondering.

Outside the whorehouse, looking like they've been beamed up from 1970, a small group of Mexican males gathers nervously. They're mostly young, but one of them is too young. Fathers regularly bring their sons to the Green Club for their first sexual encounter. The cop at the door smiles like an uncle when a terrified twelve-year-old comes under the wing of his dad. But solo, you'd have to be at least eighteen. And one of these boys is only fourteen. But he's tall, and without his glasses he looks maybe old enough.

They have gathered to buy him his first sex.

Their names are Jaime, Fausto, El Gordo, Fu Manchu, and Blondie. Blondie's other nickname is Pigfoot. But tonight, his lighter hair is more visible than his stubby feet. He's the fourteen-year-old.

It is a law: Mexican males must have nicknames. Jaime, in this group, is called El Red. There are others in their circle known as Dracula, Frankenstein, Taras Bulba, and El Chino Cochino ("The Dirty Chinaman"—he's one of the many Mexican-Chinese who inhabit the Norte). The best nickname in town belongs to a man they all fear. He's called El Quemapueblos, and I agree that it's the best nickname I've ever heard. Its pithiness can't be translated into English. The best I can do is "The Man Who Burns Down Cities."

Thank God he doesn't figure in this story, I think.

———

My father imported these strange, rangy boys to intensify the manhood factor around the house. One of them—I'll call him The Bull, a nickname he was awarded for the size of his penis—was a boxer and an athlete. Something I definitely was not. In my memory, The Bull is ten feet tall and muscular, evil, self-satisfied enough that he even sleeps with a smirk. Years later, wandering into the whorehouse, I realize with a start that he's just a little Mexican government weasel. Another Goddamned wiseguy, picking the meat off the bones of the poor, sliding illegal funds sideways into his various bank accounts. He has matted hair, jug ears, and dresses like a bad scene from an old episode of *Charlie's Angels*. All petroleum-product materials. He's only five foot eight.

I start to laugh.

"What?" he says, half-smiling but worried, afraid there's a joke somewhere that he's not in on, already partially angry that I might be laughing at him, when it has always been his right to take ferocious aim at me.

"I could break your neck," I tell him, "with one hand."

His face flushes.

His blush, in Club Verde's frosty tube lights, looks purple.

The Bull's legendary good looks have rotted and turned the color of half-cooked liver.

He is visiting his father, my uncle. We have all gathered for a family holiday. Their home is stately by village standards. It sits atop a small stationery store with the only Xerox machine in town. The machine is so old, however, that it produces weird, Cold War Xeroxes. The kind where the paper is black and the text is white—a negative copy of your document.

Over supper, he has told me, "We've got to go to the *bule* tonight. They've got a deaf-mute girl!"

He beams at this news—it's the most exciting thing he's thought of all day. I can only suppose it's the exotic nature of it that has him in a lather. It's the only new thing to do in town except for the movie, which is showing John Wayne's old nugget, *The War Wagon,* dubbed into German, with Spanish subtitles. As we talk, hundreds of little birds tumble through the air like leaves on a sidewalk.

"She's even cute," he enthuses. "And she charges thirty thousand pesos."

At the current exchange rates, I'm thinking, what—ten bucks at most.

"Just," he intones, "don't tell my wife we went."

I'm not telling anyone anything. It's my plan to get him in the graveyard and beat him senseless. I feel the rocks in my hands: I hide them under the table. I want to bury him alive out there, pour dirt in his mouth, listen to him underground as the scorpions descend.

We follow the boys inside. I feel like Blondie's father. He could be me at fourteen. The entrance is off a small courtyard. Around this courtyard, six shacks are arrayed. On the front step of one, a child plays.

"Whores' houses," my host quips.

"They live here?"

"You can't expect them to go into town! They keep to themselves."

A river of shit has run out of the spectacularly noxious toilets near the door. We all make our crossing in single file. The open door of the Green Club belches smoke and discordant electric guitar. Too metaphorical. A cop stops the boys and frisks them. He doesn't even look at Blondie. They're in.

I grab a table near them and look around.

Three women are visible. The deaf-mute, who is heartbreakingly cute, with a short hairdo and no makeup. She is using a crude sort of sign language to indicate lust to a table full of drunk men. She grabs her crotch, makes a pained face, writhes. She pantomimes masturbation as the farmers giggle like little boys and poke one another with hard black forefingers. I can see dolls in her face, and excitement over Popsicles. She looks like she's selling lemonade at a sidewalk stand in La Jolla. And masturbating.

The other woman has a face like a friendly turtle and a brassy voice that brays louder than anything in the room. My host asks, "Are you mute, too?"

She points to her ass.

"This isn't mute!" she reports. "It cuts loud farts!"

She smiles at me.

"Hola, guapo," she says.

"Good evening, *señorita,"* I reply.

She stares at me like I've said something exceedingly strange. Stops smiling.

He tries to touch her, and she yanks her arm away.

She starts to dance with a small ranchero. They look like the two ends of a horse having a seizure. The song is a Mexican version of "Rock Lobster." Some idiot on the record is bellowing: *"¡Langosta! ¡Langosta Rock!"*

The third woman, the one the young boys at the next table have obviously come for, is terrifying. She's Tina Turner—even has the same wig. Her massive eyelashes are the size and shape of tarantulas. When the boys goad Blondie into touching her—he timidly taps her on the arm with one finger—she glares at him. I'd swear she's hissing. He pulls his hand away fast and looks at the floor.

"¡Ay ay ay!" they note.

The Bull and his invasionary force came into my life with a promise of companionship and adventure. I was a Boy Scout. The scouts were the only escape from the eternal race war between my gringo mother and my *mexicano* father. It was also the only way I, raised on dirt and outhouses and barrio sadism, could hike up a mountain, see coyotes, drink from waterfalls. The cousins informed me that Boy Scouts were pussies.

If I really wanted to be *un hombre,* I'd learn to box.

Then they slapped me silly. I learned fast that my bloody noses were *funny.* I was supposed to wipe the blood off on my forearm and laugh.

I also learned an unspoken lesson about machismo.

All the toughest males, every *muy macho chingón* from deep Mexico who entered my house, was obsessed with forcing the younger children to suck his dick. Each one wanted to push his hard-on up the asses of the boys and girls of our family. But mostly, these men who were to rescue me from the unforgivable queerness of serving God wanted to ride the backs of little boys. Little boys like me.

Beside the bar there is a small shrine to the Virgin of Guadalupe. Votive candles burn at her feet, and some wilted carnations are strewn at the statue's sandals. The center of the room is a big concrete dance floor. The walls all have two doors. They are so cheap you could, if you really wanted to, look through the slats and watch the action inside.

Each door opens onto a small room. In each room, one bed and one chair. One small table holds a bowl and a jug of water, a bar of soap and a rag. Above the beds hang crucifixes.

Once, the police captain of the town fell in love with a woman who worked here. He got so jealous—and drunk on tequila—that one night he burst into the Club Verde, kicked open her door, and shot her and the unfortunate beer salesman on top of her. The Green Club didn't know what to do with the room. They considered closing it in honor of the tragedy, but ultimately changed the mattress and went on as usual.

The deaf girl—she can't be more than eighteen, I've decided—comes up to me and offers me the brother handshake. We clench hands. She looks like one of my English students. But suddenly, she gets a flushed expression, then pantomimes something going up her. She stands there and grinds at my table, hands on crotch. She's doing her little dance for me now. The Bull punches me on the arm and laughs appreciatively. Then she opens her eyes and grins at me and nods. I shake my head. She has dimples. She points at me, at my crotch, then holds her hands about two feet apart and makes an "Ooh" with her mouth.

I shake my head.

I laugh.

I hold up two fingers and hold them about one inch apart and look sad. This cracks her up. She shakes my hand and rushes off to the next table.

"You had her," my host says. "You could have fucked her up the ass!"

The man with the Macho Box comes around to the boys' table.

He's called El Maestro, "The Master," as are all workmen in the places where the old Mexican ways are still practiced. Mexico is rapidly becoming as rude as the United States, but in courtlier days, mastery was honored. Shoeshine boys, barbers, or violin virtuosos were all *maestros*. And this *maestro* brings the Macho Box, a device known to anyone foolish enough to hang out in Mexican bars for very long.

It's basically a torture device. A box with a couple of dials, a trillion batteries inside, and wires attached to two metal rods. For some reason, Mexican men can't resist holding these rods and trying to prove how much shock they can withstand. Think of it: The *maestro* actually gets paid to turn his knobs and torture men—and the torturees are the ones who pay! The really brilliant *maestros* offer, as a prize, free shocks. This is pure capitalism at its best.

Blondie has been anesthetized by his first serious gulps of tequila. He has confided to me what his friends don't know—he's too afraid of Tina Turner to try to make love to her. His buddies hook him to the machine and the *maestro* cranks it up. Blondie hangs on. After a while, he *has* to hang on because his fists are cramped onto the rods. "Not. So. Bad," he says. His arms curl and rise above his head. The *maestro* really lets him have it. But he can't give up now—everybody, even Tina, is watching. His knuckles clack together above and behind his head. He is either smiling or frozen in an electrified rictus.

The Turtle-faced Woman comes up to me.

"Writer," she says. "Look at this."

I put down my notebook and look up.

The Bull says, *"Pinche maricón. Puto. Joto.* Writing in your little diary all night."

A beer delivery man had been pestering me. He was overwhelmed with drunken filial love, you know—the kind that immediately precedes a mass slaying. He shook my hand about ten times, hanging on my table, insisting, *"Tú, amigo mío."*

She cuts him off and pulls a Polaroid out of her blouse. She's standing there naked. Smiling like she's in front of the flamingo exhibit at the zoo. In the photo, her nipples are black.

"For you," she says, "five hundred pesos."

The Bull announces, "I love this shit!"

Over at the next table, Blondie has followed his Macho Box challenge with a drinking contest with a local stud named Mauser, after the German rifle. I never ask, but I draw my own conclusions. He wins seven hundred pesos on an impromptu bet as he and Mauser chug tequila from eight-ounce tumblers. I will later learn that Blondie will spend the night with his head in a plastic bucket, convinced his bed is flying around the room, uplifted by demons. He will beg Jesus, in the classic drunk's prayer, to sober him up, and he will *never drink again.*

With the winnings, and the money pitched in by the boys, Blondie's got about enough for sex.

Tina whips her wig in the near distance, curls her lip, goes *"Chk"* with her mouth to show her disdain. But keeps her eye on him.

I watch Blondie. He's breaking out in a sweat, and it's not just the booze. Fu Manchu is almost asleep. He's lost his bridge somewhere, and his upper lip blows in and out of his mouth like laundry on a line. Fausto is fairly sober, Jaime is doing cricket imitations with his mouth. El Gordo hates his nickname. Who'd want to be called "Fatso"? His real name is Gilberto.

He leans over to Blondie and makes a drunken confession: "You're lucky," he says, "to have so much love from these guys."

"What do you mean?" says Blondie.

"You're only fourteen!" Gilberto cries. "I am twenty-one! And *I've never been laid!"*

He bangs the table.

Blondie is no fool. I can see it in his face. Inspiration.

"Boys," he says. "Boys!"

They drag their attention away from the dance floor, where everyone is wiggling around to "El Farolito."

"I love you all," says Blondie. "I do."

Drunken promises of undying love and brotherhood come from their lips in response.

"I love it that you have brought me here and given me this."

He shows them the money.

They agree that they have given it to him.

"But brother Gilberto here . . ." He touches El Gordo. "My dearest friend."

They take it in stride—in Mexico, when you're drunk, everybody's your dearest friend or deadliest enemy. Gilberto, through the magic of intoxication, is suddenly *everybody's* dearest friend.

"Fucking Gordo," they say.

"And Gilberto is twenty-one years old to my fourteen!"

This is clearly Blondie's Gettysburg Address. He will, I suspect, live longer in the town's mythology for this act than for anything having to do with Tina Turner.

"And Gilberto is a virgin!"

"No!" they say as Gilberto hangs his head in sorrow.

"It's true," Gilberto says.

"I," Blondie says, "have time. Gilberto does not."

He's a hero! The boys can't believe his loyalty to El Gordo. They buy him a beer and slap him on the back. One of them signals for Tina. She storms across the dance floor at them, looking like she's going to slap somebody. They push Gilberto at her. He holds out the money. She takes it, sinks her nails into his forearm, and pulls him away.

The little door slams.

As we leave, the deaf prostitute signs something that I can't figure out. She repeats her gestures until I understand. She is saying: "I want to come with you."

The Bull says, "You're not writing about me, are you?"

"Yes," I say, smiling.

"What?" he demands.

I continue to smile.

Bloody noses are funny, after all.

"Oye, cabrón," he warns.

"I only," I whisper, "write the truth, you son of a bitch."

He moves away from me.

Outside, the boys wait for Gilberto. When he finally comes out, his hair is a mess. He looks very sad. As they walk away, he keeps looking back at the Club Verde.

The little prostitute tugs at my arm. She gestures at herself, at me, away, to the north. She places her hands before her heart, as if she were praying. Her eyes are wet.

"Don't tell my wife about this," The Bull pleads.

My God—he's terrified of his wife. The top of his head reaches my nose. I look into the dark—the cemetery wall is barely visible across the road. A thousand dogs are barking at the moon. I put my hand on the back of his neck. It's skinny. I imagine the blows. I squeeze lightly. He winces.

"Do you remember when we were boys?" I ask.

His eyes, huge with worry, rotate in their sockets. Are they looking for escape? Then they settle on my face.

"We had fun, right?" he says.

"Not really."

The color is draining from his face.

I hug him.

He relaxes against me.

"You taught me to be a man," I say into his ear. I hug him harder. "I'm a writer now," I remind him. "And I will make you famous." I slap him on the back. "I don't need to kill you, cousin. I can make you immortal."

He pulls away.

"¿*Qué?*" he says.

"All of you. Every bit of you, *Bull.*"

I push him away.

I walk out the gate.

She is watching me. He stands between her and me. The boys are laughing in front of me. Gilberto is talking quietly. As I catch up to them, he finally says, "Do you think she would go out on a date with me?"

I stop, halfway between the graveyard and the whorehouse. The Bull is running toward me. The little whore turns and walks back inside. The boys move away, gray as ghosts. I can hear them, laughing at Gilberto all the way home.

ROMANCING

THE <u>EXILIADO</u>

Lew Wilson

RICARDO PAU-LLOSA is the author of three books of po-
etry, including <u>Bread of the Imagined,</u> from Bilingual
Press, and <u>Cuba,</u> from Carnegie Mellon University Press.
His art criticism on twentieth-century Latin-American art
has appeared widely in journals. His fiction has been
published in <u>Sudden Fiction, Iguana Dreams,</u> and <u>The
New England Review.</u> He is professor of English at Miami-
Dade Community College, Kendall Campus, Florida

I HAVE LIVED in exile since late 1960, the year my family fled communist Cuba and settled in Chicago. I was six and a half years of age at the time. Contrary to the body of superstitions that informs North American myths about newcomers (especially those who arrive here as children), exile is not a transitory state, a limbolike initiation phase of émigré consciousness. Neither is it the appropriation of politics to dignify expulsion from home, a bit of refugee chic donned in the process of stripping oneself bare before being fitted with the clean laundry of American assimilation. Exile is not the curtain one draws to secure privacy in such moments of redress. Exile is a place that shapes the temporality of identity, a stage (as in both theater and phase) one calls home, where the dialogue is not always dark. In matters of love and sex, exile is the ultimate prankster of the self.

The notion of place is intrinsic to exile. The exile is not simply another Other on the five-star menu of sappy alienation. Placement and displacement—the yin and yang of historical orientation—are what contextualize every other dimension of exilic life. Since everything always happens in a place, exile is with you no matter where you are and what you are experiencing. That includes sex and romance. Indeed, that exile should engulf the juicy matters of the heart and loins has come as yet another mild shock to one who has lived 34 of his forty years in such a state. I would have hoped that eros, at least, would have been, if not the oasis, at least the lacuna. But hope is the one distinct event that stops happening in that place called exile, if only because, whatever else happens there, hope is its substance. Hope is exile's exile, shifting in status from event to terrain, from object to environment, from caressed thigh to firm mattress.

How does what is hoped for change in this essential shift? For the first of the two types of philistines of *exilio*—those who remain stuck in its first traumatic episodes for the duration—what is hoped for is return. For the second type of *filisteo exiliado*—those who embrace assimilation regardless of how much the "natives" reject them—hope targets an impossible rebirth. For the gourmet of *exilio*—and, forcibly, that includes those thrown into exile at an early age, those who cannot remember what it is one hopes to return to or escape from—hope becomes an act of consciousness whose *noema* is a feeling of impossible belongingness; indeed, being at ease with feelings as *noemata* is a good way of telling a gourmet of *exilio* apart from everyone else. From the first configuration of this particular feeling, inextricable impossibility lies at its heart. This impossibility need not inspire sadness; it is merely a fact of that feeling.

At age twenty-one I began training to meet the demands of this hope in trips to lands that resemble the lost one—the cities and villages of the Spanish- and Portuguese-speaking world. It was in Segovia and Buenos Aires, in the Mérida of the Venezuelan Andes and in coastal villages near Rio—not in Boise or Chicago—where I was served repeatedly with the credentials of permanent foreignness, where the clear link between wanting to belong and not being able to belong were, once and for all, separated from the more primitive impulses of nostalgia and assimilation, which drive the philistine of exile. There I was, embracing and embraced by reasonable facsimiles of home ground, but to no avail. After many such trips I was finally ready for exilic hope. I was ready for love.

Before such an arrival, however, there were years in which the heart felt at home in its undiagnosed chaos. Perhaps it should have never surprised me to find I drew more interest among North American women than among *cubanas,* who had shared my history. Having attended all-boy Jesuit schools, I didn't begin dating in earnest until I started college in 1971. My first real break came in Montreal, where I attended Loyola College in 1972. At first my flawless American accent got me nowhere with women. Montreal was filled with a strange and ephemeral species— American draft-dodgers, that is to say, American exiles. Often mistaken disdainfully for one of those, I took pains to clarify that my intrinsic, Cuban, and robust commitment to historical displacement began long before North America's Vietnam debacle. The erotic reaction to my high-toned political pronouncements was, delightfully, not what I expected. I expected politically engagé coeds in Montreal to sneer at someone they would surely label a running-dog Cuban capitalist. To my surprise, I struck them as exotic. That they considered Cubans from Castro's consular corps equally as exotic, making no distinction between an exile and an apparatchik, was something I was prepared to overlook at that particularly famished phase of my erotic life. Alas, there is little ideology from the waist down.

As I grew more accustomed to swimming in melting ice, I began advertising my exotic condition with a redolent Ricky Ricardo accent—actually, I mimicked my parents' accent and broken grammar, not the clownish Desi. I started smoking cigars. And, as I vaguely recall, I even came up with a genetically flavored, jargon-laced explanation for that equine quality all males from Cuba most certainly enjoyed. At this point, of course, I had unwittingly surrendered to self-parody—I was becoming Desi Arnaz—but the more *cubanazo* I became, the more effortless dating games became. God only knows how much better I might have made out if only I had brought a Santa Barbara medal on a thick gold chain and a decent pair of bongos.

I never stopped missing Montreal, even if exotica would eventually lose its erotic magic for me. Back in Miami, I had to face a brutal reality: A Cuban was about as exotic here as a maple leaf in Quebec. My first trip back to Montreal took place twenty years later, in December 1993; I was giving a talk and a poetry reading at McGill University. The rough subterranean haunts of my student days were long gone, replaced by yuppie bars. At one such establishment near St. Catherine's, I tried to light a cigar, a votive offering to the god of lost youth. Briefly, I became a philistine exile who had replaced the Havana of his kindergarten for the Montreal of his early manhood. Where once I mimicked my father's tongue, I was now wearing his frayed nostalgias. A part of me hoped the thick smoke would camouflage the thinning hair and writer's paunch of middle age long enough to pluck a seductive glance, preferably from a woman half my age with enough literary pretensions to ease her into awe. Had it not been in Montreal where I learned to turn cigar smoke into the masculine version of Salome's veils? Alas, the crosshairs in the manager's machine-gun stare reminded me of how cruelly little room there is for the exotic in these clean-air times, so I paid my tab and climbed back into the winter from which I had descended. On the icy pavement I belonged impossibly to my strangeness once again. The cold blanched everyone's exhalations and made it seem as if a dozen strangers had joined me in a smoke. Yes, I always carry the theater props of exile in my head.

The twenty years between my two Montreal's had not been entirely consecrated to writing poems and embarking on festive travels through Latin America in search of a prosthetic Havana. Interludes with Cuban women in Miami never, to my bewilderment, got very far. Who knows what unconscious forces were driving me, and them, to pick the wrong mates within the tribe and more plausible ones outside of it. With rare exceptions, I would meet each cubana after both of us had just terminated relationships or marriages with Anglos or other foreigners (that includes non-Cuban Latins). It was as if we had met at a pit stop on the race to another extratribal affair. Of course, there was much to be said for the comfort of mating without having to expound the fundamentals of my quotidian universe. (No, black beans are not dyed that color. Don't be sad because you can't tell a mambo from a rumba. How clever of you to think Olga Guillot descended from the Frenchman who invented the guillotine. I can't imagine how poets, painters, and other citizens survived the hordes of prostitutes stampeding through pre-1959 Havana twenty-four hours a day. No, I won't sing "La Cucaracha." Of course I can tell you read *The Miami Herald*—you are so well informed about Cubans. It's Ricardo, dear, not Richardo.)

Nonetheless, a stubborn gulf would widen irresistibly with each passing day of the nascent relationship with a cubana. Could it be that we each felt at home in relationships only when we felt alien, and that in each other's company we just didn't feel odd enough to be utterly satisfied? Did each of these cubanas have an analogous Montreal experience in which, ensconced in her cultural strangeness, she had become a Tahitian nymph bedazzling a sea of horny, unblinking Fletcher Christians? Had erotic become inextricable from exotic for all the children of exile? Could it be *that* simple?

Erotic exotica, especially when played out (and exploited) within one of the cultures in which the exotic subject is fluent, permits this person to feel empowered. I never felt this in Montreal, nor did I miss it, since the focus then was entirely and youthfully on obtaining the physical gratification of sex. As sex became adult and psychological, a horizon of neurosis unique to the bicultural began to open up. This horizon is particularly acute when experienced in the context of American culture, which, despite the past fifteen years of "multicultural" chest-thumping and two centuries of individualist rhetoric, remains, and probably always will be, one of the most parochial and uniform cultures on earth.

Mainstream (invariably monolingual, ethnocentric) Americans—regardless of the degree and quality of foreign travel, level of education, ethnicity, or avowed ethnic allegiance—are, to genuinely multicultural foreigners or bicultural Americans, remarkably predictable and simple beings. The mainstreamer's cultural referents, standards, and criteria for judging anything, from the arts to morality, from food to politics, consist of a tight network of familiar causalities, reactions, and rationales that far outweigh individual quirks, histories, hopes, and traumas. At least, that is the prevailing impression of mainstream Americans that most bicultural beings and foreigners I have spoken to possess, and which my personal experiences have led me to accept as a rule with rare exceptions.

One of the more depressing manifestations of American provincialism—one that introduces itself often in any romance across ethnic lines—is that interest in foreign issues and sympathy for foreign tragedies must be predicated on how closely these mirror recent American issues and tragedies. Without the white guilt over slavery and segregation and the triumphs of the civil rights movement, I doubt Americans would have much cared about promoting an end to apartheid in South Africa. Americans show concern only for oppressed national groups whose plight is, they think, comparable to that of the American Indians. This analogy, however procrustean, has helped some Americans understand the plight of Palestinians, Kurds, Bosnians, et al. Aggression or intervention by foreign powers (e.g., Soviets in Afghanistan, Cubans in Angola, Iraqis in Kuwait) can't be condemned unless these actions are equated with American involvement in Vietnam or American interventions in Latin America. Even the recent earthquake in Kobe, Japan, was covered in the U.S. media in obsessive counterpoint with the Southern California quake one year earlier. In America, it's all sympathy by analogy.

Regrettably for a Cuban exile, Americans have not experienced life in a totalitarian state, so Castro rarely inspires condemnation by intellectuals and journalists here. *Time*'s fawning cover story on Castro (February 20, 1995) is a vivid and by no means isolated case in point. As a Cuban exile, one of the first questions that an "outsider" always and still asks—maliciously or not—is what I think of Castro and the Cuban Revolution. This enables the American interlocutor to place me somewhere in his or her simplistic political spectrum, hewn from a trivial view of how liberal versus conservative, right versus left interact on the domestic political scene.

Anti-Castro means, to them, the same thing as conservative. Period. They are invulnerable to even the calmest explanations of how their little spectrum doesn't apply, even remotely, to ethical and moral rejection of tyranny.

In a romantic context, the matter is exacerbated by the fact that the American woman most likely to be dating a Latin man defines herself as a liberal. However, the phenomenon of spectrum placement occurs as often on dates or outings with American friends as on literary panels and academic symposia. It has become the most recurrent and clearly defined experience of those I consider idiosyncratically American. Clearly, the sense of place *americanos* apply to the exile is quite different from the dynamics of time-place-identity in the *exiliado*'s psyche.

Mainstream America's parochial narcissism and thimble-sized worldview mean that, for the bicultural being (especially one whose dualities are grounded in the mind-set of exile), courting mainstreamers presents countless opportunities for bewilderment. Miami is often represented by "crackers" and other pre-Cuban exodus white "natives" as an erstwhile Eden overrun by barbarians from the Caribbean. Dating WASPish Eve's in Miami, then, begins with subtle rituals aimed at calming the feathers of ethnic vanity. Donning the casual native garb of empire—seasoned jeans and denim shirt (with cowboy boots for an extra punch in image delivery)—on a first date is advisable. If I want to impishly introduce an element that will push cultural dissonance to the surface of conversation quickly, I will put a cigar in my shirt pocket, whether I intend to smoke it during the evening or not.

After the mandatory bow to the first cliché—Freud's assurance that sometimes a cigar is just a cigar—the presence of this pocket missile will, in the more imaginative and intelligent of the native females, provoke a discussion of culturally different views of pleasure, its pursuit and expression. Even these discussions, though, usually wind up on a less-than-flattering reference to Latin inconsiderateness of civilized others' territory and rights (smoke, noise, flaunting of sexuality, cheek-kissing in salutations, et al). Among the less imaginative, the possibilities for absurdity rise dramatically. If my interlocutor is ecologically hip, she will preach about the rain forests martyred by tobacco growers. If my interlocutor is a health storm-trooper, no need to describe how the discussion might go.

In the past, a particularly Anglo aberration would occur. I would be given permission by my date to actually light the cigar, with assurance that it didn't bother her, only to watch her face curl into revolted knots as wafts of smoke came near. I confess it was amusing to see the horn-locking between irreconcilable drives to be polite and to retch. I would put the cigar out, but not immediately. Clean-air fetishism has made such coyness obsolete.

A Latin woman has always been more likely to tell you right off what she thinks of cigars. My guess is that the difference in approach is not decided by sincerity, per se, nor by the Anglo woman's diplomatic desire to avoid stomping on an ethnically sensitive habit—Latin-male cigar smoking, in this case. The Latin woman is interested in clarifying areas where spontaneous crossing-of-the-lines (as in making a pass or getting frisky) might be left in a state of hedonistic suspense, by canceling areas (like smoking a cigar) where energy might be dissipated in boring discord.

The Latina knows that being blunt about trivial matters (cigar smoking) is a form of landing-strip clearance that allows jovial or illuminating conflict about sexual agenda and intentions to come into the picture early. Once these issues are on the ground and clear of any other distractions, the conflicts in expectations can be negotiated or otherwise allowed to run their course. The North American woman, especially the feminist, long ago subtracted herself from the ranks of wily flirts, regardless of their empowering Tarzanic cries. Hence she must dissipate her territory-mapping energies across a hopelessly wide spectrum of human interactions, everything from cigars to who opens the door to sexual gate-keeping. No marker can be left unattended, and all must be guarded with equal diplomatic rigor. For the *feminista americana* it's a nearly hopeless situation; for the bicultural male who provoked the crisis in cultural dissonance, the spectacle can be either amusing or confusing, depending on his experience or the degree of awe in which he holds the woman.

Other manifestations of early feather-smoothing have to do with positions on key issues that the Anglo female has been programmed to see as litmus tests. These issues are aired after the *exiliado* has already undergone the spectrum placement described above. The list of burning issues is trite: abortion, glass ceilings, Mr. Mom skills, the Cuban-mother syndrome—the trendy plethora of gender turf discussions, victim stereotypes, and culturally influenced sex-based injustices. When the interrogations are made across culture, they become more urgent for the woman and more transparent for the man. The Anglo notion is, of course, that Latin women are the battered slaves of their machos. The Anglo hope is that the Latino specimen before her, wrapped (armored?) in reassuring denim and cowboy boots, has already been initiated into the freeing American values of sexual equality, or at least fervently hopes to be soon. The reality that cubanas in exile have generally been at par with americanas on liberation issues—and in some areas, ahead of them—is always met by the americana with ethnocentric skepticism.

I always get the feeling during these attitude-scanning interrogations that my interlocutor preens with her questions; she is certain I will see her as the model woman of the future, in stark contrast to the Latinas of the past (including those in my family), whom, naturally, I will reject now that I have seen the northern light of dignified womanhood. Winning the americana's favor by proving my egalitarian credentials is, she thinks, a kind of elevation for me, a cultural promotion, a permission to look down on the sexual power structures that stain my ethnic past. By extension, forthrightly answering her patronizing questions and waiting for the unilateral, fate-deciding conclusion she draws from my responses is one way I can liberate myself from my primitive past. The Latin male wishing to continue playing this game—to, say, get laid that night—must exhibit a carefully measured and above all humbling sign of gratitude at this point. It must be subtle. I recommend a sigh accompanied by an approving nod, as when a heartwarming lesson has ostensibly been learned from an idiotic Hollywood "masterpiece" *(Forrest Gump* comes to mind).

Is it any wonder that exotic otherness lost its allure long ago? It is a boring vaudeville act. When the exile makes the mistake of taking this swimming across the channels of cultural dissonance seriously, the exercise becomes painful. An exile in America who believes he or she will ever be anything but exotic is everyone's fool. Why, then, not simply court within the tribe? Because there is no tribe, only the illusion of one. Exile means living without a tribe. It means having to substitute a vital, social sense of belonging to a living and evolving tradition (what I mean by living in a tribe) with identifying those fellow survivors of a historical cataclysm who share essential values or interests and forming a pack with them. Not only are the horizons different, but so is the way "horizon" is defined. The native need not check where he is; the warm containment of his horizons are a given. The native is always dead center of his world. The exiliado must regularly check the hull integrity of his bubble in the midst of a complex and alien environment whose horizon, no matter how distant, is always discernible. For the exiliado, the horizon always starts with you. For the gourmet of exile—the child brought up in exile being just one of these— journeys from the margin to native space always wind up becoming journeys to a new manifestation of the margin.

A few months ago I was waiting at a red light in Coral Gables, a middle- and upper-class neighborhood full of winding streets with names, as opposed to numbers, hence particularly difficult to get around in. A female tourist pulled up next to me. At first glance, the inside of her car seemed to have been engulfed by a huge map. Only parts of her thin arms were visible. She put the passenger-side window down and waved her hand. I put my window down and smiled blandly. No use scaring the tourists any more than they already are. "Do you speak English?" she asked, more like pleaded. No doubt she had already stopped more than one foreign-tongued resident in her Gables odyssey. I looked right at her and, in my best Montreal Cuban accent, said "Jes" and lifted a hidden cigar to my grinning teeth. Blanched with fear and frustration, she quickly put her window up and began diving once again into her monstrous map. I waved at her to put her window down again, which she did halfway and with some hesitation, her left eyelid trembling a bit, bottom lip slightly bit. I dropped the accent and helped her find her joyous way. Afterward I felt as if I had just had a huge Cuban meal of pork and *moros* and yucca.

My romantic failure rate with cubanas is bound, in part, to the reality that exile is the most divisive of communal arrangements, the most fragmentary of collective conditions. Individual exiles feel tied only to those with whom they share identical strategies of healing, not just the wounds. Among exiles—particularly Cubans—the extravagance of a creative life strikes a threatening chord deep in the unconscious. The stereotyping of artists as deviants and lazy louts is all too familiar, and lamentably not an exclusively Cuban phenomenon. These culturally ingrained anti-artist biases have been augmented in exile, where survival strategies have had a lot to do with regaining economic stability, a process that is intimately identified with reconstructing the past. Ironically, the artist is fluent in pasts, but only because he seeks a vital dialogue with it from which the future will emerge. The poet-visionary among Cubans, despite the demigod status of José Martí, is simply not seen as a member of the ark-building team. The natural bonds that bind natives across professions and areas of interest are much more frail among exiles. Exile is not seen as being about myth-making or the imaginative digestion and reformulation of history—although it should be. It's about hammers and nails and buckets of tar because, as we are repeatedly informed, exile has to do with the flood at hand.

The exile of the poet from Cuban culture is similar to the alienation artists endure everywhere, especially in cultures and times in which personal and communal survival is in question. Cuba, like the U.S., was during most of this century an immigrant culture, and both nations share entrenched, philistine attitudes toward the social worth of the artist. Exile has hardened philistinism among Cubans in America, even dignified it. Every exile adores a Spartan. The "Athenian" dimension of the exilic mind—the imagination, the higher-value stuff—belongs to and is focused entirely on the lost past, as if only within trite nostalgia can the exercise of the imagination be deemed safely virile. Nostalgia is to the exile philistine what the football field is to the American mainstreamer—a parenthetical space where an activity considered deviant in everyday "real" life (e.g., body contact among males) is permitted, even extolled. Being a poet or artist, strange as this might sound, makes you less of an exile to other exiles; they see the poet as never having entirely left the past they idealize and know so little about. The poet is a traitor to the present, to its alleged urgencies. His loyalties lie in the past and the future. He is seen as belonging to a different time sense, hence he has no place among exiles, the irrepressible citizens of the now.

Ironically, being a poet among philistine exiliados means living in a double exile, and in no experience is this made clearer to the poet than when he courts a *cubana-espartana*. She can be yuppiefied or still reek of blue-collar Hialeah, it makes no difference. She can hold a Ph.D. and drive a Mercedes, even collect art and actually read good books. She can, in other words, be classified as a non-philistine by native standards. And the poet who courts her can even have a good job and make good money (although she suspects that high culture and economic disadvantage are one and the same, regardless of the empirical evidence to the contrary). The only factor in play is the fact that the foundation of her survival orientation makes her want to stay away from the man of the imagination. The same goes, of course, when the woman is the artist and the man the exiled philistine. The ark-builder's stare will always greet the artist and defeat all his or her hopes. The fragmentation and philistine agendas of exile make such romantic experiences the most alienating of all, far worse than dating a native philistine.

With the Anglo woman, you are reminded of your exile not just from Cuba but from effortless cultural participation of any kind. Your duality makes you alien, not your lack of fluency in American life and values. But then, you expect to be alien among Others. It's the double exile that is, finally, the most permanent obstacle to joy. At the Montreal bar in 1993, I was yearning only for a lost time. My father always pined for a lost time and a lost place—in his mind they were inextricable. I can never yearn for both things at once, as the person who came into exile as an adult can and must. I am sure Adam and Eve, after sharing the hardness of our world, always retained a fondness for certain fruit and snakes.

Whether I dated unapologetically philistine cubanas or gringas out to prove (and therefore disprove) their "open-mindedness," it has been in matters of love where I have felt the pain of double exile the strongest. Romance has always been a journey both to and from exilic hope, a constant return to that drawing board erected on quicksand.

ALL

ABOUT RACHEL

for Uncle Rachel,

February 1993

Scott Stoner

RANE ARROYO is the author of two poetry collections, Columbus' Orphan and The Red Bed. He is also a play-wright with productions in New York City, Chicago, and Los Angeles. His "Prayers for a Go-Go Boy" played off-Broadway in 1994. He recently completed a study on the Chicago renaissance, Babel USA. His poems have recently appeared in Another Chicago Magazine, Apalachee Quarterly, and Caliban. He teaches at Youngstown University in Youngstown, Ohio.

UNCLE ISRAEL wasn't a transvestite yet, or AIDS dead. As my baby-sitter, he told no stories. Instead, whenever Aretha Franklin came on the radio, he would make me dance with my small shadows until I collapsed into my soft arms. Once, when we were playing hide-go-seek (game that did lead me to graduate school), I cut my thigh against a knife. Uncle, known as Rachel to intimates, made me put a hand over my mouth. We didn't speak until my cut clotted. I still have a scar on that leg, pink medal of peace.

What's unbearable to me is to tell Rachel's story in a strict, narrative way. His life wasn't like that. Neither was his death. Sometimes I think of things to tell him, but his ear is now stone. Heavy planet.

Family confirms that Uncle is HIV positive or near death with "full-blown" AIDS. (*Blown* makes me think of a garden in bloom, blowout blowjobs, or glassblowers in malls.) But I just found Rachel, after twenty years. I just dedicated my play to him: *Buddha and the Señorita*. How dare he stop existing when he has at last become a named muse. His first words: *Thank God you're you. I'm me.* Mine: *Why do atheists thank God so often?* We were both alive!

Me, a poet and playwright! Rachel's son, almost. Only in *West Side Story* did I see public spaces transformed by *puertorriqueños* into resistant sites where hegemony is exposed as system and not a naturalized . . . Rachel interrupts, *Junior, I want to die. Really. Really.*

When I was young, I breathed at the movies or explored novels' labyrinths far from the world as I didn't know it. Rachel and I loved Tyrone Power (*Tyrone Power/We always have an hour for you*). A nurse cut the phone call short, gave him something new. He wanted me to sing him to sleep, but I only knew rock songs, no gospel, no psalms. I told him the story of John the Beloved.

Rachel disappeared one Thanksgiving. That's how I remember it, but I lived in dreams, then, embedded in some novel in bed, some long poem, tabloids, *Waltons* rerun. I loved John-Boy, wanting to be the man he needed me to be. Drag in flannel. Father was scared for me: black eyes because I was skinny, *pretty,* friends with Jews, smart. Father: *Israel's never coming back so you better learn about perversion.* Me: *I love Rachel the way I'll never love you.* Even then, he gave me no black eyes. What a simple and good man, whose demons have been my inheritance, dancing fools. After Israel's death, Israel and the PLO made peace. I cry as I type this. Is love greater than loneliness?

Vision of lovely Rachel: at her white wicker table, wicked woman putting on red eyeliner, wondering if the condom in her Chanel coin purse is strong enough of a parachute to support her weight, dreams, makeup, years of midnight snacks, martinis. She leans forward and kisses me, leaving a pair of lips à la Hollywood on my shy forehead. She whispers sexily: *Write the story of my life and call it "All About Rachel."* Within one hour of his death, my family destroyed all of his papers. Ashes to ashes, says the priest on cue. Curtains fall, smoky veils, secrets.

None of his memories survive. So I and Grandmother, his mother, Maria, who believes Heaven has to be real because nothing else has been so far. *Abuela,* I cried, *I won't forget him.* I have. Day by day.

Rachel died slowly, over the telephone. One weekend I was in Chicago and I had to make the drunk choice of seeing him/her or not. I chose not to because he/she disappeared on her own, Venus sinking into Atlantis, Atlantic City. I knew his/her vanity was a source of strength. Beauty remembered, like in blank faces of angels in cemeteries in winter. It's a germ-free garden of grief. There I was, miles from Rachel. I called to say something stupid, à la Frank and Nancy Sinatra. Rachel wanted to talk to God, so he gave me Beauty as a gift: *I not only made love, hijo, I kicked its ass. Good night, dream of me, as I was.* But who, what, when, where, why, and how were you, American darling (type of a fire hydrant)? I passed out in my hotel room.

Misdiagnosed with AIDS—in the eighties it was black and white, no HIV (HIVe of hurt)—I walked the Boston Common with Glenn. Buddhists in sweatpants sat on stones, heads bowed, bald. We ran through leaves, wanting to tear something that like me would never heal; then, at home, we sat in a bathtub of tears.

I now realize that the character Señorita is modeled on Rachel:

BEE:

But now, nothing is as it was and I'm not even sure anymore that what was is what I thought it was. I mean, in some ways, I am always ten years old and in another way I'm a ghost on the moon already *(Pause, a beat.)* . . . only don't tell my bones and don't tell my heart because they don't know about such things yet. They'll learn. I'm not worried about it at all. What do I remember anyway?

That play, *Buddha and the Señorita,* will never be made into a film for mall theaters. It is too interested in questions of death. *All About Rachel* is interested in questions of life. It, too, will never be a film. In cities and suburbs, black movie screens are widows' veils I wear for you, Rachel. If you must sink into stone, give up the moon you once knew for the secret sun inside the Earth. Your final blindness will fall off. Stare into red gardens where molten roses grow that we all will wear on our beautiful heads.

BLESS ME,
FATHER

Elisa V. Quintana

LEROY V. QUINTANA received a 1993 Before Columbus Foundation American Book Award for <u>History of Home,</u> a book of poetry from Bilingual Press. His other two collections from the same publisher are <u>Sangre</u> and <u>My Hair Turning Gray Among Strangers.</u> He teaches literature at Mesa College in San Diego, California.

WHAT OTHER CHILDREN took for granted when the nuns asked for information before the beginning of class meant nothing more than terror, agony, and embarrassment to me.

"What is your father's name?"

And then: "And what is your father's occupation?"

The answers came so easily!

"John."

"He's a mailman."

It was so easy, so easy for them.

I sat at my desk, frozen, trying desperately to rehearse what I would say and how I would say it when Sister Ann got to Q.

"Well," I would begin, "all I know about my father is that his name is Frank, and that only because it's written on the birth certificate that I've brought before and which you've seen, and other than that I don't know nuthin'—where he is, where he's been—so therefore I am completely unable to tell you anything about his occupation, other than he probably doesn't have one, at least according to the little my mother has chosen to reveal about him on those occasions when I've been brave enough to steer a conversation in that direction."

It seems so easy now, forty years or so later, to lay these words out just as I would've liked to then, with a "And what do you say to that, Sister?" attitude behind them.

But more than anything, what I really wanted to say, not only to the Sisters of Charity but to the entire class, was "How lucky you are! You don't have to sit at your desk, squirming yet remaining as motionless as a rock, falling so deep inside yourself you wish you would never have to come back, might never come back."

So deep inside myself I begin to emerge only thirty years later, after practicing and undergoing therapy and finishing a second master's, in counseling, because somehow I always knew that was what I needed to do to save my life.

I'd like nothing more than to glide through all this by simply uttering a name and an occupation.

Already I feel severed from classmates, teachers, parents, and most important, from myself.

It seems like forever, but soon, too soon, Sister Ann gets to *Q*. It's much too difficult, too painful to launch into any explanation of my life and circumstances. And besides, who would be interested? Who would listen? And who would care?

"Father's name?" Sister inquires.

Doesn't she have all this shit down already somewhere in my file? Why do I have to undergo this interrogation, in front of everybody? Why can't Sister Ann, who knows so much about the suffering of martyrs, see that I'm about to be crucified?

"File," I say, wanting to explain that he's my stepfather.

"Spell it, please."

"*F-i-l-e.*"

"That's *File!*" she exclaims, and now the entire class is involved. Everybody is thinking about a file and asking themselves how could anybody have a name like that. "Now, what's his name?" Sister demands again.

"File," I say again, this time with a more anglicized pronunciation.

"Phil!" she exclaims. "*P-h-i-l!*"

OK, that's fine with me, I say to myself. It's really "File" as in "Fileberto," but I'll agree to anything just to end this ordeal. Anything you say. Whatever.

I dig deeper into myself. I know what's coming.

"Occupation?"

"Roofer." The dirtiest job known to man. My stepfather is the only man on the planet that loves that kind of work. Everybody else's father seems to have a job that is much cleaner: mailman, truck driver, baker.

"Roofer?" Sister Ann asks.

Surely it can't be that difficult to figure out what the hell a roofer is. I say something about hot tar, shingles.

I think it never occurred to her that roofs just don't sprout on houses—somebody has to nail the shingles on. It's her turn to display one of those "whatever" looks. This is the land of *mañana*—so far from Cincinnati and the Mother House.

When she gets to my cousin (on my stepfather's side, which means he's not really an official, acknowledged relative in my mother's book) he answers "Rogerio" when Sister asks for his father's name.

It flies right by Sister, of course, and she asks him, in an obviously rude manner, to spell it.

"*R-o-g-e-r-i-o.*"

"That's *Roger!*" she exclaims.

And *Roger* it is. We discuss it on the way home. "It's not *Roger!*" my cousin says, angrily. Yeah, and it's not *Phil,* either, I say to myself. It's not a lot of things.

Shame, *vergüenza,* runs my life. I have too much of it. And the world, oh the world, has hardly enough.

I'm only in the seventh grade, but I've been living in pain for so long.

It's late morning and I've just been awakened by the worst of any young boy's nightmare: my uncle's high-toned voice.

I'm living with my grandparents, who for all intents and purposes are my parents. I've discovered, bit by bit, through my cousins' nosiness, that I'm the child of divorce.

I know that my mother lives in Albuquerque. I receive postcards from her. And she sends Grandma money for my first-communion suit, an Easter shirt. It doesn't occur to me until I'm older how much she helped raise me. We are poor, Lord, but not nearly as poor as most of the kids I go to school with.

I overhear whispers that are deliberately meant for me to hear. My cousins are the only family I have, but that doesn't spare me from their maliciousness. I never seem to learn that people attack the weak simply because they *are* the weak.

Whispers about an absent father followed by snickers. I learn early to ignore, or rather to pretend that I didn't hear, what was said. I'm alone, and when you are alone it's very difficult to confront. I've always been outnumbered.

It's late morning, but I refuse to get up, even though I want to, need to. I've wet my bed again. I'm soaking wet, and if I get up, I know what's going to happen: I'll walk into the kitchen and my uncle will ask, innocently enough, "*¿Cómo hace el gatito?*"—"What sound does a kitten make?"—and then quickly answer, "*Meow, meow,*" which sounds much too much like *mea'o,* a shortened form of *meado,* from the verb *mear,* which means "peed on."

But, if being outnumbered has taught me anything, it's to defend myself in less confrontive ways—by lying.

Oh, I will make my way through life hating hypocrisy but living by lies.

I make up a story about how the doctor said I had a disease, unpronounceable, of course, that caused me to wet the bed nightly and had Grandma washing sheets day after day, hanging them out like flags of surrender that my cousins could clearly see from their kitchen window.

I have, then, as role models, my grandfather, a staunch *demócrata,* a large man who can still shoulder railroad ties and who could care less about social graces. I acquire my intolerance of people from him, along with my soft-heartedness and generosity and social conscience.

And then there is my uncle, an unbelievably impatient, intolerant man who ran for office not knowing the tricks of the small-town politico, like putting spoiling meat on the tables of hungry voters on our side of town. A man who forever after ranted and thundered about how the world was going to the dogs. An abusive man, the way he teased me (in particular), but he taught me early on the meaning/s behind what took place and what really was: He was the one who questioned why the town held the yearly Kearny Entrada, an event that celebrated the entry of Stephen Watts Kearny into New Mexico with a parade and festivities. Why were we, los mexicanos, in such a fired-up hurry to celebrate the very event that had made us the colonized? Whether I want to admit it or not, I must have a good dose of my cynicism and social consciousness from him.

Also, there was my grandmother, puffing on her brown-paper *cigarrito,* telling me the old *cuentos* over and over, so patient and so loving. I owe her for being so tolerant. She forgave all my pranks and miscreant behavior. I learned kindness from her.

And finally, my *padrino,* the quiet, soft-spoken man I've strived to be all my life. A boxing champion in the army who never resorted to violence. He tried to help me save my life, but even though I listened, I paid no mind. I needed him to be closer both physically and spiritually—but he lived in another town, not too far away, but far enough so that I didn't see him that often and therefore profit from his presence. Oh, how I could have learned to be a man, a man of my own liking from him, from the very beginning!

All these were my fathers, then, had a hand in my upbringing, a role in the role/s I would play the rest of my life/ves.

And lest I forget, I too was, at any and all times, father, desperate father to that young boy learning how to survive, to endure the tragedy of growing up.

And then the day comes when I have to go live with my mother and step-father. I think I had become too much for my grandparents to handle. I was wild and I had no mind of my own. Without a doubt I would've strayed with the wild crowd and landed at the nearby reformatory.

And then the day came when I had to move away. It was the end of my childhood, and in some way the end of my life.

My mother and I were strangers to each other.

Albuquerque and the neighborhood and the children of the neighborhood were strangers to me.

I was alone, really alone—an outsider in a strange land. I began to live way down deep inside myself. I became a problem to my new set of parents—and to the nuns, who even with the help of God were unable, or unwilling, to understand me.

How angry I must have been! To be taken away from my grandparents and the sweetness of their simple lives. We had a kerosene lamp until, one day, my uncle impatiently installed electricity and then, later, indoor fixtures. But as angry as I was I was unable to do anything to better my situation. I was too much like my grandfather, who seemed to accept most events in a somewhat passive manner. I did not even allow myself the possibility of running away. Where could I go? My grandparents were two hundred and fifty miles away. (Later, when I did consider it, when I could no longer tolerate the situation, I realized two things: One, I would be brought back, by the police or whoever, and then I'd be in even worse trouble; and two, like most children who have suffered because of a broken marriage, at the same time that I was locked in conflict with my parents, I was being spoiled by them as they tried to erase or make up for any trauma I had experienced.)

So I became a behavioral problem. I wanted to rebel and tell the nuns they could and should go to Hell. On the other hand I wanted to be loved, and to belong. But to be loved and to belong you have to behave, you have to be "good." Good at books (which I had been while living with my grandparents, and could be again if I wanted to, but for what?) and a goody-two-shoes as well. I did not know how to take control of my life; I had no touchstone, no direction, no plan, no method. Nobody, and I mean *nobody,* understood me. A few tried, but I pushed them away, and I was sorry to see that they were so easily thwarted.

The way the nuns portrayed me to my parents (and to myself), I was the personification of evil. Surely I couldn't have been such a mystery. I wanted to be cool, but I also wanted to be good. Put simply, I was too brave to be a square, but not brave enough to be bad.

Oh, how I wanted (and needed) someone to protect me, to defend me by standing up to the nuns and to my parents (and maybe, more important, to me) and explain, simply explain, why I was such a *malcriado.* I understand now that that is why I had to return to school and study counseling and psychology: to save myself. I had nobody, certainly nobody I could trust, so I had to save my own life, posthumously, it seemed.

Oftentimes I hoped and dreamed of having an older brother or sister to defend me, but that's the most I allowed myself. I had hopes, opinions, and beliefs, but what did they matter? I didn't matter much to anybody, therefore I didn't matter much to me.

Stories were my salvation.

I turned to reading, to dreaming.

I began to live as far away from people, the world, as I possibly could.

Words comforted me. It was so easy for me to escape, disappear into a story.

I loved stories. Books, movies, comic books, *Mad* magazine comforted me, allowed me to escape where nobody could hurt me. On television there was *General Electric Theater* (hosted by Ronald Reagan, if I remember correctly). There was also *Playhouse 90,* and there was *Death Valley Days* (hosted by Ronald Reagan), *The Twilight Zone, Perry Mason, Paladin,* and *Alfred Hitchcock Presents* on Sunday nights, while my parents were supporting the parish by playing bingo. And there was Zorro. And when we began to climb into the middle class there was *Reader's Digest* with its

"Most Unforgettable Character," its vocabulary quiz, and its "Quotable Quotes."

Later there was *Life* and *The Saturday Evening Post*.

I loved being alone. There were no conflicts to deal with. No confrontations of any kind with the neighborhood children over not having a father; no conflicts with the nuns, who demeaned you and slapped you; no fights—especially between parents.

Going to live with a new set of parents was difficult enough, but it was compounded by the fact that they fought, and that when they fought, which was often, it carried into insults and threats of divorce, which I think I secretly hoped would be carried out so that I wouldn't have to endure any more pain, though I also worried and wondered how difficult and painful it would be not to have a "family." I was always happy when they got back together, perhaps thinking that this time was the time we were going to make it. I know now this is how and why I became a pacifist.

I remember sitting in a courtroom downtown crying uncontrollably as my parents argued, my stepfather with his family on one side and my mother (and me) on the other. It's no wonder that for most of my life I felt I had to take on the world—and did—and paid the price.

I'm hoping that the judge will do something—he seems to be so powerful—do or say something that will make these people stop fighting and look at what they are doing to me. He says something to them about me before he wraps the case up, but nothing is going to change. We walk out, warring factions awkwardly next to one another, and I don't know how I'm supposed to feel. I don't have anything against these people, but I know we have to be enemies of sorts. I have never learned how to go about getting close to someone, and something like this makes it even more difficult. My cousin (in-law) is also my best friend and I feel good and bad for liking him. I like him the way I like nobody, nobody else. And I feel badly for him, too. We walk home from school together, and even though he lives right next door he has to take one route and I another as we near home. My mother allows me to play with him, but there are times, never predictable, when she sees us together that she will say something insulting to him and we both slink away embarrassedly. I accept humiliation, and I expect it, and so it comes my way. Because I expect it, I accept it.

Eventually, my mother wins out, and so, from my stepfather, I learn how to be oppressed, but with that, I learn the kindness that only the oppressed know how to extend, a quality of mercy they are certainly entitled to but never receive.

From my mother I learn tenacity; I learn how to endure, but many years go by before I learn the good and bad side of stubbornness.

But if stories serve to heal me, words also help to cause me pain. I learn to use words, instead of fists, to defend myself. I become very proficient at using words to strike back, to deflect and inflict anger, but I never seem to learn that that gets me into even more trouble. It's the only defense I know, but I pay dearly. A person has to defend himself the best way he knows. What I knew were words, but words didn't save me. I needed to learn to shut up, not talk back, not to be a smart ass, and always, not to be a cynic. Language (in private) saved me, but language (in public) helped to destroy me.

Eventually, I isolate myself completely. I cannot deal with people. Most important, I do not want to deal with people. I do not want to get close to people. Anybody at any time can and will hurt you. Deep in my world of words I am happy without people.

But I am also very unhappy because I am extremely isolated. In order to protect myself I've had to hurt myself. I avoid people, social situations—and because I avoid people I do not become adept at small talk, gossip, social intercourse, and because I do not master the social element, I belong to no social circle to speak of. And that suits me fine, fulfills my role as rebel angry at the hypocrisies and falsehoods of society. But then, I'm also too alone—I need some kind of warmth, love, and understanding. Nobody disliked how humans acted any more than I did, and yet nobody needed to be among them, learning the games, plans, deceits, graces, compliments, kisses, shortcomings, failures, and successes more than me.

The final outcome was that I became not only a rebel, but a Zelig as well.

There are times that out of desperation, I try to fit in, go along with whatever crowd I'm in even though I do not like or believe what the rest believe. I disobey my own private philosophies and commandments. I also wander from group to group, whoever will take me, though I never stay long.

What others are born with in terms of role models, philosophies, beliefs, I have to learn, painfully, for myself. How easy, or how much easier life could have been for me if I had had someone to teach me, to point me in the right direction.

I often think that perhaps I secretly envy those who are close-minded, self-centered, and arrogant, because at the very least they believe so strongly that they are right. But I learned a lot from suffering, struggling to find myself. I learned to feel for those who are not strong or popular or powerful, and to have compassion for those who are so easily forgotten in the day-to-day rush toward riches, fame, and success.

I am learning that perhaps the best way to deal with never having had a father, never being fathered, is to learn how to be one.

After raising two girls I'm now in the process of raising an eight-year-old boy and I'm trying as best as I can to be a guide, a mentor, and, most important, a pal to him. I have delighted in the simplest of pleasures: removing the training wheels from his bike, shooting hoops, teaching him how to throw a baseball, throwing him that long pass that wins the Super Bowl over and over. I've been his protector when a problem has come up at school and I have to talk to his teacher. And I've been his worst enemy when he's had to learn his multiplication tables—that's part of the contract too.

I'm sure that all parents believe they have the best of intentions; in their hearts truly believe they have the best interests of their children at heart as they raise them, and I'm sure my parents were no different in this regard. No life can be free of pain; no life should be free of pain because pain helps us grow. It's necessary.

But fathers are necessary too. It's possible to survive without a father, but what I've been trying to get across is the amount of unnecessary pain that is caused when a father is absent. I was lucky because I was able to go to school, educate myself, and find ways to cope. This means that I don't hurt as much as I did forty or even thirty years ago, but it doesn't make my life completely easy either. I have to remember the past to heal the present and prepare me for tomorrow. There is still a hole in my life where a guiding father should have been.

Obviously there are no easy solutions. It's interesting to note that recently there has been a rash of articles on fatherhood and fathering. "Dad is destiny," began the article in a recent *US News & World Report*. I hate to think of how much pain so many children are going to have to endure because there is no father to help the mother teach them how to lead a normal and productive life.

It's not going to be easy for them. I sincerely hope that by writing this I will be able to help some young men stop and think how serious, how important it is to act responsibly. You have helped in the creation of a life, and that means, as the old people used to say, *"Ya tu vida no es tuya"*—"Your life is no longer yours."

My children don't know how much pleasure they give me each and every time they say, "Hey, Dad . . ."

THE
LATIN
PHALLUS

Layle Silbert, © 1994

ILÁN STAVANS, a novelist and critic, is the author of The Hispanic Condition, from HarperCollins, and Bandido, a study of the Chicano activist Oscar Zeta Acosta, also from HarperCollins. He edited Growing Up Latino for Houghton Mifflin. He has received the Latino Literature Prize and grants from the National Endowment for the Humanities. He teaches literature at Amherst College in Amherst, Massachusetts.

"Somos el duelo a muerte que se acerca fatal."
—Julia de Burgos

I ENVISION a history of Latin sexuality through the figure of the phallus, not unlike Michel Foucault and René Magritte's *Ceci n'est pas une pipe:* a compendium of its capricious ups and downs, ins and outs, from the Argentine pampas to the Rio Grande and the Caribbean. A brief volume, it would begin with the intimidating genitalia of the sovereigns of courage Hernán Cortés, Francisco Pizarro, and Spanish explorers like Hernando de Soto and Cabeza de Vaca. It would make abundant display of the often graphic art of the gay awakening of the early seventies, shameless in its depiction of the male organ. And it would conclude, perhaps, with the ribbing of feminists. Here, for instance, is a poem by Cherríe Moraga, for one of its last pages:

there is a man in my life
pale-man born infant
pliable flesh his body remains
a remote possibility

in secret it may know many things
glossy newsprint female thighs
spread eagle wings
in his flying imagination

soft shoe
he did the soft shoe
in the arch that separated the living
from dining room
miller trombone still turns his heel
and daughter barefoot and never pregnant
around and around and around

soft-tip
penis head he had

a soft-tipped penis that peeked out
accidentally one kitchen cold morning
between zipper stuck and boxer shorts
fresh pressed heat lining those tender white-meat loins

wife at the ironing board:
"what are you doing, jim, what are you doing?"
he nervously stuffed the little bird back

it looked like *Peloncito*
the bald-headed little name
of my abuelita's *pajarito*

Peloncito
a word of endearment
never told to the child
father
yellow bird-man
boy

Let me map the ambitions of my little book by starting at the beginning. The Iberian knights that crossed the Atlantic, unlike their Puritan
counterparts in the British colonies, were fortune-driven bachelors. They
did not come to settle down. As Cortés wrote to Charles V in his *Cartas de
Relación,* the first conquistadors were trash: rough, uneducated people
from lowly origins. Their mission was to expand the territorial and symbolic powers of the Spanish crown; their ambition in the new continent
was to find gold and pleasure. And pleasure they took in the bare-
breasted Indian women, whom they raped at will and then abandoned. A
violent eroticism was a fundamental element in the colonization of the
Hispanic world from Macchu Picchu to Chichén Itzá and Uxmal. The
primal scene of the clash with the Spaniards is a still-unhealed rape: The
phallus, as well as gunpowder, was a crucial weapon used to subdue.
Machismo as a cultural style endlessly rehearses this humiliating episode
in the history of the Americas, imitating the violent swagger of the Spanish conquerors. (This despite the Indian legends that Cortés was the
owner of a tiny, ridiculous penis.)

The hypocrisy of the Church played a role as well. Although the priest-hood bore witness to the rapacious sexuality of the Spanish soldiery, *fin-gieron demencia*—they pretended to be elsewhere. Simultaneously, they reproduced the medieval hierarchy of the sexes that prevailed in Europe: man as lord and master, woman as servant and reproductive machine. In his insightful book *Demons in the Convent,* the journalist and anthropolo-gist Fernando Benítez eloquently described how the Church in the sev-enteenth century established an atmosphere of repressed eroticism. The archbishop of Mexico City, Aguiar y Seijas, a demonic man who walked with crutches and nourished a thousand phobias, *detested* women: They were not allowed in his presence. If in a convent or monastery a nun walked in front of him he would *ipso facto* cover his eyes. Only men were worthy of his sight—men and Christ. In the religious paraphernalia of the Caribbean, Mexico, and South America, Jesus and the many saints appear almost totally unclothed, only their private parts covered with what in Spanish is known as *taparrabo;* whereas the Vírgen de Guadalupe, the Vírgen de la Caridad, the Vírgen del Cobre, and a thousand other incar-nations of the Virgin Mary are fully dressed.

In a milieu where eroticism reigns, my volume on the Latin phallus is ob-viously far from original. In Oscar Hijuelos's Pulitzer prize–winning novel, *The Mambo Kings Play Songs of Love* (1989), the male organ plays a crucial, obsessive role. The narrative is a sideboard of sexual roles in the Hispanic world. Néstor and César Castillo, Cuban expatriates and musi-cians in New York City, personify Don Quixote and Sancho Panza: One is an outgoing idealist, the other an introverted materialist. Throughout Néstor's erotic adventures, Hijuelos refers to the penis as *la cosa*—"the thing." Its power is hypnotic, totemic, even. When men call on women to undo their trousers, women reach down without looking to unfasten their lover's buttons. The novel's libidinal voyeurism even extends to incestuous scenes, like the one in which Delores, Hijuelos's female protagonist, finds herself in touch with her father's sexuality.

In imitation of her mother in Havana, Delores would cook for her father, making do with what she could find at the market in those days of war rationing. One night she wanted to surprise him. After he had taken to his bed, she made some caramel-glazed *flan,* cooked up a pot of good coffee, and happily made her way down the narrow hallway with a tray of the quivering *flan.* Pushing open the door, she found her father asleep, naked, and in a state of extreme sexual arousal. Terrified and unable to move, she pretended that he was a statue, though his chest heaved and his lips stirred, as if conversing in a dream. . . . He with his suffering face, it, his penis, enormous. . . . The funny thing was that, despite her fear, Delores wanted to pick up his thing and pull it like a lever; she wanted to lie down beside him and put her hand down there, releasing him from pain. She wanted him to wake up; she didn't want him to wake up. In that moment, which she would always remember, she felt her soul blacken as if she just committed a terrible sin and condemned herself to the darkest room in hell. She expected to turn around and find the devil himself standing beside her, a smile on his sooty face, saying, "Welcome to America."

For a culture as steeped in sexuality as our own, it is strange that the substance of our masculine identity remains a forbidden topic. But it does. We are terrified of exposing the labyrinthine paths of our unexplained desire of engaging in what the Mexican essayist and poet Octavio Paz once called "the shameful art of *abrirse*"—opening up and losing control, admitting our insecurities, allowing ourselves to be exposed, unprotected, unsafe. We are not Puritans; our bodies are not the problem. It is the complicated, ambiguous pathways of our desire that are too painful to bear. We have adopted the armature of our Spanish conquerors: Hispanic men are machos, dominating figures, rulers, conquistadors—and, also, closeted homosexuals. In *The Labyrinth of Solitude,* Paz has been one of the lonely few to criticize male sexuality:

The macho commits . . . unforeseen acts that produce confusion, horror and destruction. He opens the world; in doing so, he rips and tears it, and this violence provokes a great, sinister laugh. And in its own way, it is just: it reestablished the equilibrium and puts things in their place, by reducing them to dust, to misery, to nothingness.

Unlike men, Hispanic women are indeed forced to open up. And they are made to pay for their openness: They are often accused of impurity and adultery, sinfulness and infidelity. We inhabitants of the Americas live in a nest of complementing stereotypes: On one side, flamboyant women, provocative, well-built, sensual, lascivious, with indomitable, even bestial, nerve and intensity; on the other, macho men. Both seemingly revolve around the phallus, an object of intense adoration, the symbol of absolute power and satisfaction. It is the source of the macho's self-assurance and control, sexual and psychological; it is also the envy of the Hispanic woman. Our names for the penis are legion; besides the *pajarito* of Cherríe Moraga's boxer-short reverie it goes by *cornamusa, embutido, flauta, fusta, garrote, lanza, masta, miembro viril, pelón, peloncito, pene, pinga, plátano, príapo, pudendo, tesoro, tolete, tranca, verga,* and *zurriago,* among many others.

Where to begin describing the multiple ramifications of the adoration of the phallus among Hispanics? In the Caribbean mothers rub a male baby's penis to relax him, to force him out of a tantrum. In Mexico the charros (*guasos* in Chile, *gauchos* in Argentina) are legendary rural outlaws, independent and lonely men. Their masculine adventures—clashes with corrupt landowners and politicos—live on through border ballads, known on the U.S.-Mexican border as *corridos;* and through *payadores,* a type of South American minstrel who accompanies himself with a guitar. (The fantastic no-budget film *El Mariachi* is a revision of this cultural myth.) The Latin man and his penis are at the center of the Hispanic universe. Ironically, more than one rebellious Hispanic artist including Andrés Serrano, has equated the Latin penis to the crucifix. Which helps us understand what is perhaps the greatest contradiction in Hispanic male sexuality: our excessive machismo—"an exaggerated sense of masculinity stressing such attributes as courage, virility, and domination," according to the dictionary. Take bullfighting, an erotic event like no other, supremely parodied in Pedro Almodóvar's film *Matador.* Where else can the male strike such provocative sexual poses? Carlos Fuentes described the sport in his book *The Buried Mirror:* "The effrontery of the suit of lights, its tight-hugging breeches, the flaunting of the male sexual organ, the importance given to the buttocks, the obviously seductive and self-appraising stride, the lust for blood and sensation—the bullfight authorizes this incredible arrogance and sexual exhibitionism." Essentially bestial, the *corrida de toros* is a quasi-religious ceremony unifying beauty, sex, and death. The young bullfighter, an idol, is asked to face with grace and stamina the dark forces of nature symbolized in the bull. His sword is a phallic instrument. A renaissance knight modeled after Amadís de Gaula or Tirant Lo Blanc, and parodied by Don Quixote, he will first subdue and then kill. *¡Viva el macho!* Blood will be spilled and ecstasies will arrive when the animal lies dead, at which point the bullfighter will take his hat off before a beautiful lady and smile. Man will prevail, the phallus remains all-powerful, and the conqueror will be showered with red flowers.

The Hispanic family encourages a double standard. Few societies prize female virginity with the conviction that we do. But while virginity is a prerequisite for a woman's safe arrival at the wedding canopy, men are encouraged to fool around, to test the waters, to partake of the pleasures of the flesh. Virgins are *mujeres buenas:* pure, ready to sacrifice their body for the sacred love of a man. Prostitutes, on the other hand, are hedonistic goddesses, *mujeres malas,* safeguards of the male psyche. Like most of my friends, I lost my virginity to a prostitute at the age of thirteen. An older acquaintance was responsible for arranging the "date," when a small group of us would meet an experienced harlot at a whorehouse. It goes without saying that none of the girls in my class were similarly "tutored": They would most likely become women in the arms of someone they loved, or thought they loved. But love or even the slightest degree of attraction was not involved in our venture. Losing our virginity was actually a dual mission: to ejaculate inside the hooker and then, more important, to tell of the entire adventure afterward. The telling of the story—the matador defeating his bull, the conqueror's display of power—was more crucial than the carnal sensation itself. I still remember the dusty Art Deco furniture and the blank expression of the woman. She was there to make me a man, to help me become an accepted member of society. Did we talk? She asked me to undress straightaway and proceeded to caress me. I was extremely nervous. What if I were unable to prove myself? The whole ceremony lasted twenty minutes, perhaps less. Afterward, I concocted a predictable cover, announcing to my friends that the prostitute had been amazed at my prowess, that I had made her *very* happy, that she had been shocked at my chastity.

We told tall tales to compensate for the paucity of our accomplishments. After all, a prostitute is an easy triumph. Even consensual sex is an unworthy challenge for the aspiring macho. Courting women with serenades and flowers, seducing them, undressing and then fucking them, *chingárselas,* only to turn them out: That's the Hispanic male's hidden dream. *Chingar* signifies the ambiguous excess of macho sexuality. Octavio Paz's exploration of the term concludes that the idea denotes a kind of failure. The active form means to rape, subdue, control, dominate. Chingar is what a macho does to women, what the Iberian soldiers did to the native Indian population, what corrupt politicos do to their electorate. And the irreplaceable weapon in the art of chingar, the key to the Hispanic worldview, is *el pito,* the phallus.

Not long ago, while writing on the Chicano movement of the late sixties, I came across the extraordinary figure of Oscar "Zeta" Acosta, defender of the dispossessed. Born in 1936 in El Paso, Texas, Acosta became a lawyer and activist well acquainted with Cesar Chavez, Rodolfo "Corky" González, and other political leaders of the era. An admirer of Henry Miller and Jack Kerouac, and a close friend of Hunter S. Thompson's, whom he accompanied in his travel to Las Vegas (Acosta is the three-hundred-pound Samoan of *Fear and Loathing in Las Vegas)*, Acosta wrote a couple of intriguing novels about the civil rights upheaval in the Southwest, *The Autobiography of a Brown Buffalo,* published in 1972, and *The Revolt of the Cockroach People,* which appeared a year later. Both volumes detail man's rite of passage from adolescence to boastful machismo. A cover photograph by Annie Leibovitz showed Acosta as a Tennessee Williams type, a perfectly insecure macho with flexed muscles and spiritual desperation in his eyes. He is in an undershirt and stylish suit pants, fat, the lines in his forehead quite pronounced. He is thirty-nine years old and looks a bit worn out. Besides this picture, nothing is certain about him, except perhaps the fact that in the early seventies he went to Mazatlán, a resort area and port on Mexico's Pacific coast, and disappeared without a trace.

The moral of Acosta can be used to understand what lies behind the ostentation and bravado of the macho: a deep-seated inferiority complex. The size and strength of the penis is the index of masculine value, as well as the passport to glorious erotic adventure. Inevitably, then, it is also a boundless source of anxiety. He is an emblem of the insecure Hispanic male. His machismo could not hide his confusion and lack of self-esteem. He spent his life thinking his penis was too small, which, in his words, automatically turned him into a fag. "Frugality and competition were my parents' lot," he writes, describing his and his brother's sexual education. "The truth of it was [they] conspired to make men out of two innocent Mexican boys. It seems that the sole purpose of childhood was to train boys how to be men. Not men of the future, but *now.* We had to get up early, run home from school, work on weekends, holidays, and during vacations, all for the purpose of being men. We were supposed to talk like *un hombre,* walk like a man, and think like a man." But Acosta's apprenticeship in masculinity was undermined by the embarrassment of his tiny phallus. He perceived himself as a freak, a virile metastasis:

> If it hadn't been for my fatness, I'd probably have been able to do those fancy assed jack-knifes and swandives as well as the rest of you. But my mother had me convinced I was obese, ugly as a pig and without any redeeming qualities whatsoever. How then could I run around with just my jockey shorts? V-8's don't hide fat, you know. That's why I finally started wearing boxers. But by then it was too late. Everyone knew I had the smallest prick in the world. With the girls watching and giggling, the guys used to sing my privates song to the tune of "Little Bo Peep" . . . "Oh, where, oh where can my little boy be? Oh, where, oh where can he be? He's so chubby, *panzón,* that he can't move along. Oh, where, oh where can he be?"

Acosta is a unique figure among male Chicano novelists in that his bitter, honest reflections do nothing to enhance his machismo.

I lost most of my religion the same night I learned about sex from old Vernon. When I saw the white, foamy suds come from under his foreskin, I thought he had wounded himself from yanking on it too hard with those huge farmer hands of his. And when I saw his green eyes fall back into his head, I thought he was having some sort of seizure like I'd seen Toto the village idiot have out in his father's fig orchard after he fucked a chicken.

I didn't much like the sounds of romance the first time I saw jizz. I knew that Vernon was as tough as they came. Nothing frightened or threatened him. He'd cuss right in front of John Hazard, our fag Boy Scout leader as well as Miss Anderson [our teacher]. But when I heard him OOOh and AAAh as the soap suds spit at his chest while we lay on our backs inside the pup tent, I wondered for a second if sex wasn't actually for sissies. I tried to follow his example, but nothing would come out. With his cheering me on, saying, "Harder, man. Pull on that son of a bitch. Faster, faster!" it just made matters worse. The thing went limp before the soap suds came out.

He advised me to try it more often. "Don't worry, man. It'll grow if you work on it."

Taboos die hard, if they ever do. After emigrating to the United States in 1985, my identity changed in drastic ways. I ceased to be Mexican and became Hispanic, and my attitude toward homosexuals underwent a metamorphosis. Still, that transformation took time. Even as homosexuals entered my peer group and became my friends, I was uneasy. At times I wondered whether having homosexual friends would make others doubt my sexual identity. Though I've never had an intimate encounter with another man, I have often wondered what I would feel, how I would respond to a kiss. As José Ortega y Gasset said: *"Yo soy yo y mi circunstancia"*—"I am the embodiment of my culture."

My father had taught me to show affection in public. When departing, he would kiss me without inhibition. But as I became an adolescent, I heard my friends whisper. Was I secretly a deviant? To be a Hispanic man was to hide one's emotions, to keep silent when it came to expressing your heart. We are supposed to swallow our pain and never cry *como una niña*— like girls. Keep a straight face, suck it up—*sé muy macho*. Many Hispanic adolescents still find role models in the confident and aggressively reserved stars of the Golden Age of Mexican film, black-and-white celebrities like Pedro Armendáriz, Jorge Negrete, and Pedro Infante, Hispanic analogues of James Dean and John Wayne. These figures were classic macho: ultra-masculine Emiliano Zapata mustaches, closely cropped dark hair, a mysterious Mona Lisa smile, thin, well-built bodies, and an unconquerable pride symbolized by the ubiquitous pistol. Vulnerability means cowardice. Deformity was not only evidence of weakness but a sign of unreadiness to face the tough world. In spite of his verbal bravura, Cantinflas, the Charlie Chaplin of Spanish language films like *Ahí está el detalle,* was anti-macho: poorly dressed, foul-mouthed, short, unhandsome, without a gun and, hence, probably possessed of a tiny phallus.

Among Hispanics, homosexuals are the target of nigh-well insurmountable animosity. If the Latin phallus is adored in heterosexual relations, it is perceived as wild, diabolic, and uncontrollable for homosexuals. Reinaldo Arenas, the Cuban novelist who died of AIDS in New York City in 1990, argued that Latin society comprises five classes of homosexual: the *dog-collar gay,* boisterous and constantly being arrested at baths and beaches; the *common gay,* who is sure of his sexual identity but who never takes risks save to attend a film festival or write an occasional poem; the *closeted gay,* a man with a wife and children and a public profile, who is reduced to sneaking off to the baths without his wedding ring; the *royal,* a man whose closeness to politicians and people of power allows him to be open about his sexual identity, to lead a "scandalous" life, while still holding public office; and finally the *macho,* whose cocksure bravado is intended to fend off questions about his sexual identity. It goes without saying that most gay men are forced to assume the less public personas.

In his second book, *Days of Obligation,* Richard Rodríguez includes an essay, "Late Victorians," about AIDS and his own homosexuality. He ponders the impact of the epidemic: "We have become accustomed to figures disappearing from our landscape. Does this not lead us to interrogate the landscape?" Very few in the Hispanic world have dared to address the subject: Hispanic gays remain a target of mockery and derision, forced to live on the fringes of society. To be gay is to be a freak, mentally ill, the sort of abnormality José Guadalupe Posada, the celebrated turn-of-the-century Mexican lampooner, often portrayed in his sarcastic cartoons: a creature with legs instead of arms, a dog with your eyes. And yet homosexuality, a topic few are willing to address in public, is the counterpoint that defines our collective identity. Despite the stigma, homosexuals have been a ubiquitous presence in the Hispanic world, a constant from the Cuban sugar mill to the colonial *misión,* from Fidel Castro's cabinet to the literary intelligentsia. And, like Saint Augustine's attitude toward the Jews, the established approach toward them follows the maxim: Don't destroy them, let them bear witness of the lawless path of male eroticism. They are the other side of Hispanic sexuality, a shadow one refuses to acknowledge—a "they" that is really an "us." Again, the language betrays us: the panoptic array of terms for homosexual include *alabado, adelito, afeminado, ahembrado, amaricado, amujerado, barbalindo, carininfo, cazolero, cocinilla, enerve, gay, homosexual, invertido, lindo, maría, marica, mariposa, ninfo, pisaverde, puto, repipí, sodomita, volteado, zape,* to name only a few.

In the Mexico of the seventies in which I grew up, common sense had it that machos were the unchaste victims of an unsurpassed inferiority complex. Unchaste victims—impure, yes, but sympathetic characters and commanding figures. Homosexuals, on the other hand, were considered oversensitive, vulnerable, unproved in the art of daily survival. At school, the boys were constantly made to taste their muscular strength. Girls were allowed to cry, to express their emotions, while we *men* were told to remain silent. If to open up was a sign of feminine weakness, to penetrate, *meter,* meant superiority. Sex—fucking—is how we prove our active male self, subduing our passive female half. Physical appearance was fundamental to this regime: obesity and limping were derivations from the norm, and hence effeminate characteristics.

I recall an occasion some years ago in which a Mexican publisher sat with me and a gay friend of mine from Venezuela. In a disgusting display of macho pyrotechnics, the man talked for the better part of an hour about the size of his penis. His shtick was full of degrading references to homosexuals, whom he described variously as kinky, depraved, and perverted. The presence of a self-identified "queer writer" at the table only stimulated his attack. He suggested that the United States was the greatest nation on earth, but that sexual abnormality would ultimately force its decline. Days later my Venezuelan colleague told me that the publisher had made a (successful) pass at him that very night. They shared a hotel room. This sort of attitude isn't uncommon. The Hispanic macho goes out of his way to keep up appearances, to exalt his virility, but he often fails. Sooner or later, his glorious masculinity will be shared in bed with another man.

Who is gay among us? It's a secret. We simply don't want to talk about it. Although a few essays have been written about Jorge Luis Borges's repressed homosexuality, the topic is evaded in Emir Rodríguez Monegal's 1978 biography. Borges lived most of his life with his mother and married twice: once, briefly, in his forties, and then to María Kodama, a few months before his death in 1986, in order to turn her into the sole head of his estate. His writing is remarkable for its lack of sexuality. When his stories do verge on the intimate, they portray only rape or molestation. Still, the matter is hushed up, the details of a life subordinated to the dense lyricism of an oeuvre. Undoubtedly concern for the master's reputation can explain some large part of the silence.

Take the case of John Rechy, whose 1963 novel, *City of Night,* a book about hustlers, whores, drugs, and urban criminality, garnered him accolades and a reputation as one of the most promising Chicano writers of his generation. Shortly thereafter, Rechy's book was categorized as a "gay novel," a stigma that tarred the book for Hispanic readers in the United States. It is only recently, since the onset of the North American gay rights movement, that Rechy's achievement has been reevaluated. And then there's Julio Cortázar, the celebrated Argentinean novelist and short-story writer responsible for *Hopscotch.* In 1983, at the peak of his fame and just a year before his tragic death, he made a trip to Cuba, and then New York, to address the United Nations about the *desaparecidos* in South America. Cortázar was alone and lonely as a strange sickness began taking over his body. He lost his appetite, became thinner, became susceptible to colds. After his divorce from Aurora Bernárdez some fifteen years previous, he had been involved with a number of women and men although he tried desperately to keep his homosexual encounters secret. In the depths of his solitude, he told Luis Harss, he began to lose confidence in his writing. A symbol of liberation for many Hispanics, Cortázar had probably contracted AIDS. He died in Paris on February 12, 1984, when the epidemic was still largely unrecognized, its details elusive to scientists and never openly discussed. A number of Cortázar tales deal with homosexuality and lesbianism, including "Blow-Up," "The Ferry, or Another Trip to Venice," and "At Your Service." The last, the story of an elderly servant woman working as a dog-sitter in a wealthy Parisian home, moved a Cortázar specialist to ask him about his own homosexuality. He answered quite impersonally, with a lengthy dissertation on the general subject, a history of homosexuality from the open love of the Greeks to the present-day climate of ostracism and homophobia. "The attitude toward [it]," he suggested, "needs to be a very broad and open one, because the day in which homosexuals don't feel like . . . persecuted animals . . . they'll assume a much more normal way of life and fulfill themselves erotically and sexually without harming another one, by being happy as much as possible as homosexuals male and female." He concluded by applauding the more tolerant atmosphere of select North American and European societies. One might assume that the profound questions of sexuality and repression broached in this discussion would have had severe, productive, repercussions in the critical work of one of the giants of Latin American literature. But Cortázar's gay life, like Borges's, remains a forbidden issue.

Since the sixties, gay artists in Latin America have worked to put Latin homosexuality on the map. They have devised strategies to name the unnameable and trace a symbolic picture of our collective erotic fears. The Argentine Manuel Mujica Láinez's 1962 novel, *Bomarzo,* for instance, equates the male organ, and homosexuality in general, with the monstrous. Thanks to him and to many others (José Ceballos Maldonado, José Donoso, Carlos Arcidiácono, as well as Reinaldo Arenas, José Lezama Lima, Richard Rodríguez, Manuel Puig, Virgilio Piñera, Severo Sarduy, Hector Bianciotti, Xavier Villaurrutia, Calvert Cassey, Luis Zapata, and Fernando Vallejo), a small window of vulnerability has been created, a space for the interrogation of suffocating, monolithic sex roles. The most significant of these, to my mind, are Puig, Arenas, and José Lezama Lima. *Kiss of the Spider Woman,* Puig's most celebrated work, directed for the screen by Héctor Babenco, portrayed a forced male relationship in an unspecified prison south of the Río Grande. The film made waves from Ciudad Juárez to the Argentine pampas with its startling conclusion—a kiss between a macho Marxist revolutionary and a gay man—and the suggestion that the characters complemented each other.

Puig is one of the principal characters in the long history of homophobia and gay bashing in the Hispanic world. In the early seventies the committee for the prestigious Seix Barral award in Spain selected his first novel, which the filmmaker Néstor Almendros and the Iberian novelist Juan Goytisolo openly endorsed. But the publisher, Carlos Barral, rejected the recommendation of the selection committee because of Puig's and the book's sexual orientation. He was similarly stigmatized in his native country, where the Peronists banned his work, calling it "pornographic propaganda."

Puig died in his mid-fifties in 1990, in Cuernavaca, Mexico, during a bizarre (and suspicious) gall bladder operation. Was it AIDS? Puig chose to keep silent about his impending demise. At the time, I was preparing a special issue of *The Review of Contemporary Fiction* about his oeuvre and had been in contact with him. I last saw him at a public reading at the Ninety-second Street Y just a few months before his death; he looked thin but energetic. There was no mention of an illness. Of course, having been burned so many times before, it was unlikely that he would open up now. Two years after Puig's death, Jaime Manrique, the Colombian author of *Latin Moon in Manhattan* and a close friend of Puig's, reconstructed the gay subtext of Puig's life in a moving reminiscence "Manuel Puig: The Writer as Diva" for *Christopher Street.* After considering the possibility of Puig opening up, *abrirse,* in public, Manrique concluded that whatever honors Puig could still hope for were infinitely more secure with his personal secrets kept hidden. In the end he had moved back to Cuernavaca with his beloved mother, spending the last months of his life "busy building his first and last home in this world," a fortress closed to strangers, filled with Hollywood memorabilia. Puig's death is emblematic of the fate of the Hispanic gay.

Puig's work was remarkably tame, at least with regard to the representation of the Latin penis: He feared the persecution of the Argentine military and depicted its image only in a short section in the novel *Blood of Re-*

quired Love. Like most gays in the Hispanic world, Puig was trapped between his sexual preference and the prejudices of the larger society. And yet, what is distinctive about him and the literary generation that came of age in the wake of the sixties is the desublimation of the phallus. Puig and other gay writers began a process of *apertura:* They have named names, celebrated and mocked Latin masculinity and the omnipresent phallus.

Reinaldo Arenas is probably the best known openly gay writer from Latin America. His writings explore Latin sexuality and the phallus with eloquence. His final years prior to his suicide—years marked by extreme fits of depression, a chronic and abrasive pneumonia, paranoia, and increasing misanthropy—saw him complete a surrealist novel, an autobiography, and the last two installments of the *Pentagonía,* a five-volume novelization of the "secret history of Cuba." *Before Night Falls,* the autobiography, is destined to become a classic. It traces Arenas's birth in Holguín in 1943, as well as his rural childhood; his difficult transition to Havana; his friendships with Virgilio Piñera, José Lezama Lima, Lydia Cabrera, and other important Cuban artists and intellectuals; his "youthful loyalty" to Castro's socialist regime and his subsequent disenchantment with the revolution; his betrayal by a family member; the persecution, "re-education," and imprisonment he suffered in Havana's infamous El Morro prison because of his homosexuality; his participation in the 1980 Mariel boatlift and his bondage experiences in Florida and Manhattan.

Dictated to a tape recorder and then transcribed by friends, *Before Night Falls* is one of the most incendiary, sexually liberating texts ever to come from Latin America. Published posthumously in 1990 shortly after the long-suffering author committed suicide in his New York City apartment, it appeared in English in 1993. Its confessional style and courageous depiction of homosexual life make it a remarkable and haunting book. Its impact in the Spanish-speaking world, including Spain (where it appeared under the prestigious Tusquets imprint), has been enormous. "I think I always had a huge sexual appetite," writes Arenas. "Not only mares, sows, hens, or turkeys, but almost all animals were objects of my sexual passion, including dogs. There was one particular dog who gave me great pleasure. I would hide with him behind the garden tended by my aunts, and would make him suck my cock. The dog got used to it and in time would do it freely."

Guillermo Cabrera Infante, a fellow Cuban, summed up Arenas's career in an obituary published in *El País:* "Three passions ruled the life and death of Reinaldo Arenas: literature (not as game but as a consuming fire), passive sex, and active politics. Of the three, the dominant passion was evidently sex. Not only in his life but in his work. He was a chronicler of a country ruled not by the already impotent Fidel Castro, but by sex. . . . Blessed with a raw talent that almost reaches genius in his posthumous book, he lived a life whose beginning and end were indeed the same: from the start, one long, sustained sexual act. . . ." And indeed, Arenas repeatedly describes his sexual intercourse with animals, family members, children, old people, friends, lovers, and strangers. The volume ends with a personal letter, written shortly before Arenas's death, in which he bids farewell to friends and enemies. "Due to my delicate state of health and to the horrible emotional depression it causes me not to be able to continue writing and struggling for the freedom of Cuba, I am ending my life," Arenas writes. "Persons near to me are not in any way responsible for my decision. There is only one person to hold accountable: Fidel Castro."

The autobiography details his multifarious sexual encounters. He recalls the fashion in which he was abused by his grandfather, his close attachment to his mother, a woman who left Cuba early on in the child's life to make money for the family by working in Florida. What's remarkable is the fact that the book comes out of the Spanish-speaking world, where erotic confessions are few and seldom related to politics.

> In [Cuba], I think, it is a rare man who has not had sexual relations with another man. Physical desire overpowers whatever feelings of machismo our fathers take upon themselves to instill in us. An example of this is my uncle Rigoberto, the oldest of my uncles, a married, serious man. Sometimes I would go to town with him. I was just about eight years old and we would ride on the same saddle. As soon as we were both on the saddle, he would begin to have an erection. Perhaps in some way my uncle did not want this to happen, but he could not help it. He would put me in place, lift me up and set my

butt on his penis, riding, as it were, on two animals at the same time. I think eventually Rigoberto would ejaculate. The same thing happened on the way back from town. Both of us, of course, acted as if we were not aware of what was happening. He would whistle or breathe hard while the horse trotted on. When he got back, Carolina, his wife, would welcome him with open arms and a kiss. At that moment we were all very happy.

Arenas's other major work, the *Pentagonía* quintet, is similarly obsessive about sex and politics. Though the text has fascinated critics for some time, it continues to scare lay readers. An exercise in literary experimentation modeled after the French *nouveau roman,* the first three volumes—*Singing from the Well, The Palace of the White Skunks,* and *Farewell to the Sea*—display a fractured narrative and convoluted plot that often make them appear impenetrable. *The Assault,* the fifth installment, is the most accessible. A compelling exercise in science fiction, it is structured as a tribute to Orwell's *1984* and Kafka's *The Castle.* It is narrated by a government torturer, a leader of the so-called Anti-Perversion Brigade who spends his days visiting concentration camps and prisons looking for sexual criminals to annihilate. The book's nightmarish landscape is a futuristic Caribbean island deliberately similar to Cuba under Castro's dictatorship. At the heart of the book is the torturer's search for his mother, whom he glimpses from afar but seems unable to approach. He is passionate and inscrutable in his hatred for her, ready to undertake any action that might lead to her destruction. The book opens: "The last time I saw my mother she was out behind the National People's Lumber Cooperative gathering sticks." Approaching her, the narrator thinks to himself: "This is my chance; I knew I could not waste a second. I ran straight for her, and I would have killed her, too, but the old bitch must have an eye where her asshole ought to be, because before I could get to her and knock her down and kill her, that old woman whirled around to meet me." With macabre echoes of Luis Buñuel, the allegory is not difficult to decipher: Pages into the book, the reader comes to understand that the torturer's mother is Castro himself. As the search for her continues in various "Servo-Perimeters" of the land, Arenas prepares us for a colossal encounter, savage and profane. In the final scene, Arenas's protagonist fearlessly employs his penis one last time: He fucks and then kills his lover, whose identity is dual—his own mother, whom he describes as a cow, and The Resident, Fidel Castro himself.

> With my member throbbingly erect, and my hands on my hips, I stand before her, looking at her. My hatred and my revulsion and my arousal are now beyond words to describe. And then the great cow, naked and horrible, white and stinking, plays her last card; the sly bitch, crossing her ragged claws over her monstrous breasts, looks at me with tears in her eyes and says *Son.* That is all I can bear to hear. All the derision, all the harassment, all the fear and frustration and blackmail and mockery and contempt that that word contains—it slaps me in the face, and I am stung. My erection swells to enormous proportions, and I begin to step toward her, my phallus aimed dead for its mark, that fetid, stinking hole. And I thrust. As she is penetrated, she gives a long, horrible shriek, and then she collapses. I sense my triumph—I come, and I feel the furious pleasure of discharging myself on her. Howling, she explodes in a blast of bolts, washers, screws, pieces of shrapnel-like tin, gasoline, smoke, semen, shit, and steam of motor oil. Then, at the very instant of my climax, and of her final howl, a sound never heard before washes across the square below us . . . While the crowd goes on moving through the city, hunting down and destroying to the accompaniment of the music of its own enraged whispering, I tuck the limp mass of my phallus (now at last spent and flaccid) into my overalls. Weary, I make my way unnoticed through the noise and the riot (the crowd in a frenzy of destruction, like children, crying *The Resident is dead, the beast at last is dead!*), and I come to the wall of the city. I walk down to the shore. And I lie down on the sand.

It is the singular achievement of the gay Cuban writer Lezama Lima (1912–1976) to have provided an accounting of the Latin phallus equal to its inflated importance in the Hispanic world. Lima was the author of *Paradiso,* published in 1966, a book hailed by Julio Cortázar and others as a masterpiece. It is a remarkable text: In the words of the critic Gerald Martin, the text renders "both classical and Catholic imagery, lovingly but also scandalously, achieving the remarkable double coup of offending both the Catholic Church and the Cuban Revolution through its approach to eroticism in general and homosexuality in particular." Chapter VIII details the promiscuous sexual adventures of the young Casanovas Farraluque and Leregas, whose penis, which would swiftly grow from the length of a thimble to the "length of the forearm of a manual laborer," becomes legendary among his classmates:

Unlike Farraluque's, Leregas's sexual organ did not reproduce his face, but his whole body. In his sexual adventures his phallus did not seem to penetrate but to embrace the other body. Eroticism by compression, like a bear cub squeezing a chestnut, that was how his first moans began. The teacher was monotonously reciting the text, and most of his pupils, fifty or sixty in all, were seated facing him, but on the left, to take advantage of a niche-like space, there were two benches lined up at right angles to the rest of the class. Leregas was sitting at the end of the first bench. Since the teacher's platform was about a foot high, only the face of his phallic colossus was visible to him. With calm indifference, Leregas would bring out his penis and testicles, and like a wind eddy that turns into a sand column, at a touch it became a challenge of exceptional size. His row and the rest of the students peered past the teacher's desk to view that tenacious candle, ready to burst out of its highly polished, blood-filled helmet. The class did not blink and its silence deepened, making the lecturer think that the pupils were morosely following the thread of his discursive expression, a spiritless exercise during which the whole class was attracted by the dry phallic splendor of the bumpkin bear club. When Leregas's member began to deflate, the coughs began, the nervous laughter, the touching of elbows to free themselves from the stupefaction they had experienced. "If you don't keep still, I'm going to send some students out of the room," the little teacher said, vexed at the sudden change from rapt attention to a progressive swirling uproar.

The chapter becomes increasingly daunting as the florid prose continues.

An adolescent with such a thunderous generative attribute was bound to suffer a fate according to the dictates of the Pythian. The spectators in the classroom noted that in referring to the Gulf's currents the teacher would extend his arm in a curve to caress the algaed coasts, the corals and anemones of the Caribbean. That morning, Leregas's phallic dolmen had gathered those motionless pilgrims around the god terminus as it revealed its priapic extremes, but there was no mockery or rotting smirk. To enhance his sexual tension, he put two octavo books on his member, and they moved like tortoises shot up by the expansive force of a fumarole. It was the reproduction of the Hindu myth about the origin of the world.

The phallus remains an all-consuming image for Hispanic society whether as the absent animating presence in the *repressive* culture of machismo or the furtive purpose of the *repressed* culture of homosexuality. It is the representation of masculine desire, a fantastic projection of guilt, shame, and power. Hyperactive bravura and suppressed longing are its twin modalities.

I envision an open book on the phallus, steeped in the infinite richness of reality. A Borgesian volume of volumes incorporating every detail of every life of every man and woman in the Hispanic world, alive and dead—the record of every innocent or incestuous look, every masturbatory fantasy, every kiss, every coitus since 1492 and perhaps even before. The book is already in us and outside us, simultaneously real and imaginary, fatal and prophetic, *abierto* and *cerrado*. As a civilization, we are such a history—a living compendium of our baroque sexual behaviors. From Bernal Díaz del Castillo's chronicle of the subjugation of Tenochtitlán to Mario Vargas Llosa's novella *In Praise of the Stepmother;* from Carlos Fuentes's climax in *Christopher Unborn* to José Donoso's *The Obscene Bird of Night* and his untranslated erotic novel *La misteriosa desaparición de la Marquesita de Loria;* from Lope de Vega's Golden Age *comedias* to Sor Juana Inés de La Cruz's superb baroque poetry and Cherríe Moraga's *peloncito,* the tortuous history of our sexuality is the story of the Latin phallus. In a continent where tyranny remains an eternal ghost and democracy (the open society, *la sociedad abierta*) an elusive dream, the phallus is an unmerciful dictator, the totemic figure of our longing.

MY

LITERARY FATHERS

Al Rendon, © 1992

RAY GONZÁLEZ is the author of <u>Memory Fever,</u> a book of essays, and four books of poetry, including <u>The Heat of Arrivals and Cabato Sentora,</u> both from BOA Editions. He is the editor of sixteen anthologies, most recently <u>Currents from the Dancing River: Contemporary Latino Fiction, Nonfiction, and Poetry,</u> from Harcourt Brace. He received a 1993 Before Columbus Foundation American Book Award for Excellence in Editing. He is assistant professor of English and Latin American Studies at the University of Illinois in Chicago.

I HAVE NOT SEEN my father in eight years. He and my mother divorced in 1982 after thirty-two years of marriage. Since then, I have seen my father three times, each visit not lasting more than fifteen minutes. Two of them were in his office in downtown El Paso when I came to see how he was doing. When I walked into the old brick building, a clothing warehouse he managed, I didn't recognize my father. It was 1985 and my first visit to see him after the divorce. The man that rose from behind the desk was bone thin. My father had always been husky and overweight. He now wore his black hair long with thick, wavy curls hanging on his forehead—a contrast to his crewcuts I had known as a boy. I was told later by my sister Pat that our father now had the habit of dyeing his gray hair. The most startling detail I noticed about my father was all the jewelry. Both of his hands were covered with expensive-looking gold and silver rings. A huge, shiny gold chain hung on his neck. He wore a long-sleeved silver shirt, the kind you see men wearing on the disco dance floors. I was stunned at the transformation that had happened to a fifty-six-year-old man, even though my mother and sisters had hinted that he had really changed since the divorce and seemed to be searching for his "second youth."

The last time I saw my father was 1988. It was a brief hello. He came by my mother's house during one of my trips to my hometown. We embraced awkwardly and he asked me if I needed any money. I shook my head. We said we were both doing fine, and he left. In recent times, I have made a point to call him two or three times a year. The phone calls are short. We exchange awkward hellos and how-is-it-going's. Then, his familiar, "Good talking to you. I'll call you." We hang up. My father has never once called me on the phone. Each time I call him, he makes it a point to ask me for my phone number, explaining that he lost it and needs it so he can call me. During my last few visits to El Paso, I have made attempts to see my father. A couple of times, I couldn't get hold of him because he and his second wife move quite often from house to house around town. Other attempts to see him have ended in frustration when he has not shown up at the place we have agreed to meet, or he found an excuse of being busy during my brief stays in El Paso.

Since August 1994, I have been calling him more often and have tried to extend our phone conversations from five or six minutes to over ten. For me it is progress toward a closer relationship because I have had more to talk to him about since that summer. The reason is that a longer period of family alienation came to an end that August when my wife, Ida, and I went to Sacramento, California, to visit my Uncle José, my father's older brother. I had not seen José, his wife, Violeta, or my cousins in thirty years. The last time I saw them was 1964 in El Paso. I was eleven years old. My uncle was on leave, between assignments in the army, and brought his family for a visit to his hometown.

My uncle made the initial contact by calling me in January 1994. I was still working at The Guadalupe Cultural Arts Center in San Antonio. One morning, I found a phone message in my box that said, "Call José González. Your father's brother," then the number. I was startled, thinking something had happened to my father. I didn't even know where José and his family lived. I was nervous, but called him from my office. There was no answer the first time. I tried several times but didn't reach him until I got home later that day. When he answered, the similarity in his voice to my father's was reassuring and painful to hear.

"Hey, Ray! This is your Uncle Joe. Remember me? I was talking to your father the other day. He sent me a copy of the article. Congratulations!"

At first, I didn't know what he was talking about, but we had no trouble having a friendly conversation. It was as if we had been talking for years. The reason he called was that my father had recently sent him a newspaper clipping from the *El Paso Herald-Post*. It was a review of my book of essays *Memory Fever,* which had been published the previous fall. I was surprised to hear my father had taken the time to contact him about me. As far as I could recall, it was the first time my father had acknowledged my accomplishments as a writer.

My uncle told me, "Your father is proud of you and so are we. Hey, when are you coming to Sacramento?"

My eyes started to water as I spoke to my uncle. I was very uncomfortable because I was not used to having my father talk to anyone about me as a writer. My uncle did not know yet that *Memory Fever* contained several pieces that referred to my parents' divorce and the breakup of our family. I was proud of the book because it had been very difficult to write.

The essays were not only about the desert Southwest, but about my childhood, and later attempts to come to terms with the way I was raised with
such emotional isolation. Essays about my mother's strict Catholicism and
me wandering the barrio streets of El Paso filled the book.

As I told my uncle I would send him a copy of the book, I wondered if
he would still be friendly after reading it. The essays that mentioned my
parents were clearly slanted in favor of my mother. I painted my father as
the bad guy in their troubles, even though my love and longing for him
was expressed in compassion for his plight as a very isolated and with-
drawn person. In "My Father's Pool Hall," a piece on a failed business my
father had in the early sixties, I wrote:

> By 1966, my father was struggling as a used-car salesman, barely
> bringing home enough money to buy groceries. I didn't know it
> then, but I believe now that the pool hall was a turning point in my
> parents' marriage. After the business failed, they worked hard to
> pay off the debt, the loans, struggling to put food on the table for me
> and my three sisters. For years after, I watched my father work hard
> at sleazy used-car lots and waited with my mother, late at night, for
> him to come home, exhausted, so she could feed him a late-night
> dinner. It was the beginning of the end, a crumbling that took al-
> most another twenty years to complete.

Several essays referred to feeling like I had lived only half a life in El
Paso—one that was influenced by historical events around my mother's
side of the family. Her father worked in the Yaquí railroad camps of Arizona before World War II. His wife, my grandmother Julia, raised me as
a baby in El Paso and influenced my religious and spiritual life. The result was a childhood shaped from a dominating mother and a distant, passive father who carried his secrets with him, intimate details of his own
youth in a small border town in the middle of a vast desert.

One story my father did share with me, when I was a boy, was about
him having to shine shoes on street corners at the age of five. He told me
this several times over the years, emphasizing that he made pennies and
nickels from shining the shoes of strangers near the railroad station and
outside of dingy bars so he could eat. He always claimed his father, José,

Sr., was a miser who threw his kids into the streets to fend for themselves after his wife, Josefina, died. My grandfather José also worked for the railroad. My father retold his shoeshine story with pride and would remind me how tough it was for a man to make a good living. I referred to the five-year-old shoeshine boy in my book. Later, during my visit to Sacramento, my uncle reprimanded me on this, insisting his father was a generous man who took good care of his family. He insisted it was not true that my father had to survive on the dirty streets of El Paso during the thirties. José, as my father's older brother, was responsible for the younger Ramón and told me he took care of him when their mother died in their youth. This contradiction between the two brothers would not be the first I would find as I learned more about the González family.

Despite my misgivings about having a close member of my father's family read my autobiography, I was excited that, at last, the González side of the family was recognizing my writing. I promised my uncle that my wife and I would come visit him that summer.

We ended our phone conversation with him saying, "Hey, it's good to talk to you. I've always asked Ray about you. Keep in touch. Your cousin Tony told me he heard you on the radio a few months ago. We all want to see you."

I thought it was ironic he brought up my radio presentation, because it was about my father. After *Memory Fever* came out, I was contacted by NPR to do a commentary based on my essays. Their editor had read my book and asked me to condense "My Father's Pool Hall" to three minutes. It took about twenty takes at the local public radio station to finally tape a shorter version of the piece. Many people around the country have told me they heard the national program. To this day, I wonder how such a personal view of my father managed to make it onto NPR.

After I hung up the phone, I sat on the living room sofa and cried. I told Ida about my father sending a copy of the review to his brother. I cried because it was a sudden turn in my relationship with my father. I also wept because I believed my uncle when he told me my father was proud of me, something I knew my father could never tell me to my face. When I first started writing seriously, back in the early seventies, the only thing I heard from my father then was "Well, why don't you get a real job? You can't make any money from poetry!"

It was a strange sensation to have someone on my father's side of the family talk to me. A certain pressure had been taken off my shoulders, though it ate at me every day of my life. I had not seen my father in years, but there I was talking to his brother, whom I had not seen in thirty. The mere fact that my uncle took the step of calling changed something. Suddenly, there were new possibilities. I felt as if the scope of my role as my father's son, and as a writer trying to leave his past behind, had widened. It energized me and frightened me at the same time.

This anxiety had to do with my parents' divorce. I assumed my father's adultery was the final catalyst for the end to what must have been years of a miserable marriage. It was the disintegration of a life together that, as a boy who believed the family circle was utopia, had never been evident as I was growing up. Writing the very personal and painful essays in *Memory Fever* helped me to understand the mysteries of childhood. As I got off the phone with my uncle, I knew I had written only one half of the story.

The other side involved the history of my father's family, which I knew nothing about. It was built around my father's silence and his inability to be close to me and talk to me when I was a boy. My most vivid memories include him driving us to the movie theater downtown without saying a single word to me. I would sit in the passenger seat and look out the window at the passing cars. We sat in the dark theater without saying a word. I also remember when he tried to make me a baseball player. For several weeks one summer, we played catcher and pitcher. He bought me a glove and ball and made me pitch it to him hard, dozens of times. He told me he wanted me to go out for the local Little League team and I should be the pitcher. After weeks of throwing him the ball as he crouched in the catcher's stance, I went out for the team. The coach immediately stuck me in right field and cut me and two other boys from the team one week into practice.

One of the most unforgettable memories has to do with the senses. It is tied into the passage I quoted about my father being a used-car salesman most of his adult life. I can never forget the late nights waiting with my mother for him to come home. When he showed up very tired, he would eat, then go lie down. He would take off his shoes and socks and turn on late-night television. I would sit on the edge of my parents' bed and watch

TV with him. He would sigh, sometimes ask me what I did that day, then gaze off at the black-and-white screen. He would lie there and not move as a powerful smell filled the room. To this day, the memory of the tired car salesman brings back the sweaty smell of his shoes and socks. The odor of his feet was overpowering and hangs in my mind and nose as the eternal scent of a man who worked hard, made little money, and grew farther away from his family. I will always equate the smell with the weariness of my father. Smell as a lingering memory becomes a cloud I would give anything to experience again because it is repelling and endearing. It is me sitting on the edge of the bed, wanting him to say or do something for me. It is the smell of love, compassion, and distance. It is the odor of men.

The puzzle of how our family dynamics came together and fell apart could not be truly understood until I learned more about the Gonzálezes. It was hard to admit I had been under the deep and complete control of my mother when it came to the details and reasons for their divorce. For years after the breakup, she forbade my three sisters and me from having anything to do with my father. When I would mention that I spoke on the phone with him, she would get upset and claim I was conspiring against her.

"Your father doesn't care about his children," she would say. "When was the last time he called or asked how you were doing?"

If I told her I just wanted to say hello, she would contradict herself and tell me she didn't care if I talked to him. Then, I would hear a brief rundown of how he cheated on her, took her money when he left, and how he would pay for his sins someday. By the end of the conversation, the guilt set in and I would go months without making the next call to my father. Since 1982, a slow process developed where my sisters and I widened the distance between us and my father in order not to hurt my mother and protect our relationship with her. It didn't help that my mother and father were the kind of people they were. For years, my mother refused to accept that she had to go on with her life. The bitterness over the divorce made her ill and kept her in a self-made trap of hatred and pity. It is only recently, thirteen years later, that I have noticed she talks about him less and deals with other realities of life instead.

On the other hand, my father is guilty of adultery and of abandoning his family to go live another life. He didn't want anything to do with us after the divorce. My sisters and I were adults, but still his children. My frustrating attempts to start a dialogue and try to see him were created by my mother's control over my actions and my father's unwillingness to have a good post-divorce relationship with his son and daughters. At the time I first talked to my uncle, I had no idea the visit to Sacramento would help me in trying to break the pattern of being caught between my mother's guilt trips and my father ignoring me.

My uncle's reintroduction of the González family filled me with anticipation and with the fear of being let down again. Even though I looked forward to the summer trip to Sacramento, I was afraid my uncle would disappoint me, just like my father had many times. Things had started on a positive note because this sudden contact, after thirty years, had come about because of my writing. The day after the phone call, I sent several copies of *Memory Fever* to my uncle because he told me my cousins wanted to read my book. I enclosed a brief note saying I looked forward to seeing him later in the year.

I called my father a few days after talking to his brother. The first time, I got the usual answering machine with his wife's voice on it. I had left messages before that were never returned, so I hung up on the machine. I tried again the following day and got hold of him. We had our usual short talk, which I was able to extend by a few minutes when I told him about José.

"Yeah, I sent him the newspaper," he told me. "He's always asking me about you. He said your cousin Tony heard you on the radio. Send me a copy of your book and I'll buy it from you."

I was taken back by this, even though I was used to my father always bringing up money. I told him I would send him one, but I never have. To this day, I do not believe my father has seen a copy of *Memory Fever*. I am still unable to share it with him. The failed billiard parlor, the smelly socks, and the small boy waiting for his father to say something inside the movie theater are all there. My mother has not seen it, either, though one of my sisters ordered a copy last year. I have written a book about my life in El Paso, but have not been able to share it with my parents. Are the childhood incidents so damaging that I do not want to hurt those responsible for many of them? As a writer, am I truly free to write in an autobiographical mode without considering how my confessions will affect those whom I love? And, if I do consider them, do they naturally create an inner process of self-censorship that shapes what is revealed in the writing?

I have dozens of books of poetry by male writers who write about their fathers. The "father poem" has become a cliché in itself. There are a handful of anthologies of father-and-son poems. Robert Bly is one of the best writers of this genre. I have written at least one hundred poems about my father. Several appeared in my first two published books of poetry. My third book, *The Heat of Arrivals,* contains a crucial section of nothing but father poems. The central poem in the section, "The Energy of Clay," ends with this stanza:

Of my father, he lives in two worlds—
land of the digger and the cave of clay,
territory he never inhabits because
his houses were built from harder ground,
mixture of the bitter cottonwood and the thorn,
formed with the isolation of walls where all fathers,
in their son's clay, lie down to forget.

My fourth book, *Cabato Sentora,* is centered entirely around building and destroying family myths and how they keep the male writer from truly understanding where he came from and why he writes. Despite the publication of these two books by a major press, I am tired of writing father poems. They are a small fraction of the entire body of poetry I have written, but are the most disturbing pieces. They continue to pop up when I am in the middle of creating new poems. I can't get away from writing about my father and the rest of my family. My creative process is ingrained with my past. The continuing family poems may be the lost conversations I never had with my father when he drove us to the movies. They are the shameful lines of defense I used to explain to him why I got cut from the baseball team. They are the images of an exhausted man, whose smelly feet melt into the heat of the desert, only to be molded out of clay, again, by the trembling hands and sharp language of his son.

The subject of fathers in poetry came up in the spring of 1994 when I gave a poetry reading in Indiana. A friend of mine and fellow poet, George Kalamaras, invited me to read at the university in Fort Wayne, where he teaches. I spent several days there. Besides the reading and a workshop, the visit gave George and me time to catch up on things as old friends from our Colorado days.

One evening during dinner, George told me about making contact with his father, whom he had not talked to or seen in twenty years. George's parents divorced years ago. In his case, it happened when he was a young boy. He grew up with a stepfather. The subject came up because we were eating in a diner across the street from another restaurant in downtown South Bend. George pointed to the building and told me he recently found out it was owned by his father, who is a businessman in Chicago. He stumbled upon the information after overhearing workers in the restaurant mention the owner by his last name. George and his wife, Mary Ann, had been eating in the place, but no one knew who they were. A couple of days later, he called the place. He was told by the manager that the restaurant was one of several owned by a Dennis Kalamaras from Chicago. It was his father. For a couple of weeks, George tried to reach him at the restaurant in Chicago, where his father's office was located. He left several messages.

"Tell him it's George, his son," the messages said. "I just want to say hello. I live in South Bend."

Weeks passed without a response. George came home one day to catch the phone ringing. After twenty years of not knowing each other's where-abouts, his father returned his calls.

"I didn't know what to say to him," George told me. "What do you say to your father you haven't seen since you were a kid?" George said this without any sign of emotion.

They had a pleasant conversation, but George could tell his father was hesitant to see George and his younger brother, Karl, who also lived in Chicago. His brother had not seen his father since he was a tiny boy. By coincidence, Karl lived just a few blocks from his father's office, but had never known they both resided in the same city.

A reunion in one of Mr. Kalamaras's restaurants was scheduled. "It was one of the hardest things I have ever done," George whispered to me over

his salad. "My father looked just like I remembered him. I couldn't believe it. He was older, but he still had that overwhelming Greek presence.
I could tell he was used to being the boss. His waiters waited on Karl and
me hand and foot."

The father and two sons were polite to each other and managed to tell
each other about their lives. They promised to stay in touch and see each
other again. He even offered to have one of his drivers come pick up
George and his wife and bring them for a visit sometime.

George and Karl experienced short-lived elation because, a few weeks
after the reunion, Dennis canceled plans to see them. One of the last conversations George had with his father on the phone had to do with Dennis's reluctance to have his first sons come back into his life. He told them
he had a second family and a wife who didn't even know about his first
marriage. His sons from the second marriage helped him run his business.

"I don't know what it was," George said. "I think he thought my
brother and I were contacting him after all these years because we wanted
money. He was probably afraid we wanted a cut of his restaurants. He
was real defensive."

George paused and looked toward the diner across the street. "I'll
never forget him telling me that if I ever needed anything to call him.
Well, what Karl and I needed had nothing to do with what he had."

George's father said good-bye for good one year before my visit to Indiana. The two have not talked since. I was surprised at the lack of emotion George showed in telling me his story. In its own way, it was more
extreme than my situation with my father. I told him about my phone
conversation with my uncle and how I was counting the months before
my trip to see him.

George's story about his father haunted me for several days after I returned to San Antonio. I told it to Phil Woods, a friend of George's and
mine who lives in Denver. Phil, too, had traumatic experiences with his
father. Phil wrote "Fathers and Sons," one of the most moving and haunting poems about fathers I have ever read. The following stanzas from the
long poem are most memorable:

I can see his face, now,
staring at me,

full of inquisitiveness,
trying so hard to connect

So he starts telling me
old Air Corps stories
from his young manhood
in the Big War,

a couple of new ones that
I was too tired to remember.
He apologizes for telling them
and calls himself dumb.

I say, "No, don't do that.
You don't have to apologize.
I've always liked hearing
your stories."

Phil wrote the poem as a tribute to his father, who died in 1980. The poem does not make references to several nervous breakdowns Phil's father experienced over the years, dark states of mind that deeply affected his son. Mr. Woods worked at the army depot and was a laborer in the steel mill in Pueblo, Colorado, for many years. Later in the poem, Phil admits what every son writing about his father has to admit:

We both grow quiet.
It is a moment, I'd
like to have back.
I'd hug him and
tell him the truth.
Maybe not. That's the way
it is with fathers and sons.
They can't ever get down to it.

This was not the first time Phil and I had talked about fathers and how our relationships with them shaped our poems. As our friendship grew over the years, we were willing to admit the topic was difficult to talk to other people about. For me, it was harder talking about my father than writing about him. We were familiar with Bly's work and often debated the impact of the men's movement. Our discussions always came back to the poems.

Despite honest attempts by many males to come to terms with the kind of men they had for fathers, we don't completely understand why so many of us are blocked from having good relationships with them. We can go as far as to say it is not our fault our fathers were screwed up and had lived very different lives than our own. As young men, their values were different and family roles were not what they are today. We could point out certain events in our parents' lives that affected us as kids, but we could not completely understand why it was so damn hard to reach out to the male parent and pay such a high cost for doing it. To me, the fact my father lost his mother at the age of five has a great deal to do with this whole story. But, since I am not a psychologist, I can't describe every implication of not having a mother to nurture your natural instincts and help sustain the positive road toward maturity.

At the opposite extreme, it was harder to close the gap between me and my father because my mother was a dominating force in our domestic history. She didn't want me to be athletic because she was afraid I would get hurt playing sports. During the sixties, I could not grow my hair long—she insisted I cut it. We had terrible fights over this. She didn't want a "decadent" hippie in her house. If I went to hang out with one of my friends, sooner or later, there would be a phone call at the guy's house for me to come home. In those days, I subscribed to the *L.A. Free Press,* a pioneering underground newspaper of the sixties. It was full of ads for strip joints and massage parlors. Each time the new issue came, my mother grabbed it from the mailbox and took it into her room. She kept a box of black crayons in there, which she used to cross out every ad photograph of a topless woman. I read about the cultural life of California in a newspaper smeared with greasy black lines—page after page of them. I got used to seeing photos of women with black bars across their chests.

My father went along with all of this. I recall my parents often arguing about things I could or couldn't do, but my mother always won. She was overly protective, feared the wrath of God, and was going to make sure her son did not show any sign of independence. My father quit telling her

I needed to grow up and be allowed a normal life as a boy. He surrendered to her crushing wall of control and it amplified his distance from me. As I became a teenager and could look at my father more deeply, I realized he had totally backed off in his support of me against her.

In the midst of our confusion over our families, Phil and I agreed the only solace we found was in our writing. Being a writer means I buy time to live and survive my "family of distance." It means surrounding myself with a private language that has taken years to shape into public speech other people can relate to. As a poet, I respond to the world my parents gave me by isolating past and present existences within the life of the poem. Not all my poems are about family history, but my entire poetic output comes from what happened long ago. My identity as a man, a husband, and a person in the community was shaped by having a father who rarely spoke to me as a child. I don't know what it is like to sit down and have a long, pleasant visit with my father. I have never shared a meal with him, just the two of us, in a public place. I wouldn't know how to ask for any advice from him on anything having to do with women, jobs, politics, or any semblance of a spiritual life. I have no idea how my father sees the world or what kind of inner philosophy drives him. Who knows what demons have been eating away at him for years? He has never allowed me close enough to find out.

This silent power he has over me defines the obedient son. What I obey from a distance, and feed into, is this mute way of being. He lives in his world and keeps it from his children. I live in mine and write about it. When I cast my writing into the public arena, I risk being judged by my audience. Sharing my personal stories in a universal manner is why I got a good book review in the El Paso paper. The positive response is why my father sent it to his brother. The critical acclaim is why my uncle is curious about my life as a writer. It is why my father poems and essays keep me alive.

Phil and I know how family history drives a poem or essay into creation. We feel the weight of carrying our fathers' presence in our chests, in our wide bellies, and in the hidden, secret language that churns inside us. I like to refer to this secret language as the "code of silence." It thrives between fathers and sons. It is a deep and wounding silence that gives life to the relationships among men like myself, George, Phil, and our fathers.

As sons, we are used to having fathers that don't want to be near us. We accept that part of the code. We are confused because we don't have all the details about how our fathers became wealthy businessmen, or secret adulterers, or mentally ill individuals. The code feeds its own circle. Our families will go on somehow.

As sons, we act like our fathers without knowing it. I don't mean we act out every destructive act of our fathers. What we are capable of doing is inheriting this code of silence. Then, we apply it to our interactions with our children, our wives, and our community. This hit home for me after struggling for several years to build a good relationship with my stepson, Charlie. He lived with his mother and me for six years of our marriage before moving back to Denver to live with his father. I always had difficulty talking to him. If we went anywhere, I felt self-conscious as I tried to start a conversation with him. When it came to discipline and Ida asking me to speak with him, my determination to set the rules would turn into shouting matches and angry confrontations. All of this just like my father. It was uncanny. It is something still unresolved in me.

We may not repeat every mistake our fathers made, but our inner turmoil, weaknesses, and strengths come from the same fibers of that code. Before we know it, we have our identity as men. It has been passed down from one generation to another. If we know this, how do we stop it or change it? How do we turn toward a more rewarding existence, when the most life-sustaining force we have—our lives as artists—has been greatly shaped by the flaws of our fathers? We are poets, so we know how to feed and starve that silence. When we can't take it anymore, a father poem comes out. It saves us temporarily, adds to our body of work, but turns around to reinforce the unsaid things between us.

My wife and I flew to San Francisco in August and drove a rental car to Sacramento. I had been to the Bay area many times, but never felt as apprehensive as I did that summer. My visit with my Uncle José and his family was a combination of wonderful leisure time playing tourists, along with intense conversations about my father. José is seventy-one, five years older than my father. He is retired from the military after forty years of service and five bullet wounds in his head. He received them in three major wars. During one of our talks on his patio, he told me he killed eighty-two Japanese soldiers during World War II. He also killed forty-two North Koreans and Chinese in the Korean War. The figure that made me stare at him for a long time was the 140 Vietnamese men and women he killed in North and South Vietnam.

José showed me dozens of medals he got as a hero. He revealed that he served in the U.S. Army Special Forces. It is how he tallied nine Purple Hearts, five head wounds, and 264 kills. He told me there are many things he did as a soldier he can't talk about, but admitted he was a secret U.S. advisor at Dien Ben Phu, the 1954 battle where the Vietnamese defeated the French forces. There weren't supposed to be any Americans in Vietnam during that time. He was also part of the Phoenix Program, where U.S. Special Forces and South Vietnamese agents killed thousands of Viet Cong and North Vietnamese in the late sixties. My uncle told me he was so good at his job that he and his partner, working in two-man teams behind enemy lines, had a high monetary price placed on their heads by the North Vietnamese.

In 1987, after already having retired, it caught up with him. He was hospitalized with a large brain tumor. He almost died and spent months in the veterans hospital in Sacramento. The doctors told him the tumor was caused by the shape his brain was in after five head wounds. My uncle is an intelligent and articulate man. He speaks in a normal voice. He is doing fine now and enjoys his retirement. He does volunteer work at a number of charities in Sacramento.

I describe what I know of his military life because what he told me still shocks me and is a factor in how I see him and my father. In their own distinct ways, they are lonely heroes. My uncle did it for his country and survived. My father, who served in the navy between World War II and Korea, has survived in a less dramatic fashion on the home front. Either way, it seems both of them have played out the lives of two loners. I couldn't have reached these conclusions before my visit to Sacramento. My uncle's experiences in the Special Forces and his years spent away from his family tie into the code of silence my father bears. The things my uncle told me about himself gave me the ability to see my father and his family in a more realistic light. After all these years, I made a start in moving out from under my mother's control over the kind of family the Gonzálezes were supposed to be. I could love them completely, at last.

My uncle's sad and brutal accounts of his military actions, and how his wife and children went months without knowing what part of the world he was in, fit the characteristics of González men that are never going to change. While my uncle's January phone call came with great potential, his revelations about his secret life told me to bring him down off the pedestal I placed him upon after he called me. His forty years of being gone from his family, and a certain disturbing pride he expressed in remembering his war tales, told me he was not that different from my father. Both of them had lived a major portion of their lives without the immediate love and attention of family. My uncle even told me that during the infamous Cuban missile crisis of 1962, he disappeared for six months without contacting Violeta and his children once. Military intelligence didn't allow for such contact. Despite these sobering facts, I knew I had done the right thing in coming to Sacramento. Perhaps there was a growing crack in the code of silence that kept my uncle in military service for so long. If I could have longer phone conversations with my father after Sacramento, it might mean we were weakening the code.

While Ida and I visited, my uncle was very generous. He told me he liked my book, but added that it was very one-sided. I felt self-conscious talking about it. I got excited when he promised to send me the González family tree and other information about how my father's ancestors settled in New Mexico in the mid-nineteenth century. One evening, I interviewed him about the great-great-grandparents and other family members I knew nothing about. I took pages of notes. Our talks about the family tree led to conversations about my father.

The day after he told me about his military career, he shared several things about his brother. He said my father had always been very quiet and it was hard for him to tell me he was proud.

"Did you know Ray had a heart attack in 1988?"

"What?" I shook my head.

"He didn't tell you about it?" My uncle frowned and looked down at his coffee cup. "He was in the hospital for several days."

"No," I swallowed. "I didn't know."

It was shocking and disturbing news because I never knew about it and neither did my mother and sisters. I could see how such things could happen without anyone from his first family finding out. After the divorce, my father became very good at going for long periods of time without us knowing where he lived or what he was doing.

One of the most memorable conversations José and I had was about the two brothers' childhood in El Paso. José laughed about how he always led the way for my father. He protected him from neighborhood bullies on the streets of El Paso during the Great Depression. Their mother, Josefina, died when my father and José were small boys. José told me that the day after her funeral, he and my father were walking down a street in south El Paso. They came to a busy intersection. My uncle took his brother's hand so they could get across the street. As they waited for a chance to cross, José looked toward the opposite corner and saw his mother standing there, pointing at her sons. He motioned to his brother. My uncle claims they both saw their mother standing in the middle of a crowd, trying to cross toward them. By the time both boys stepped onto the busy street and dodged several cars to get across, she was gone.

My uncle swore this incident was true. He told me to ask my father about it sometime. I haven't asked him. I know the ghost of my father's mother has come back because she has appeared in several of my poems. I have written about her because I have dreamed of her. I always know who she is, even though I never knew her. These dreams occur every now and then. So far, they have all taken place before my trip to Sacramento and my uncle's story. The grandmother I never knew has appeared in my dreams, just like she appeared to her sons after her death. Perhaps, now, I know why.

Dreams have dominated my poems for many years. Some of them contain strangers I know are family members from the past. Talking to my uncle gave my family poems a different edge that does not disturb me. A few of the dreams have ended with feelings of suffocation—the distress of a nightmare. I don't know why some of them have concluded in that manner. In some of those dreams, these people are trying to harm me.

My uncle's tale about his mother was one of the last ones he shared before my wife and I returned to Texas. The four days we spent with him went by quickly. There were times during our talks, as we sat at his kitchen table, that I swore I was talking to my father. They look very much alike, even though I can't really say what a man I haven't seen in eight years looks like now. They both have broad foreheads and dark, wavy hair. My father once told me his brother's hair turned completely white after his brain operation. José showed us a photo from World War II, when he was twenty years old. He is very thin and looks like Elvis Presley. My wife claims the González men have very feminine facial features. The round cheeks and dark eyes run in the family.

We said our good-byes. My uncle invited me and Ida to come back again. I asked her to drive most of the way back to San Francisco because I was weeping. I had not cried that hard over anything in years. The rush of sobs came from the rich information I had gathered about my father and the grief I encountered over his family's past, which had been kept from me. The crying also came from knowing I was ending a part of my isolation. I grieved because I was going to have a different relationship with my mother. She was no longer in control of the official family record. I had to accept that the new relationships I formed with my relatives were not going to bring my father back to me the way I wanted him. It was up to me and my father to do that.

Since my visit to my uncle, my phone conversations with my father last longer than before. I have more to tell him, but also wait to see if he has more to say to me. Most of the time, he does not. It is up to me to enlarge those moments. I am the one that has to do it, in order to finally step beyond the moment of the father poems I have written. Whatever desires and pain I express in those poems now have to come from my heart and my mouth—a truly oral sounding that has to go beyond the silence of language. They can no longer come from a small boy yearning blindly for his father. I can't depend on my gift as a poet for everything. Sharing these things about men with George and Phil have taught me that. We can't stay on the same page forever. Talking longer to my father also means I have more things to write about.

One of the last things my uncle told me was to call my father more often. He said my father loves to hear from me. Some of my calls have resulted in my father calling José to tell him he heard from me. This was a real surprise. I always thought my uncle did the calling and made the attempts to stay in touch with him.

I called my father a few days after we returned home. I said how much I enjoyed seeing my uncle. I repeated some of the names he had given me from the González family tree. My father remembered some of his ancestors and was curious about others. I told him I found out about his heart attack of a few years before.

My father paused over the line. "That's not true. I never had a heart attack," he said quickly, then laughed. "Your uncle doesn't know what he is talking about."

He changed the subject to the usual, "I'm glad you're doing okay. Why don't you give me your number so I can call you?" I repeated it, as I always do, and we said good-bye.

Even though I was angry at his denial and believe my uncle, I let it go. It was too much to expect. Like George's father, mine is also a businessman. My uncle revealed that my father owns several houses and real estate in El Paso. They both inherited properties when my grandfather died eight years ago. I didn't know that. Perhaps my father denied ill health in fear that my mother, sisters, and I would line up to get what is his. Telling truths between fathers and sons is too much to expect, even if our poems and essays point us toward those truths. Without my book of essays, my father never would have contacted my uncle about me. Without their pride in my literary accomplishments, I doubt my uncle would have called me. Those truths took thirty years to reach me. The truths about love, family, and history my father and I need to share might come the day we finally break the code. One form of its silence is presently in its eighth year. These truths that build great distances between fathers and sons are as old as any poem a son can write. They are as ancient as words shared between friends who don't understand their fathers. They are as eternal as the ghosts that rise from the pages of father poems. They haunt our dreams while they point to boys trying to cross the street without letting go of each other's hands.

ON

MACHO

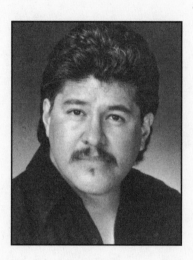

LUIS J. RODRÍGUEZ is an award-winning poet, as well as a peace activist in barrios throughout the country. He is the author of two books of poems, including <u>The Concrete River,</u> from Curbstone Press. His latest book is the widely acclaimed memoir <u>Always Running: La Vida Loca, Gang Days in L.A.,</u> from Touchstone Books. He directs Tía Chucha Press, a publisher of socially engaged poetry, in Chicago, Illinois.

"What is madness but nobility of soul at odds
with circumstance."
—Theodore Roethke

I AM A MAN. This is a fact I've carried with me for some forty years now. But as a fact it says little of what being a man is all about, little about the essence, the complete meaning and sense of *manness*. Little about the heart or the truth of it, the lie or distortion of it.

For most of my life, I've been a man consumed by a certain madness. Madness of spirit, *mi vida loca;* madness of spirits, the bottle; madness of body, rage eternal; depth of sea, sea of pain. Sea of madness. A man to be a man is to live a lie, I'm told. The lie of manhood, the mask, the carica-ture. A man to be a man must live the truth of man-being, the power of it. Beyond the madness, into the manness.

In January 1994, I attended my first men's conference amidst the scorched Malibu terrain—acres had recently been consumed by fire—just outside Los Angeles, where days before the Northridge earthquake had rocked this earth.

I had until then little knowledge of the so-called men's movement in this country—I'd read a bit about it, and I knew some of Robert Bly's work, including *Iron John*. Once, when Bly read at the 1991 International Book Fair in San Antonio, he mentioned that a poem in my book *The Concrete River* had interested him. The following excerpt is from that poem, "Always Running":

I sat down on the backsteps,
gazing across the yellowed yard.
A 1954 Chevy Bel-Air stared back.
It was my favorite possession.
I hated it just then.
It didn't start when I tried to get it going
earlier that night. It had a bad solenoid.
I held a 12 gauge shotgun across my lap.

I expected trouble from the Paragons gang
of the west Lynwood barrio.
Somebody said I drove the car
that dudes from Colonia Watts
used to shoot up the Paragons' neighborhood.
But I got more than trouble that night.
My wife had left around 10 p.m.
to take a friend of mine home.
She didn't come back.
I wanted to kill somebody.
At moments, it had nothing to do
with the Paragons.
It had to do with a woman I loved.
But who to kill? Not her—
sweet allure wrapped in a black skirt.
I'd kill myself first.
Kill me first?
But she was the one who quit!
Kill her? No, think man! I was hurt, angry . . .
but to kill her? To kill a Paragon?
To kill anybody?
I went into the house
and put the gun away.

For years, rage had governed many of my actions and inactions; it had
accompanied many of my defeats and sorrows. In that poem, I sought to
deal with the uncontrollable pull of this inexplicable fury. Other times I
dealt with it through drugs or alcohol.

At the end of the poem, after the gun is back in a closet, I end up at the
Los Angeles River and then run along its concrete banks for hours—to
heal, to think, to cleanse as a way to salve the hurt, without needing to
hurt in return. I could see why Bly might have liked the poem.

I came to the men's conference in Malibu as a teacher/elder, invited by
master storyteller and men's movement veteran Michael Meade. His Mosaic Foundation had by then sponsored a number of multicultural men's
conferences around the country.

My misgivings at the time came from a perception—not that far off the mark—that the men's movement consisted of Anglo therapists, stockbrokers, teachers, and doctors, mostly privileged men who felt rootless, spiritless, vulnerable to elements and powers beyond their grasp. They were seekers, trying to traverse a tumultuous internal sea of conflicting realities and philosophies, often race and class based, most of which served to disorient or diffuse their ideas of what it meant to be a man in a fragmented culture that distorted and devalued the essence of both men and women.

They needed this, I figured. But what about me?

As a Chicano male, the men's movement as I envisioned it failed to engage me. What did it have to do with my pain? I was not like those guys! I had been a member of a violent barrio gang. I had shot and stabbed people. I had firebombed people's homes. I had done car thefts, burglaries, and armed robberies, been in and out of jails. Many of the homeys from my youth were dead or in prison. What program could get close to this!

I remember as a teenager participating at a Brotherhood Camp sponsored by the National Council of Christians and Jews where a number of young people from L.A.'s poorest neighborhoods were to strike at a stuffed footstool with an inflated rubber hammer. Most played it like a game. Some were shy. Others only said a few things about the issues that tore at them. But when I got to the footstool, I began to strike it, and something alien, like another hand, began to pounce on it with that hammer. I yelled, I cried without concern about those around me or whether I could even stop.

This incident scared me, as I'm sure it scared others. I never wanted this kind of anger to erupt again, but it often did, and mostly I was unable to do anything about it. The raging animal within me—the beast, as I later learned to call it—helped break up relationships and marriages (I'm officially married three times, but I lived with two other women as common-law wives, and had three platonic relationships).

The drumming, the chanting, and the "sharing" I had linked to men's gatherings in the woods just didn't appear to have anything to do with me and this beast.

Few Chicano men had participated in these events up until that time. But Ed Carrillo, a Vietnam War vet and social worker I'd known for many years, had attended and recommended me to Meade. I also found out that a person whom I had great respect for, Haki R. Madhubuti of Chicago, an African-American poet, thinker, and activist, and longtime theorist on black male rage, had been part of Mosaic's events in the past. And one of Meade's sons, Fian, had read my memoir, *Always Running: La Vida Loca, Gang Days In L.A.,* and told his father about my possible participation.

I first met Michael Meade in Seattle in the summer of 1993, where I was commissioned to do a weeklong poetry workshop with about thirty inner-city children for Centro de La Raza and the Bumbershoot Literary Arts Festival. He impressed me as someone with experience and knowledge of important aspects of myth, story, and men's lives, and I wanted to work with him. I agreed to be on the teaching staff for the Malibu event.

The conference turned out to be an immensely important, life-transforming event. Since then I have attended a few more, including weekend events with Meade and company on Vashon Island in the Puget Sound, where Mosaic has its offices.

What so affected me was the intense level of probing and dealing with the life-and-death issues that gnawed at all of us. Many of the young men who attended that conference in Malibu were from South-Central Los Angeles and East L.A., not long after the 1992 rebellion and its aftermath.

A few of the older men were Vietnam veterans, former prisoners, and former gang-bangers. It proved to be the first place where I had a level of comfort in which to share some dark and deep concerns. I got particularly close to one of the men, a former Ohio farmboy who had been made into a meticulous killing machine in Vietnam and then let loose on a world that had no place for him. We shared some wonderful poetry together.

I had never been able to truly open up to the source of my own rage before, except through writing poetry and the memoir, undergoing counseling with my oldest son, Ramiro, and through participating in a recovery program two years ago for my drinking.

At the men's conferences, it all seemed to fit into place. A year later, nineteen-year-old Ramiro, and two of his homeboys from Chicago, attended a conference in North Carolina, which helped open up new possibilities for them about their own pain and manhood.

I am now in the process of involving other Latino men—Puerto Rican, Central American, and Mexican—who work with gangs in Chicago, as well as gang members themselves, in men's retreats around the country.

When I wrote this, a couple of situations were hanging over my head. A fifteen-year-old friend of our family had his best friend stabbed to death in his home. The facts of the case were not all in then, but the fifteen-year-old's mother came by our house in tears so we could take care of her younger daughter while they attended the wake.

The violence of men. It appears so senseless, so random, but if we look deeply at the culture, at the spiritual losses and the capitalist relations that place property rights over human rights, material goods over spirituality, then the violence begins to make a lot of sense.

On top of this, my son Ramiro was sitting in the maximum security section of the Cook County Jail, one of the world's largest and most dangerous facilities. In one of the retreats on Vashon Island, in December 1994, Meade and I both had sons undergoing intense conflicts. Urgent phone calls to the camps from our families put a damper on our abilities as teachers to address the other men's concerns. Meade, holding back tears, read a poem by Li-Young Lee about the kind of helplessness fathers often have in relation to their sons. I sobbed silently in my seat.

The men, however, rallied to our needs. They gave us support and prayers. They built fires on which I placed wood and sage in the name of my son. Meade and I knelt in front of shrines created by the men and said our own prayers.

Ramiro presently faces many years in prison, if his cases don't work out as we hope. He has pretty much done what I had done at his age. But now there are fewer options for him, fewer resources from which he can draw the strength to carry on in this life with autonomy, dignity, strength, and courage. He wrote this poem while incarcerated:

The day the world took my life away
The day I took my life away from the world
I opened up my eyes
To a world that has chained me to this dying earth
My heart has been broken

Not for the love of someone else
But for the love I did not have for myself.

I still believe in him. He has made many mistakes, too many to outline
here. But I also know he is a beautiful human being, capable of great poetry, great transformations, great battles. Just before his arrest, Ramiro
was excited about attending Columbia College, where he had just registered for classes. He had gone to speak at public schools and other meetings with Chicago's Rogers Park Youth Congress, sponsored by the Jew-
ish Council on Urban Affairs. He had reactivated himself in the Youth
Struggling for Survival meetings, a group we founded with more than
one hundred gang and nongang kids in August 1994.

On the phone recently, Ramiro tells me he is now seeing things more
clearly, or more like what I had been telling him for years. But he has to
find all this out in his own way, in his own time—I just wanted him to do
so before he hurt himself or others.

This had required that I be there for him and with him, not to have en-
abled his afflictions, but to have kept providing him a pathway out of this
stage of his life once he matured intellectually and emotionally. I believe
he is getting there, but he may still have to pay a heavy price before he can
do something with this newfound knowledge and power.

Unfortunately, there haven't been many other things out there for him
or other youth like him. I learned in the men's meetings that a father cannot do it all (although fathers are critical). I had tried for two years to or-
ganize a number of his own homeboys, and other gang youth in Chicago,
so they could envision and create a meaningful alternative to their pain
and fears.

I worked with people who had years of youth work experience. I even
set up a special council of gang youth workers in the city to pool resources,
share experiences, and just to bounce off ideas. This group is very interested in the spiritual links missing from our lives. Many of these youth,
particularly the Mexicans, are of indigenous blood. Yet they have been totally cut off from their ancestral and native ways.

Presently, many sectors in society are talking about mentors. Working
with Meade helped me understand the importance of this concept. A
mentor is one who above all imparts skills or crafts knowledge. It comes

from *The Odyssey:* Athena sends Mentor (a navigator, a helmsman, a steerer among rocky seas) to Odysseus's son Telemachus to help him find his father.

I'm convinced we need a mentor-type system of guidance and education. All human beings are capable of being great artists at something (as the saying goes, "Artists are not a special kind of people; we are all a special kind of artist"). A good mentor is more than just a friend or a father substitute. Methodology is key here, in the sense of mentors who help awaken the artist, the poet, in everyone.

Poetry became my path to healing. At the men's conferences, my major contribution was to read poems addressing my conflicts, my doubts, and my rage. I remember reading a poem about my father that elicited some sorrow from other men. The poem, "Deathwatch" (from *The Concrete River),* ends like this:

All around the room are mounds of papers:
Junk mail, coupons, envelopes (unopened & empty),
much of this sticking out of drawers,
on floor piles—in a shapeless heap
in the corner. On the wooden end
of a bed is a ball made up of thousands
of rubber bands. Cereal boxes
are thrown about everywhere,
some half full. There are writing
tablets piled on one side, filled
with numbers, numbers without pattern,
that you write over and over,
obsessed.

For years your silence
was greeting and departure:
a vocal disengagement.
I see you now walking around in rags,
your eyes glued to Spanish-language *telenovelas,*

keen to every nuance of voice and movement,
what you rarely gave to me.
This silence is now comfort.

We almost made it, eh Pop?
From the times when you came home late
and gathered up children in both arms
as wide as a gentle wind
to this old guy, visited by police and social workers,
talking to air, accused of lunacy.
I never knew you.
Losing you was all there was.

My father died of stomach cancer in 1992; he was eighty-two years old.
His time had come. That poem, however, was written a few years before
his death. We never really communicated. We never shared intimate moments, or even the word *love* between us. Some ten years before his death,
he began to lose his mind; there was little time to make up for the words
unsaid between us. The poem was about the closing of his mind, and
thereby his heart, to me.

When I called him the last time—he was on his deathbed—I told him
I loved him very much. He couldn't speak then, but my mother says his
eyes brightened, his lips moved, and I knew he was telling me how much
he loved me. In fact, his heart had not closed.

The patriarchal Mexican culture had helped build a wide breach between my father and me. The silent and strong man—perhaps such a di-
chotomy could exist, but it also had vestiges of deceit—was revered.
Waited on. Accepted. My grandfather drank his manhood away, beating
up his wives, demeaning his children. My mother learned to hate, to talk
a blue streak so she could defend herself. As a child, I often felt her wrath
when she beat me and my brother.

Mexicans are a traumatized people. We still maintain some of our indigenous traditions, yet only a small percentage know—or even care—
what tribes they originated from. Our genetic stock is mostly native to this
soil, but our language, our names, our customs—even if transfigured with
native ones—are from Europe. Yet despite our history of *mestizaje,* in the

United States we cannot assimilate—not as long as we suffer an imposed second-class citizenship, race and class exploitation.

It's true many of us become "Anglicized" whether we like it or not, but no one fools anybody. This is mostly strategizing one's way in the world. Besides, the so-called Anglo culture is multicultural at its core. North America is not a pure culture (neither is Europe). The issue, then, is not to assimilate, but to get rooted again, to honor our ancestors, our rituals, our men and women. To know our real names. Our real languages. To celebrate our diverse histories, stories, tongues, faces, and songs.

I once received a letter from a twenty-eight-year-old homeboy from my old neighborhood. I'll call him Johnny (for our purposes, this is not his real name). He was incarcerated in a California state prison at the time. For most of his life, he has been behind bars; a heroin addict for about as long. It turns out his father was a member of the same club in the South San Gabriel area of Los Angeles County that I was connected to. Johnny's life has been dictated by one fact: His father was murdered by police.

I know Johnny has done many terrible things in his life. He has murdered. He has hurt people. But his letter indicated that even for the Johnnys of the world, there is great possibility. Here's an excerpt:

> *Qvole Carnal,* How are you homes? . . . A lot of what you had to say hit home. Especially about sobriety being a political act (you ain't lying bro). It's even spiritual. In a society that is spiritually dead, that systematically isolates brown men from the mainstream of society and conditions them through various ways to commit self-destruction, for a barrio boy to take all of this sober is nothing less than heroic. . . . Our new breed of leaders must not only demonstrate different patterns of behavior, they must shed that shell of their lesser selves to become all together new men. Only then can a new age of intelligent brown warriors be not only efficient and effective, but most of all triumphant.

Over the past two years since my memoir has been out, I've talked to thousands of young people throughout the country: in schools, alternative programs, juvenile facilities, and recovery programs. I've been corresponding with a number of them in prisons. They include Puerto Rican,

Mexican, African, and Anglo youth. A few women. They are the ones this society has written off. Yet the seeds of spiritual renewal and social revolution are also in their grasp.

About the time of Johnny's letter, I received another letter from a leader in the Almighty Latin Kings Nation in the northeast part of the country. He too is incarcerated. What he has to say has some relevance for the need of Latinos to deal with what it means to be a man in this profit-motivated, oppressive environment called America:

> You cannot imagine the immense joy I felt when receiving your scribe. Being an individual of eclectic upbringing I am prone to know who are the dilettantes in the struggle and who are the ones with the deep rooted concerns for the present plight of the "ALANA" (African, Latino, Asian, Native American) peoples . . . You informed me of a movement which you had founded in '94, like yourself I am hoping that my leadership in the A.L.K.N. (a.k.a. Latin Kings) will have the impact as you have had. I was of two minds with the "L.K.'s," on the one hand I saw the violence and narcotics negativity which constantly seems to surround the Nation and on the other hand I envisioned that with strong determination among other things, the Nation could become a catalyst for Revolutionary Progress.

As these letters indicate, Latino men everywhere are seeking the necessary spiritual changes and transcendent pathways for living. For us, it is perhaps more urgent. We have lost too many of our numbers, too many of our warriors to gang wars, drugs, and incarceration. Some 40 to 60 percent of California's penal population—the largest in the world—is made up of Latinos (although Latino percentages on college campuses are minuscule). Our numbers in penal institutions throughout the United States are just as disproportionate.

We are losing many leaders. We are losing many fighters. We are losing much of our future. A Latino men's movement to regather our energies, to recall and honor our ancestors, that can make peace and sobriety acts of courage, respect, and struggle, and that can reconnect us to our mother nature, and thus to the women we have long shunned and often hurt, is extremely vital for us today.

I've come to realize, in my dealings with elder-teachers such as Meade, West African shaman Malidoma Somé, and Guatemalan healer Miguel Rivera that a society loses its equilibrium when the youth are neglected, but also when the elders are not listened to or honored.

Somé once said, "When youth are abandoned, and elders are abandoned, everything in the middle spins into various orbits. The youth and elders hold a community together."

In our barrios, I see the monstrous chasm between our elders and the past, and our youth and a future. We need the fire of youth. We need the fire of the elders. Fire to meet fire. When youth do not see the light from the elders, when they are not warmed by their fires of wisdom along a windswept and cold road, they lose sight of their aims, they lose heart, they get confused and sidetracked.

Many of our youth have created their own structures, such as gangs, to fill the vacuum. In a gang, they receive the initiation rites missing from community. They establish the rituals, rules, and hierarchies to make sense of a world that makes no sense. But too often they become heroes of descent, of going down, of dying in a blaze of bullets. There's no feasible path toward becoming heroes of ascent, of struggle, of a revolutionary service to life. For this we need elders.

Chicano men have been at war for generations. People have said we are good at it. During World War II, Chicanos garnered the largest number of medals of any other ethnic group. In Vietnam, our casualties were far beyond our numbers as a people (almost 25 percent of the war's casualties were Latinos, at a time when we made up less than 6 percent of the population). And when they returned back to the barrios, the wars never stopped. A full half of all the gang members in this country (estimated at some 250,000 young people) are Latinos. We don't need to prove to anyone that we are prepared to fight.

This is why I say peace in our communities would be a dangerous proposition for the powers-that-be in this society. It's also true for drug and alcohol addiction, which strikes our communities in disproportionate numbers. True community sobriety can't help but be political. There are far more options to kill, hurt, and deaden the pain than there are to be a contributing and valued human being. It's so easy to fall into a life of crime and addiction where I'm from, but quite difficult to get a decent education or meaningful work.

I'm pleased that Latinos and other people of color are increasingly participating in men's conferences. But I'm only in it for their revolutionary potential, for the life-liberating qualities of transformation embodied in them. Who needs to just feel good? Who needs to have an ego massaged, guilt explicated, and pain removed, only to go out in the world and keep doing the same old thing?

As Meade once said, "Healing is a revolutionary act," but I would also add that the act of revolution is healing. We need more people socially active, socially questioning, socially contributing to the lives of our youth, both male and female, to our communities and in our workplaces.

I believe the answer has always been within our reach. Human beings have long created wondrous rituals and laws and rules for how to live in peace, embracing the individual while ensuring the well-being of all. As we enter the first stages of a revolutionary epoch, in which technology has developed to such a level that all people's basic needs can be met, all their physical wants can be provided, then we have to ensure that our human capacity for imagination, for spirit, for consciousness is also given full dominion.

With community, with links to our myths, stories, and rituals, we can turn youth gangs around. We can stop the rising violence and suicide among the young. It means keeping them on track, in the direction where their pain and structures are already taking them. That's why even people like Ramiro, my homeboy Johnny, and the Latin King leader are important—they are proof that transcendence is possible for all. They need elders to guide them, to teach them, to show them the way.

I also believe we must challenge some sacred cows if we are to advance in this regard—I mean the so-called market system and capitalism as a whole. This is not a system ordained by any power other than man. This system engenders more exploitation, more repression, and more violence. It lives off the alienation and divisions between races, nationalities, sexual orientations, and, of course, the genders. It survives on scarcity, even if imposed, pushing social production to where the money is—not according to need, but to who can afford to pay. Billions are starving in this world for the sake of this parasitic system. The massive glut of cities, the destruction of earth's key resources, the impending battles over the basic resources for life on the planet—this is what capitalism has wrought, and we can do without it.

And finally, I have to address an important aspect of men coming to terms with themselves, with their inner workings, their mistakes, their strengths, their vulnerabilities. And that is that no man can find his essence, can get a hold of his own true self, as long as he participates, whether willfully or not, in a world that is predicated on man's power over woman.

I may have achieved a level of peace within myself and with those I live with, but I was also capable of great destruction, including almost killing my first wife. We can't lie to ourselves. A free and spiritual man can never be a user or exploiter of women. For us, *macho* does not mean the bully, the jock, the knucklehead. He is warrior, protector, defender, and lover. He is artist, hero, father, and elder. Nowhere does this imply or indicate a relation of superiority or strength over the only being that can define, limit, and even set him free: woman. This, I believe, must be integral to any activity by men in finding themselves.

And this is why, after all these years, I've begun a spiritual and political quest that has allowed me to once in my life have a *compañera,* María Trinidad, mother of my youngest sons, my comrade, fellow writer and thinker, with whom my reconciled rage, my nondrinking future days of focused social energy for true change, will now be shared.

FATHERS
IN THE
MIRROR

VIRGIL SUÁREZ was born in Havana, Cuba, and moved to the U.S. in 1974. He is the author of three novels, including <u>Latin Jazz,</u> from William Morrow, and <u>Havana Thursdays,</u> from Arte Publico Press. He is the co-editor of <u>Iguana Dreams: New Latino Fiction,</u> from HarperCollins, and <u>Paper Dance: 54 Latino Poets,</u> from Persea Books. He teaches literature at Florida State University in Tallahassee.

BITTERNESS

My father brings home the blood of horses on his hands, his rough, cal-
loused, thick-fingered hands; he comes home from the slaughterhouse
where the government puts him to kill old, useless horses that arrive from
all over the island. On his hands comes the blood encrusted and etched on
the prints and wrinkles of his fingers, under his nails, dark with the dirt
too, the filth and grime, the moons of his fingers pinked by the residue,
his knuckles skinned from the endless work. Sticky and sweet scented is
the blood of these horses, horses to feed the lions in the new zoo, which is
moving from Havana to Lenin's Park, near where we live. Dark blood,
this blood of the horses my father slaughters daily to feed the zoo lions. I,
being a child, ask how many horses it takes to feed a single lion. This, of
course, makes my father laugh. I watch as he washes and rinses the dried-
up blood from his forearms and hands, those hands that kill the horses,
the hands that sever through skin and flesh and crush through bone because tough is the meat of the old horses. Feed for the lions. So my father,
the dissident, the *gusano,* the Yankee lover, walks to and from work on
tired feet on an aching body. He no longer talks to anybody, and less to us,
his family. My mother and my grandmother; his mother. But they leave
him alone, to his moods, for they know what he is being put through. A
test of will. Determination. Salvation and survival. My father, under the
tent on the grounds of the new zoo, doesn't say much. He has learned how
to speak with his hands. Sharp are the cuts he makes on the flesh. The
horses are shot on the open fields, a bullet through the head, and are then
carted to where my father, along with other men, do the butchering. He
is thirty (the age I am now) and tired and when he comes home his hands
are numb from all the chopping and cutting. This takes place in 1969.

Years later when we are allowed to leave Cuba and travel to Madrid—to
the cold winter of Spain—we find ourselves living in a hospice. The three
of us in a small room. (My grandmother died and was buried in Havana.)
My father, my mother, and I, and next door is a man named Izquierdo,
who keeps us awake with his phlegmy coughs. From the other side of the

walls, his coughing sounds like thunder. We try to sleep; I try harder but the coughing seeps through and my father curses under his breath. I listen to the heat as it *tic-tacs* coming through the furnace. My father tries to make love to my mother. I try now not to listen. The mattress springs sound like bones crushing. My mother refuses without saying a word. This is the final time she does so tonight. There is what seems like an interminable silence, then my father breaks it by saying to my mother, "If you don't, I'll look for a Spanish woman who will." Silence again, then I think I hear my mother crying. *"Alguien,"* my father says, meaning "someone," "will want to, to [fuck him]." And I lay there on my edge of the mattress, sweat coming on from the heat. My eyes are closed and I listen hard and then the sound of everything stops. This, I think, is the way death must sound. Then my father begins all over again. The room fills with the small sounds . . . the cleaver falls and cuts through the skin, tears through the flesh, crushes the bone, and then there is the blood. All that blood. It emerges and collects on the slaughter tables, the blood of countless horses. Sleep upon me, I see my father stand by the sink in the patio of the house in Havana. He scrubs and rinses his hands. The blood dissolves slowly in the water. Once again I build up the courage to go ahead and ask him how much horse meat it takes to appease the hunger of a single lion.

JICOTEA (TURTLE)

They arrived in *yute* sacks. Their carapaces forming lumps as they pushed against the weaved string of the brown sacks. Once my father put down the sack on the cemented patio of the house in Havana, I walked around the lumpy pile, intrigued. I was still at an age where guesswork led to endless questions. My father said he'd gotten lucky this time at La Cienega de Zapata, a pocket of the province of Las Villas. My father was from this swampy area of the island of Cuba.

What is it? I asked. *Jicoteas,* he said and smiled, then reached into his shirt pocket for a cigarette. This was the time when my father still smoked, even though he suffered from asthma. *Jico*—I began but my tongue stumbled over the word—*teas? Tortuguitas, let me show you one.*

He opened the mouth of the sack and reached into it the way a magician might into his hat to pull out a rabbit by the ears.

It appeared: a turtle. Startled, waving its claws? Feet? Legs? In the air as if making a futile attempt at a swim/escape. *See?* my father asked. *Surely you've been shown pictures at school.* (At school we'd only been shown pictures of Camilo Cienfuegos, Che Guevara, José Martí, Karl Marx, Máximo Gómez, Vladimir Lenin, etc.)

Give me a hand, he said. At first I was reluctant, but then my father turned the sack upside down and let about thirty of these turtles free. *But they'll get away,* I told him. And again, he smiled, then blew smoke out of his nostrils.

No, no, no, he said. *See how they move? They are slow. They can't get away fast enough.*

Get away from what? I thought. Indeed, these *slowpo* creatures tried to make a path on the cemented patio—and I swear—making little scratch sounds with their nails against the surface.

My father crushed the cigarette under his shoe, reached to the sheath tied to the side of his right thigh, and pulled out his sharp machete. *This is what I want you to do, son,* he said and showed me.

He grabbed one of the turtles, stepped on it so that it couldn't move, then with his free hand he pulled and extended the neck of the turtle. *Like this, see?* He stretched . . .

I looked, not catching on yet. Then, to my surprise, he swung the machete downward so fast. There was a loud, crushing sound. There was a spark as the machete sliced through the turtle's neck and hit the hard concrete underneath.

The creature's neck lay on the floor like a piece of rotted plantain. It was still twitching as I looked up at my father, who was saying, *It's that simple, you grab and pull and I chop.*

As reluctant as I was, I did as I was told. I grabbed every one of those thirty turtles' necks, pulled without looking into their eyes, and closed my eyes each of the thirty times the machete came down. Turtle, after turtle, after turtle. All thirty.

After this you help me clean up, no, my father was saying. *We need to re-move the shells so that your mother can clean the meat and cook it.*

Yes, we were going to eat these turtles, these jicoteas (the sound of the word now comes naturally), and there was nothing I could say on behalf of the creatures I had helped my father slaughter.

And so the idea of death had been inflicted upon me quickly, almost painlessly, with the sacrifice of thirty jicoteas.

THE GOAT INCIDENT

One of the biggest scars from my childhood comes to me at my most vulnerable moments. My parents—I'm still clueless about the reasons, though I have speculated: the government's torment of my father (he was going crazy, I remember, once having tried to set the house on fire, though that's another scar), the friction between my mother and father due to my grandmother's illness, the fact that my parents had been trying to leave the island for the past few years, since 1962 (the year I was born)—left me in the care of my maternal grandparents in the little town of San Pablo, somewhere in the province of Las Villas. I cannot remember how I got there, whether my parents took me up or somebody went to Havana and then brought me up. Funny how memory fails one.

But the goat incident I remember well from all the years that I've had to carry it blazoned in my memory, though I once tried to purge myself of it in one of my books, my first novel, in fact, a pseudo autobiography, not mine, but my father's. I claim this because I was too young to go through any of what the main character, Julian Campos in *The Cutter,* goes through. But my father did. It is his life mostly that I try to capture in that book. Anyway, I wrote a chapter about the goat incident, which I liked and my agent liked—she thought it added dimension—but when it came to my editor, he thought it didn't fit. So, I cut it out. In cutting it out of the final draft and printed text, I didn't resolve the scarring, so I've carried it with me since. I've carried it since 1968, when I was six and had somehow ended up in the care of my maternal grandparents.

The incident begins very much like the chapter I wrote in *The Cutter,* with an unknown voice. An unknown, unseen voice saying: "Let's go, let's go, there's a fight. Let's go see it."

My grandfather, Domingo, white haired then as he is now, more than twenty years later, climbed on top of his horse. My mother's brothers were there and they too got on their horses. I was looking up at these giants sitting on top of these beasts. I wanted to go too. I voiced so to my grandfather. He turned the horse a few times, then he reached down and in one swoop, he pulled me up and I found myself sitting behind him, holding on to him.

They wasted no time going up to wherever it was the fight had broken out. I braced my grandfather. I could feel the horsehair sneaking in through my pants and irritating the skin on my legs.

In the novel, the incident takes place at night, but such violence is better seen by a child at night and attributed to nightmares, but in broad daylight . . . what torment. We arrived in a clearing that was surrounded by *bohios,* which are thatched huts. A crowd of men made a circle. There were two men, that much I saw. They stood in the circle, bare-chested, shoeless.

The circle of men expanded and contracted as the pushing and shoving continued. Again, the men in the circle. Another glimpse revealed the men, sweating, bestial, fighting each other with goats.

With goats over their shoulders. Both goats had not made it. They were limp in death. One of the animals was white. The other spotted, or was that blood?

My grandfather dismounted, pulled me down, and told me to move away with his horse. Both my uncles had already entered the circle and were pushing their way in.

I ran to a nearby *guayaba* tree, tied my grandfather's horse, and climbed up high on to one of the branches. A part of me didn't want to see, but the other did and so I climbed higher, scraping the insides of my thighs against the knobby branches of this *guayaba* tree. I went up high enough to get a perfect view.

Inside the circle of spectators, the two men went about their fighting slowly. The fight had been going on for quite some time now. They moved sluggishly, as if tired and worn.

One of the goat's belly had been gutted open by the horns of the other. The pink and reddish entrails dangled like rope out of the gaping wound. They oozed over the bare-backed man. The other goat had its fur stained. Their heads hung limp.

"I'll kill you," the man with the gutted goat said. "I'll teach you to re-spect a man."

The other man did not respond. He charged and struck the other man with the goat. The other man lost his balance. He fell on his knees, but then got up quickly and charged.

No one made an attempt to stop the two men from fighting. I hung tightly, wondering when my grandfather and uncles would come to the rescue. For the goats, they had already come too late, but not for the men.

Someone threw in a knife; the man with the spotted goat flung the car-cass off his shoulders and picked up the knife. The men continued with their death dance. The man with the knife kept stabbing at the goat. More blood, more entrails.

Then a machete was thrown in to the other man. He let go of the man-gled goat and grabbed the machete. Both men swung at each other. The one with the knife swung low at the other's stomach, each time missing, coming close the next.

This went on and on until one of the men lost his balance, perhaps out of exhaustion, and fell on his back. The other man, the one with the ma-chete, swung and cut the man on the arm. The sharp of the blade cut through the flesh. The crowd held its breath. For one long moment all sound escaped the scene.

Then my grandfather fired a shot and the crowd parted. My uncles took their place by both men. Why my grandfather waited so long to fire, I still don't know. He and my uncles stood in the center of the circle and kept both men from starting again. My grandfather told everyone to go away, to go back to their homes. The men did reluctantly at first, but then, seeing how my grandfather and uncles were serious, more quickly.

Then I can't remember much else, other than my looking down and re-alizing how high up the tree I had climbed. How would I get down? I started to inch my way slowly. My hands became tired and cramped.

Slowly I descended, my inner thighs on fire, scraped and bruised. I made it down and grabbed the horse's bit and pulled him away from the tree.

My grandfather and uncles returned. We all got on the horses and rode back to my grandparents' house. I rode back holding on to my grandfather's waist, my head against his chest. I listened to him as he talked to my uncles about what had happened. Why the men had fought.

The one man had caught the other with his wife. My uncles laughed and nodded their heads. "These *guajiros,*" my grandfather said, "they have too much time on their hands." My uncles nodded in agreement.

We arrived at the house and the men told nothing to the women. The women, my aunts and grandmother, had heard the shots, so they wanted to know what happened. "Let's eat," my grandfather said.

I wanted to hear it again, the whole story. Over dinner, my grandfather spoke up and told of what had happened, but I couldn't make it out, the conversation being too adult for my understanding then. But I kept waiting and waiting for him to mention the goats, but he didn't. I kept hearing about violence, the violence of these men so secluded from society. This was the kind of violence, my grandfather must have said, that was brought about by the system.

And much later that night I thought about the goats. I had, like so many other countless nights, thought about the dead goats. The way their heads dangled, eyes wide open, tongues sticking out from the corners of their mouths.

Years later, when I saw Francis Ford Coppola's *Apocalypse Now,* the scene where the natives killed the oxen during a ceremony, I thought of the goat incident again, then realized what I believe about violence now: It is all irrational and it isn't supposed to make sense after the fact, after so many years, even words, language, fails what really did happen, what memory chooses to carve out into some part of ourselves.

GUTIÉRREZ

My father's friend who owned the rusty, noisy Indian motorcycle and came to visit the house a couple of times a week. He'd arrive and help my father with the animals. Often, he'd let me sit on the motorcycle and pretend I was riding it. Even though my father never said so, Gutiérrez was the closest friend my father came to having in those uncertain days after the revolution.

Gutiérrez, a short, stocky, dark-skinned man with a crown of graying hair around a big bald spot. Gutiérrez of the big cigars and the scent of his smoke, which followed him everywhere he went; sometimes, if the wind was right, the smell preceded his appearance. He'd arrive and park his motorcycle in front of the house. "Take good care of it, *muchacho,*" he would say to me as he passed by on the porch and entered the house.

Soon enough some of the other kids from the neighborhood appeared and I would brag to them about how one day the bike, Gutiérrez's bike, would be mine. It seemed then like the only way to regain their respect, or make them jealous for having treated me like an outcast at school, like the antisocial element the government had named us.

My father smoked cigarettes in those days, so he and Gutiérrez, after doing whatever it was they did in the patio, sat and smoked and talked about politics and the revolution in a roundabout way. Sometimes they communicated without really speaking, with sounds like hums and *tsk-tsk* and laughter. Or nodded some truth or another into being. Both he and my father were counter-revolutionaries, or *gusanos,* which was what the government came to call people who were not on the side of the revolution and who had applied for exit visas to leave the island.

They sat on the porch steps next to the banana trees and planned ways of leaving and taking their families out. But Gutiérrez couldn't really leave because he was married to Teresa, "the witch," as he called her. They had children together and because of that he couldn't leave. Teresa, he told my father often, was a stubborn woman—he hated her with a passion, or so he said.

Sometimes he caught up to me at the beginning of our block and gave me a ride home. I held on tight against his damp back. Straddling the seat, I felt the grunts and rumbles of the engine vibrate through me as we rode over potholes and rocks. Ah, the excitement of the first push and then there was movement as we rolled over the pebbled dirt road up past all the houses on our street. I knew well that the other children heard the sound of the motorcycle and ran to their windows to look out, to watch me pass by, riding on Gutiérrez's bike.

He'd pick up the speed right before we got to the house. Then he would wave to my father and ride off. Of course, long after I went inside, I could still smell the smoke of Gutiérrez's cigar everywhere. Those were the days when I wanted nothing more than to be a spy and ride a motor-cycle.

I remember that when I joined my father and Gutiérrez on the porch, the cigar smoke was so potent that it made me dizzy. Both he and my father claimed it kept the mosquitos away. Other bugs too. "How about frogs?" I'd ask, having developed one of my many childhood-adulthood lasting fears. "Frogs too," Gutiérrez would say and then wink at me.

He and my father sat there, wrapped in the smoke and aroma. They talked of the possibilities and what if's. Then, after what seemed like a long time, Gutiérrez would point to me and say to my father, "He needs a better future." My father would nod in agreement. "It'll be a shame if this kid ends up in the military. Who knows what'll happen to him then."

My father grew serious because he often entertained the possibility of my getting involved in the regiment at the age of fifteen. Once he thought about it too much, it didn't matter if he was finishing a cigarette or starting a new one, he placed the thing under his foot and would grind it out. *"Hijos de puta,"* my father would say under his breath, smoke leaving his nostrils. "No way they'll get their hands on my boy."

To change the conversation because he stood up to leave, Gutiérrez would ask me if I wanted a ride on his bike. Thus the long-awaited moment through the riddles of conversation and hypnotic smoke. Yes!

He'd climb on first and kick the pedal and start the engine, then pull me up and over behind him. I held on to the belt loops on his pants, and off we rode up and down the blocks several times until he dropped me off again, then waved good-bye. How many times did I not stand there and watch him fade into the distance.

Gutiérrez stopped coming by the house one day and I overheard my father tell my mother the reason why. Teresa, the wife, and Gutiérrez were getting divorced and he was going through hard times. "She's accused him," my father told my mother, "of counter-revolutionary activities. The police came and arrested him."

After that my parents never mentioned Gutiérrez again, at least not in my presence, and Gutiérrez never rode by again and never came to visit. My father went through a moody period when all he did was sit on the porch and smoke his cigarettes and curse at nothing under his breath. He and I knew it was no use; without Gutiérrez there was something missing. Hopes in conversation for my father; for me the chance to show off on his motorcycle.

Many years later when my parents lived in Hialeah, Florida, and I was visiting them from college, there was a knock on the door. I answered it as I was on my way out. It was a man who claimed he knew my father. I called my father and he came to the door. Just when I was about to leave, I saw my father and this man embrace. The man started to cry. My father invited him in. "Do you know who this is?" he asked me. I hadn't the slightest clue.

"This is Gutiérrez's son," he said. I shook the man's hand and out of respect I followed them inside and sat with him and my father. I sat there looking for resemblances, but there were none. The man in front of me looked nothing like the father I knew in my childhood. He told my father that Gutiérrez had gone insane and that he had died in the asylum. "It was a terrible thing," the son said. The three of us sat in silence and then my father asked me, "Do you remember Gutiérrez?"

There was more silence because remembering was easy, then the son asked me, "Do you? Do you remember my father?"

"I remember his motorcycle . . ." I began.

His son smiled, then grew serious and said, "They took it away from him. They confiscated it. They stole it like they stole everything from everybody."

But not the memories, I thought, those we keep, like Gutiérrez on his bike, heading uphill, into the horizon, riding on into the distance, against all forgetting.

In pace requisquat. En paz descanse.

IZQUIERDO

The phlegmy coughs resounded and echoed in the lazy afternoon hours when I was home from school. Izquierdo in nothing but shorts and a stained undershirt—who, no matter the weather, always sat on the sofa of the hostel rooms he and his wife, Eloisa, and my parents and I shared—dying of throat cancer, but he wouldn't stop smoking cigarettes and, whenever he wanted to make his wife suffer, cigars, the cheap, stinky kind that left an awful stench on all my clothes.

He sat on the sofa in silence, smoking and nodding at the plumes of smoke that whirled into his eyes. He continued to smoke, even when the doctor had told him not to do it anymore, even when he knew it was too late to stop because he was dying. But he didn't *want* to stop. "Period," as he would put it. *"¡Punto y aparte!"* And Eloisa would leave each time he sat there smoking, for she couldn't stand the sight of him killing himself.

My parents didn't know it but many an afternoon I would spy on Izquierdo smoking and nodding and sometimes muttering to himself in his native Cuban Spanish, once in a while a *coño* becoming audible. All he ever talked about was what he had lost—his homeland . . . his house . . . his/his/his.

I would spy on him to make sure that he would not be using the bathroom any time soon, since I was twelve and afternoons had become my time to masturbate. This was my secret. The way Izquierdo smoked, I masturbated. Through the bathroom door I would hear him cough, loud grinding and wheezing cough.

Izquierdo sat there throughout the winter, spring, and well into the summer smoking, smoking, smoking—leaving a trail of ashes and tobacco all over the living room and hallway that ended at the entrance of his and Eloisa's room door.

Eloisa once told him that if he saved all the cigarette butts of cigarettes he had consumed, he could fill many buckets. "You've filled your lungs," she said to him one afternoon, "with that poison, and I want no part of it. *¿Me oyes?"*

That was the same afternoon that I went into the bathroom for the last time (I didn't know it would be the last time I would masturbate in the bathroom, that bathroom, anyway) and I closed the door.

There came a great silence while I put my hands to work. Left first, then right, then both. Those were days of ambidexterity. Suddenly I heard footsteps approach on the other side of the door, then they stopped. Izquierdo, I thought. He tapped on the door and said, "We're going to have to put *cascabeles* around your wrists." Then he walked away.

I didn't know what he meant, but I did stop and stood up and raised and buckled my pants and walked out of the bathroom a little embarrassed, as if he had been able to see what I was doing through the door.

Next time he saw me, which was a couple of days later, he smiled behind a few puffs of smoke, looked at me from across the smoke-filled room, and said, "Good afternoon, Cascabeles."

I returned to the room I shared with my parents and sat on the bed confused, for I was beginning to understand what he had meant. *Jingle bells.*

ANIMALIA

As a child the games to break boredom included a certain cruelty of which only children are capable. Plucked wings from flies, caught lizards and geckos, trapped fireflies in jars. I kept my distance from the frogs, which the other kids in the neighborhood, aware of my terror, insisted in putting down the back of my shirt or pants. We caught *lagartijas* with long grass stems & noosed them around their necks, then lowered the lizards into the black recess of a spider's hole—like fishing, the spider bit the lizards & dragged them down. The trick was to pull the spider out of its hole, then one of us would smash it with a rock. We hated everything that crawled on so many hairy legs. We encircled a scorpion in a ring of gasoline & set fire to the ring to watch how the insect stung itself in an act of suicide. Once, I slashed the tires of my brand-new bike (a bicycle my father had stood in long lines to buy), and I made a double-banded slingshot, the best all the kids in the neighborhood ever saw or held. They were envious, all right. A group of us went out into the backyard to shoot at sparrows. I killed my first as it perched on the clothesline preening its feathers. The pebble shot from my new slingshot broke its breastbone & the bird plummeted to the ground like a rotted mango. Fueled by the violence of those days, I became an expert at killing—I had learned well from watching my father & uncles slaughter so many animals in our backyard. Pigs, chickens, goats, rabbits, turtles. The pigs my father knifed in the heart while they ran—"It's the only good way," my father would say, "so they don't squeal." The goats bleated & kicked as they hung by rope from a roof beam, their necks about to be slashed. My father sliced through in one swift motion. Their throats opened & so much blood flowed. Then there were the countless chickens & ducks & guinea fowl whose necks my mother wrung, lending meaning to "running like a chicken with a bro-ken neck." Then there were rabbits, turtles, pigeons, turkeys, fish, both from the rivers & the ocean—all killed & gutted in the eyes of so many children. So many times stray dogs followed me home from school, mangy, filthy & hungry; my mother wouldn't let me keep any of them as a pet. In those days, as now, people would kill & eat anything in Havana, Cuba, and I think she feared the temptation. We raised & kept animals in our yards. So did everyone else in the *barrio*. Even after severe sanitation laws were passed, we took our chances. People hid their animals in their bathrooms, bedrooms, closets. One time the military came to our neigh-borhood & confiscated all the animals. Rounded them up and led them to a huge pit a bulldozer had dug at the corner. All the animals were herded into this pit & set on fire. Ah, the carnage & the wail of so many burning animals. In school field trips they took us to the chicken hatcheries & showed us how male baby chicks were ground to make feed for the zoo animals. My father, who was a *gusano* then & made to work voluntarily as a killer of horses to feed the lions & tigers at the zoo, never confirmed the story about the baby-chicks-as-feed. He did tell us about the monkey that played & teased a cage full of tigers until one day when it slipped & fell & the tigers quartered it immediately. My father smuggled home some of the horse meat from the horses he killed & then there were the sexual per-versions stories told by the neighborhood punks, with goats, pigs, dogs, even chickens. My father told me that when he was a kid & his uncle wanted to get him out of a conversation, he would send my father to *ten-tar las gallinas,* which meant that my father would have to go into the chicken coop & stick his pinkie into the chicken's ass to feel for the next morning's egg. I had a bunny that a couple of fierce neighborhood dogs caught & mauled. Cats, too, suffered in our neighborhood. They died reg-ularly in *yute* sacks hung from trees & beaten up like piñatas. Or they were left in bags on the railroad tracks. Such cruelty makes the mind's eye burn, the heart flutter . . . We fished the rivers, roamed the woods for every-thing & anything edible. Doves, quail, even rats. When my parents sent me off for the summer to San Pablo in the province of Las Villas, to my maternal grandparents, it wasn't any good either, no escape from people & their slaughter of animals. Though within the context of a farm, the killing makes some sense. Becomes less disturbing. I witnessed the castration, quite brutal, in cold blood, of pigs & bulls. My grandmother chopped the heads off guinea fowl. Then she put me to pluck the feathers & clean each bird. Then in 1970, the madness stopped, when we left for Spain, where the only animals I saw were ones people kept as pets. Of course there were the carcasses at the markets, but people no longer killed & ate their pets—they didn't have to. I too kept my first animals as pets: goldfinches, goldfish, hamsters, a turtle. I kept them throughout my youth in Madrid & later when we moved to Los Angeles, California. After so many years I came to appreciate creatures well kept & alive. My friend Wasibi caught a frog once & dissected it for a science project, then he removed its flesh by dunking the thing in Clorox. . . .

That was many years ago; now I've become a responsible adult. These days I have a dog (more on him later) & a garage full of canaries. I've become quite a canariculturist. During the breeding season sometimes it becomes necessary, because of genetic disasters, to dispose of a canary chick. Often, if things go wrong, a chick might be born without a limb, or, as was the case recently, without eyes. To have to cull is to return to the violence I experienced in my youth, but to leave such a creature in pain is unpardonable, so we have to cull, which means I drown the chick quickly in a glass of water. Recently at a bird show I asked several bird keepers what humane methods they utilize. The discussion turned into a heated argument about the best way being no good at all, but the majority of us agreed that to kill a bird quickly is to, like a chicken, snap its neck—the process by which this is done varies from the cruel & macabre to the quick & painless. Now about the dog, our basset hound, Sir Mongo of Tallahassee, who though AKC registered is far from being a champion specimen. Our dog. Our dog, who has been howling & crying at night since we brought him home as a puppy. His nocturnal whimpering & wheezing is enough to test anyone's patience, and I won't mention his lack of intelligence. Sometimes when he can't stop crying, I get out of bed, naked or clothed, & I walk to the kitchen to plead with the dog for a little silence, a little rest. But it is no use. He whimpers & cries more. We keep him behind a gate in the kitchen, & when he isn't making noise, he is busy at mischief. He will search & destroy almost everything he can reach, from cereal to fruit to thawing meat to coffee. It's worse when we have visitors. He once stole a friend's pair of glasses & chewed them & possibly ate glass & plastic, for we found only half of the frames. But nighttime is the worse, & so there's nothing to do but rage—once I let myself go & I beat up Sir Mongo of Tallahassee so that he did stop, but only briefly to catch his breath. It was during this moment that I caught a glimpse of myself, half naked, in the window—myself a creature, nocturnal & afraid like any other, driven mad by lack of sleep. When I looked across the dark expanse of the yard, I saw the neighbors' lit kitchen window & it was then I realized I had a problem that would not be easy to explain. I imagined a person there awake at the same hour, up for a glass of milk, and then—then the same image I saw in my kitchen window: a man half naked fighting with his dog. What would you think?

JUST TALK

Father says the birds in Mexico City fall amid flight from the polluted skies. They fall from the trees in the parks. On the sidewalks. We talk about the situation all over Latin America. Sendero Luminoso in Peru massacres innocent people, even the Indians. Guatemala, too, suffers from guerrillas' havoc. And those cocaine wheelers & dealers in Colombia and Bolivia. And let's not forget the macho dictators who know the secrets of power longevity, who know how to break down the opposition by crushing their families first: Castro in Cuba (always Castro in Cuba . . .), Pinochet in Chile, Somoza in Nicaragua, Noriega in Panama. And take Argentina, for example; for a president they have a smooth talker with funny-looking sideburns who looks like a tango dancer straight out of the ballroom. Things are bad, Father says, everywhere. Be thankful to live here in the USA. My turn comes and I think of all the hatred & violence on the streets. The way people die quickly in eight-to-five jobs, like Thoreau said, living lives of quiet desperation . . . Father gives me his best you're-full-of-shit look. I may not know what I'm talking about but I know what I see & I don't like it, so being ill at ease with poorly chosen words I try to make my point. I say . . . I say daily here in the great El Norte I witness people's souls rot like uneaten fruit and they, too, fall to the earth, yeah, like those birds of Mexico City. Some too shrivel up slowly and sure ok people die all over the world. Young. Because of wars. Star-vation. Over God. & sure ok unnatural causes but here in the good old US of A they wilt, wilt I say, and die slow painful humiliating deaths. I tell my father, I say I saw this old lady in a Melrose convalescent home. Yes, some son or daughter must have put her in there. It was past midnight and she was slumped over asleep on the sofa of the lobby in front of this big window whose sign read WE TAKE CARE OF YOUR LOVED ONES. Father says, he says what's your point son? I say, I tell him Hell, the best we can hope for here is that when our turn comes to drop dead that a hungry crow or mocking bird pecks out our heart first.

MY FATHER
AND THE SNOW

Davey Photo

ALBERTO ÁLVARO RÍOS received the Walt Whitman Award for <u>Whispering to Fool the Wind,</u> his first book of poems. He is the author of four other collections, including <u>Teodore Luna's Two Kisses,</u> from Norton. He received a Western States Book Award for his first book of stories, <u>The Iguana Killer,</u> recently reprinted by Confluence Press. His second short story collection, <u>Pig Cookies,</u> was published in 1995 by Chronicle Books. He teaches literature and creative writing at Arizona State University in Tempe.

MY FATHER IS DYING. There it is, openly said.

It is a long and slow worm, this thing of dying in the way that he is. But it is his dying, his alone and no one else's, and that is the particular—toward which end can be fairly said that he has been an ordinary man who has colored outside the lines of all of his lives, and of the lives around him, and in doing so has written with his life a striking story for himself, worthy in its words and too fleet on its pages.

But what a serious-sounding debris of words. It's just that there's nothing else to say or to use. When I talk to my father these days, I think I am not very good with words. The reason is simple—when we used to talk together, we never talked very much about him, not the inside him. We looked at his architecture, but not who lived in it.

The outside him, the structure, the public him, that's what he gave me, and that's what much of my own literary work has been about. He was born in Tapachula, Chiapas, Mexico, on the border of Guatemala, where there's a great deal of trouble right now, and where perhaps there has always been trouble. When he was born, the volcano Tacaná erupted, and I remember my grandmother telling me how all the birds from the surrounding jungle flew in through the open windows of their house, and the noise they made was confused for her with the noise my father made as he was being born. The stories about my father, and about his father before him, are like that.

But the quieter sense of himself, that is something else. I don't finally understand very much about it. Nothing I can say about him, about his inside, comes easily or with authority. But I know the signs, the dodges he has used through the years, the small glimpses and half-looks, perhaps because I have inherited them in one form or another for myself. If I have seen him look to the side for a moment, in a particular circumstance, I have been able, sometimes, to know why, though not from anything he has ever told me.

I take as measure against these recent days the fine drama and big lives of my parents together—that's where my father is still big. He, as I say, was born in Mexico, and my mother was born in England. How they met is another story altogether; what matters is that she came by herself across the ocean halfway around the world to be his wife, even though in her life up to then she had never been more than two train stops away from home.

Guglielmo Marconi, the inventor of the wireless telegraph, sent the single letter *S* through the air across the Atlantic in the 1800s. It was a first ephemeral traveler through an air of mystery. When I read this, I thought of my mother, how she was this one letter coming from one place to another and hoping she would find a like alphabet, a place for herself, someone to reach up and catch her out of the air. Both the sending of the letter and my mother's coming over to this country were fleeting, even capricious acts, but they changed forever the worlds they would find.

That she would come, that he could catch her in flight, that he could hold on—this as well is something of the measure of my father, how by understanding something of my mother I understand something more of him. I don't for a moment diminish my mother in all of this; what is simply remarkable for me is this way of understanding—of understanding her, of course, but of understanding him too. He simply, in fact, did these things, and it is a real measure.

The escape velocity of an object from earth is seven miles per second. If my father is revving up for his own act of travel, and I believe he is, it's hard to see because he seems to be moving so slowly. But the movement, I think, is all within, which says something about the inside of this man. That inside is a strong place. That is not something he ever needed to tell me.

Watching my father now I am too much reminded of this place where my parents, my brother, and I have lived these many years, of its quieter and more secret underside, an underside one would only know by living here and paying attention. In this place that we live—my West, my father's North, and my mother's new hemisphere—rabbits in a burning field of grass can catch on fire. They run to a clear place, where there is no fire, but in doing so light it up because their fur is burning. That way, in trying to save themselves, they spread the fire more. Dying like that is a difficult thing to watch; in slow motion, it is cruelty. And it spreads to everyone.

I got news last night that my father was not doing well. My mother called, and she sounded clear—a rarity, as my parents like to put on the speaker-phone and have everybody talk. It never works out quite right, though, and my mother has a hearing aid anyway. So everybody shouts, and no-body hears, and sentences always go about half their intended distance. But that's family.

My mother wasn't on the speakerphone, though, and she said my fa-ther was sleeping. Of course he wasn't. He was listening from the couch—I could see it, like I'd seen it a hundred times in that house. He has dia-betes, fully engaged, and had a stroke awhile back, which required that he have eye surgery. But this wasn't that.

He had been short of breath for a couple of days, so my mother—who was a nurse and still is, most days, except when my father can talk her into giving him just a little something, a little something he shouldn't be eat-ing, which really he can do any time he likes, that's the truth of it, the good truth, my mother saying "a little piece like that," she's sure it won't hurt his diet—my mother took him to the doctor, her former employer, who right away put her to work.

The nurse there had taken my father's blood pressure, but the doctor wanted my mother to take it. What he really wanted was for her to *feel* it, something he knew she'd understand, so that he wouldn't have to tell her something like 220 over 120, which was so much nothing. She felt it, all right. And that meant my father felt it, too, them having been married so long.

The doctor ordered blood work, an EKG, and some small stuff, and then sent them to the hospital for a chest X ray, just to be on the safe side. They went and got it done. Just to be on the safe side.

The results were in by afternoon. The EKG showed what it had shown before, the stroke, the little strokes before that. The X ray was okay, show-ing the scarring around the heart from the stroke. But the blood work. "That was the thing," said my mother.

"His kidneys are only working at twenty percent," she said, quiet and matter-of-fact.

I don't know what you do with information like that. I have worked in a hospital; I know things. But none of that helped now.

"So, what do you think?" I asked.

"Well, the doctor has put him off salt and off potassium. No more banana bread for a while. No more chile either."

"No more chile?"

"No, can you believe that?"

I knew my father was listening, the way she said this one.

"Then they're going to do it all over again on Friday. We'll know more then. I just wanted to call you because I thought you should know."

"Yes, that's right. I'm glad you called."

"I don't think I'm going to call your brother yet, do you think? I don't want to get him worried."

"No, no, you don't need to do that. We should see what happens on Friday." She knew I would call him.

Then my mother moved a little on the couch. I could hear it.

"Oh, your father's awake. Do you want to talk to him?"

"Sure."

"I'll just put this thing on so he can hear you. There. Can you hear?"

"Hi, son."

"Hi." I realize, every time, that I still don't know what to call him. "How are you feeling?"

"A little under the weather."

"I guess so. No salt, huh?"

"No salt. You should be careful."

"I will. Maybe I should think about no salt too. Well, I'll call on Friday."

The process of diabetes is different for everyone, but ultimately and inexorably fierce, as it has been for my father. He has had a stroke, and kidney failure, dialysis, congestive heart failure, and all the rest, underscored by an itching all over that cannot be scratched enough. My father has finally lost his sight, and much else.

But it has been the loss of his sight that he cannot reconcile. He describes it as having woken up one day and suddenly not having been able to get his bearings, and no matter how hard he rubs his eyes, fully expecting that the film will lift, they do not come back. He has kept trying for months, maybe now a year. He knows the center, from so many years of having been there, but he can't get back to it.

The way these things go is predictable enough, and any single day becomes the gauge.

The next time something happens, it's like the last time, only more. He has a blood infection, they said months later, but it's under control. The only thing we have to hope now is that he doesn't get another fever.

But of course, once said, that was the next thing.

And the next.

He has a heart problem, said the cardiologist. Cardiologist. I didn't even know he had a cardiologist.

It's an act of translation, the cardiologist said, like this: If you can understand what the diabetes has done to his eyes, that's what it's doing to his heart.

The diabetes has made him blind. I see that. What happens to the heart is more difficult to articulate, but not hard to understand. I see that, too.

This last trip my father did what he's been doing for most of our last trips—he slept. He sleeps more than possible, maybe less than necessary. We talk around him in his chair and do things that need doing, but it's all small. My aunt calls, long distance, and my father says a few words, but that's it. All of this is how things are now. That, and with us thinking a little too far ahead.

My mother is getting the house fixed up. She has had several slabs of concrete poured, an addition to the garage put up, a small fence added to the front yard. She can't stop fixing the house. And this thing of fixing the house—it works. It works and it's something she can do. She can't fix my father.

My mother has also been putting whipped cream on her doughnuts. And for dinner the cafeteria people at the hospital made her a fresh big batch of french fries, and she had only a little piece of pumpkin pie for dessert. She tells me this and things like this in bits and pieces of conversation, when she can't quite hold all the food in and it comes out as conversation.

My mother was a nurse, and that turns out to be a good thing for my father. But for all those years of working, she could always go home at the end of a day. She can't go home now, not like that. Hers has become a curious retirement, as if she never left work at all, and can't. It's like a dream, that way. And with arthritis as the electricity that powers it.

She would never call this whole thing with my father a *bad* dream. It's not in her. But she's been hard at work filling in those places in her that might have started to think it.

My father always told me a story about snow, and how he encountered it for the first time when he visited Nogales, Arizona, from all the way down in the tropics. He thought at the time that the sky was falling, and that perhaps he was responsible in some way. But his mother laughed and told him it was snow. Snow, however, in Spanish, is the word *nieve,* which is also the word for ice cream.

The stories he told when he got back to the tropics became legend, especially as he had brought back a postcard with a house surrounded by snow. In the United States, *nieve* comes down from the sky, really. That's when he would show the postcard. It comes down in *vainilla* up there, he would say. And in later years, sometimes in *chocolate* as well.

This last time I saw my father in the hospital, he looked snowed upon. These days his hair seems even whiter, his skin a little darker, so that this time his hair seemed to be placed there, almost to have fallen onto this place rather than to have grown out of it. That was the first thing I noticed. But the second thing was his eyebrows. His eyebrows, too, had turned a white I had not seen before. They were big enough before this, but now, with their white kind of neon, they looked tremendous. This was the snow even more, and he looked like he had just stepped in from the outside, like his brow held the snow the way an overhanging roof does.

This moment, all this snow, it was a kind of England again, from all the stories my parents had told me together. It was from another place in that moment.

I was reminded of an event several years ago. I was a visiting writer at Vassar College, and the college was gracious enough to fly my family out to be with me for my last week there. My son was instantly on fire in all of the wonder of the cold. Having grown up all of his six years in Arizona, he was an energy matching up to the newness of this landscape.

He was quiet enough about it. This was his secret. But he had found something, and it was big.

On the night before we were to leave, it was snowing. We put him to bed and said our things. A little later that evening, I heard quiet but insistent sobs coming from his room. I went in and found him in tears. He said he didn't want to leave, and I understood him profoundly at that moment.

We talked awhile, and said some more things, and did what could be done. But I knew what had happened, I knew what the crying was about, and I have been haunted by it ever since. He had no name for what he felt. Instead, because he could not yet articulate his feelings, he let his body do his talking, and what it said, it said elegantly, and spoke beyond itself, as any honest word invariably must.

He met snow, and when he knew he had to leave it, he cried for beauty.

In that moment, I did not want to be my son's father. I did not want to be the one who took him away from something he had found. It's a hard thing to explain.

Like that, my father too has been hard to explain. I can't say that my father was a father the way fathers are fathers, the way they are in books, in movies, even in songs—that's way too much father. My grandfather was that kind of father, and my father didn't want to be that. My father had run away from home, after all. At fourteen, he had run away from his own larger-than-life father, from *Papá,* from *Papi,* from San Luis Potosí, where they were living, to Nogales, on the border of a new country and a new world in a new time, from the good and the bad and the middle of it all. So, when the time came for him to be *Father,* it had to be something different.

But that's the rub. My father became something inside the word, and around and between the word. He found a place in it that worked for him. But it wasn't *Father,* exactly.

All of which is all right with me, except that now I don't know what to call him, and I haven't for a long time. Probably because of the English of my mother, or because it was the fifties and it's what people said on television, and to be sure that it was not his old *papá* in a new world, I grew up calling my father *Daddy,* and my brother still can say it with ease. But somewhere along the way, that became a hard word for me to say. The thing is, I could never replace it with anything equal. When I had to write something, or found some other circumstance that compelled me to call him something, I mumbled or said *Dad* or took a left turn. I still do it, every telephone call and every visit.

Maybe after everything, this is my own discovery. This is my snow. I don't know what to call my father. Somewhere in my life he was *Daddy* with authority and arms and life. It was simple and easy and it worked. I need an honest word like that to call him. I need back the ease of saying it right out of my mouth without a second thought.

ACKNOWLEDGMENTS

"Me Macho, You Jane" by Dagoberto Gilb. Copyright © 1996 by Dagoberto Gilb. Used by permission of the author.

"From the Land of Machos: Journey to Oz with My Father" by Elías Miguel Muñoz. Copyright © 1996 by Elías Miguel Muñoz. Used by permission of the author.

"Guatemalan Macho Oratory" by Omar S. Castañeda. Copyright © 1996 by Omar S. Castañeda. Used by permission of the author.

"How to Live with a Feminista and (Still) Be a Macho: Notes Unabridged" by Juan Felipe Herrera. Copyright © 1996 by Juan Felipe Herrera. Used by permission of the author.

" 'I'm the King': The Macho Image" by Rudolfo Anaya. Copyright © 1996 by Rudolfo Anaya. Used by permission of the author.

"The Puerto Rican Dummy and the Merciful Son" by Martín Espada. Copyright © 1996 by Martín Espada. Used by permission of the author.

"Of Cholos and Surfers" by Jack López. Copyright © 1996 by Jack López. Used by permission of the author.

"Whores" by Luis Alberto Urrea. Copyright © 1996 by Luis Alberto Urrea. Used by permission of the author.

"Romancing the Exiliado" by Ricardo Pau-Llosa. Copyright © 1996 by Ricardo Pau-Llosa. Used by permission of the author.

"All about Rachel" by Rane Arroyo. Copyright © 1996 by Rane Arroyo. Used by permission of the author.

"Bless Me, Father" by Leroy V. Quintana. Copyright © 1996 by Leroy V. Quintana. Used by permission of the author.

"The Latin Phallus" by Ilán Stavans originally appeared in Transition #65, Spring 1995. Copyright © 1995 by Ilán Stavans. Used by permission of the author.

0805